REMEMBERING VANCOUVER'S DISAPPEARED WOMEN

Settler Colonialism and the Difficulty of Inheritance

Between the late 1970s and the early 2000s, at least sixty women, many of them members of Indigenous communities, were found murdered or reported missing from Vancouver's Downtown Eastside. In a work driven by the urgency of this ongoing crisis, which extends across the country, Amber Dean offers a timely, critical analysis of the public representations, memorials, and activist strategies that brought the story of Vancouver's disappeared women to the attention of a wider public. *Remembering Vancouver's Disappeared Women* traces what lives on from the violent loss of so many women from the same neighbourhood.

Dean interrogates representations that aim to humanize the murdered or missing women, asking how these might inadvertently feed into the presumed dehumanization of sex work, Indigeneity, and living in the Downtown Eastside of Vancouver. Taking inspiration from Indigenous women's research, activism, and art, she challenges readers to reckon with our collective implication in the ongoing violence of settler colonialism and to accept responsibility for addressing its countless injustices.

AMBER DEAN is an assistant professor in the Gender Studies and Feminist Research Program and the Department of English and Cultural Studies at McMaster University.

AMBER DEAN

Remembering Vancouver's Disappeared Women

Settler Colonialism and the Difficulty of Inheritance

UNIVERSITY OF TORONTO PRESS
Toronto Buffalo London

© University of Toronto Press 2015
Toronto Buffalo London
www.utppublishing.com
Printed in the U.S.A.

Reprinted 2016

ISBN 978-1-4426-4454-0 (cloth)
ISBN 978-1-4426-1275-4 (paper)

Library and Archives Canada Cataloguing in Publication

Dean, Amber Richelle, 1975–, author

Remembering Vancouver's disappeared women : settler colonialism and the
difficulty of inheritance / Amber Dean.

Includes bibliographical references and index.
ISBN 978-1-4426-4454-0 (bound) ISBN 978-1-4426-1275-4 (paperback)

1. Native women – Violence against – Social aspects – British Columbia –
Downtown-Eastside (Vancouver). 2. Women – Violence against – Social aspects –
British Columbia – Downtown-Eastside (Vancouver). 3. Missing persons –
British Columbia – Downtown-Eastside (Vancouver) – Social conditions.
4. Memorials – Social aspects – British Columbia – Vancouver. 5. Collective
memory – Social aspects – British Columbia – Vancouver. 6. Missing persons
in art – Social aspects – British Columbia – Vancouver. I. Title.

HV6250.4.W65D42 2015   362.8808209711'33   C2015-905833-3

This book has been published with the help of a grant from the Federation for
the Humanities and Social Sciences, through the Awards to Scholarly Publications
Program, using funds provided by the Social Sciences and Humanities Research
Council of Canada.

University of Toronto Press acknowledges the financial assistance to its
publishing program of the Canada Council for the Arts and the Ontario Arts
Council, an agency of the Government of Ontario.

Canada Council
for the Arts

Conseil des Arts
du Canada

ONTARIO ARTS COUNCIL
CONSEIL DES ARTS DE L'ONTARIO

an Ontario government agency
un organisme du gouvernement de l'Ontario

Funded by the
Government
of Canada

Financé par le
gouvernement
du Canada

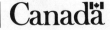

Canada

For Sharon,
who lives on in countless ways
and for
Howie and Drew,
who imagine otherwise

We inherit not "what really happened" to the dead but what lives on from that happening, what is conjured from it, how past generations and events occupy the force fields of the present, how they claim us, and how they haunt, plague, and inspirit our imaginations and visions for the future.

Wendy Brown, *Politics Out of History*

When you see, in a photograph or in a hat or in a foot print, the hand of the state, the other door, the water and what is down there, you have seen the ghostly matter: the lost beloveds and the force that made them disposable. When you have a profane illumination of these matters, when you know in a way you did not know before, then you have been notified of your involvement. You are already involved, implicated, in one way or another, and this is why, if you don't banish it, kill it, or reduce it to something you can already manage, when it appears to you, the ghost will inaugurate the necessity of doing something about it.

Avery Gordon, *Ghostly Matters*

Contents

Illustrations

Acknowledgments

This research project now spans more than a decade of my life, and in that time I have benefited from countless rich and challenging conversations about this work – conversations that have profoundly shaped and sometimes radically altered my thinking. For all the gentle pushes, sparks, challenging criticism, and deep engagement I have received, I am eternally grateful.

This book would never have been written without the encouragement, support, and nearly illegible but copious feedback offered by Dr Sharon Rosenberg on numerous early drafts. It was Sharon who first prodded me to consider doing extended research on memorials for the disappeared women of Vancouver's Downtown Eastside, and I am profoundly indebted to her thoughtful, often difficult but always generous engagement, as well as her own scholarship. Losing her in 2010 has forever altered my understanding of the gifts we receive as scholars from our mentors; nothing can replace the impact she had on my thought. This book is enriched by all that she contributed to my thinking while she was still with us, and impoverished by all the questions and concerns that I could not discuss with her after her death. And yet, it is also true that she lives on in countless ways, and every time I revisit her writing I discover new thoughts and realize anew how indebted my own thinking remains to her brilliance.

For conversations and collaborations that have also profoundly shaped my thought and kept me sticking with this project over the years, I am indebted to two key interlocutors: Kara Granzow and Phanuel Antwi. For the generosity of their friendship, the richness of their own scholarship, and for their unwavering support, I can only offer insufficient thanks.

It was Daphne Read who first informed me, after reading an early version of my Introduction, that I was in fact writing a book. I am grateful to her for encouraging me to conceive of the project as a book early on and for guiding and supporting me through some very difficult moments in my doctoral program. Thanks to Daphne for also prompting me to give more thought to the implications of the language of witnessing. Many thanks are also due to several scholars who contributed to the project in its early incarnation as my doctoral dissertation at the University of Alberta, especially Julie Rak, Cressida Heyes, Michael O'Driscoll, and Teresa Zackodnik.

For our rich conversations while editing a 2007 special issue of *West Coast Line* (41.1) on "Representations of Murdered and Missing Women," for her own writing and scholarship, and for her critical engagement with an early draft of chapter 3, I remain deeply grateful to Anne Stone.

It is impossible to remember all the many conversations over the years that have had an impact on this book, but an enormous thank you is due to all the people who have taken time to talk with me about the ideas it contains. Big shout-outs are due to Terra Poirier, Louise Croft, Colleen Mangin, Emily Aspinwall, Paul Ugor, Shawna Hohendorf, Daniel Coleman, Rick Monture, Vanessa Watts, Nadine Attewell, Chandrima Chakraborty, Angela Failler, Shawna Ferris, Sarah Brophy, Janice Hladki, Margot Francis, Melinda Gough, Jennie Anderson, Jessie Forsyth, Vilma Rossi, Ian Jarvis, Cole Gately, Jannet Geddes, Meaghan Ross, Sarah Mann, Kristin Smith, and all the people involved with Big Susie's (Hamilton's Sex Worker advocacy organization) and the sadly now-defunct HAND (Hamiltonians Against Neighbourhood Displacement). For their expert mentorship and generous support of my work at McMaster, I'm so grateful to Susan Fast, Peter Walmsley, and Mary O'Connor. Special thanks to Susan for making the "No Comment" moments of university life bearable. I am also grateful to my students at Capilano College in Vancouver and McMaster University in Hamilton for dialogues in and out of the classroom that constantly challenge and enrich my thinking. Special thanks to Shaun Stevenson for his work on the manuscript as a research assistant, for his thoughtful engagement with my work, and for his own scholarship.

For an early email exchange that pushed me to confront the ethical implications of critically analyzing memorials, and for being ever willing to allow me to reprint excerpts of her sister Sarah's writing, I am very grateful to Maggie de Vries. For his assistance over a decade now with tracking down particular articles or images, and for his work maintaining the important digital archive missingpeople.net, huge thanks are also due to Wayne Leng.

I remain so grateful to my loving family, many of whom have continued to read my writing and share their thoughts across a couple of decades now of my academic life. With love and thanks to mom, dad, Erin, Tyler, April, Anthony, and Scottie. So much love and gratitude are due to Howie and Drew Dean-Rowe and to Will Rowe, for their willingness to tolerate much grumpiness and distraction all while continuing to fill my life with so much joy.

For their expert help with the selection of an image for the book's cover, I'm so grateful to Terra Poirier and April Dean. I couldn't have dreamed of a better image to grace the cover than the photograph of Jaime Black's remarkable REDress project (to learn more about the project, see theredressproject.org). Thanks so much to Jaime Black for her generous permission to use this image of her work. Enormous thanks to my editor at UTP, Siobhan McMenemy, for many years of guidance and patience, and to everyone at UTP who contributed to the book.

The following presses kindly granted me permission to reprint excerpts from the book that have been previously published: short excerpts from the preface, introduction, chapter 1 and chapter 4 first appeared, in different form, in my book chapter "Inheriting What Lives On from Vancouver's Disappeared Women," published in *Not Drowning but Waving: Women, Feminism and the Liberal Arts*, edited by Susan Brown, Jeanne Perreault, Jo-Ann Wallace, and Heather Zwicker and published by the University of Alberta Press in 2010. An earlier, shorter version of chapter 1 was published as "Space, Temporality, History: Encountering Hauntings in Vancouver's Downtown Eastside," in *The West and Beyond: New Perspectives on an Imagined Region*, edited by Sarah Carter, Alvin Finkel, and Peter Fortna and published by Athabasca University Press in 2010. Excerpts from chapter 2 and my conclusion also appear as "Inheriting What Lives On: The 'Terrible Gift' of Sarah de Vries' Poetry," in *Torn from Our Midst: Voices of Grief, Healing and Action from the Missing Indigenous Women Conference*, edited by A. Brenda Anderson, Wendee Kubik, and Mary Rucklos Hampton and published by the Canadian Plains Research Centre in 2010. Finally, portions of chapter 5 were previously published in "Can Names Implicate Us? The Memorial-Art of Rebecca Belmore and Janis Cole," which appeared in *Public: Art, Culture, Ideas* 42 (2010): Traces, a special issue co-edited by Chloe Brushwood Rose and Mario Di Paolantonio.

I am also grateful to the Arts Research Board at McMaster University for a scholarly publications grant and to the Social Sciences and Humanities Research Council of Canada for funding that has supported this research.

Preface

In the spring of 2000 I acted on a long-standing desire to move to the city of Vancouver, British Columbia, located on unceded Coast Salish territory and renowned as one of the world's most "liveable" cities. Vancouver topped the *Economist*'s "liveable city" rankings for most of the 2000s, but dropped to third place in 2012, apparently due to a twenty-two-hour highway closure that summer on Vancouver Island (a ninety-minute ferry ride away from the city of Vancouver itself). And yet, in 2002, the year the city made international headlines for the arrest of a man suspected of murdering dozens of women from its Downtown Eastside neighbourhood, Vancouver remained tied for first place on the *Economist*'s list. Questions about *for whom* the city is made so liveable and at what cost to others' lives are not concerns that this index purports to measure. But beyond a doubt, a city containing a neighbourhood so often described as "Canada's poorest postal code" cannot be equally liveable for all of its residents.[1] In fact, a significant number of women from that particular neighbourhood are not finding the city of Vancouver liveable at all.

I began teaching some of the books, essays, and newspaper stories about murdered or missing women from the Downtown Eastside in classes I was giving at Capilano College in Vancouver in 2004. At that time it seemed unnecessary to provide much by way of background information about the story of "Vancouver's Missing Women" before assigning these texts, as most of my students seemed at least somewhat familiar with the events they discussed. By 2008, teaching now in Haudenosaunee territory in Hamilton, Ontario, I was caught off-guard when I discovered that I could no longer assume my students had heard anything about the large number of murdered or missing women from

Vancouver's Downtown Eastside. Proximity and time seem to make all the difference – if I was still teaching in Vancouver, even today I would assume that most of my students might know at least something about the disappearance and murder of such a large number of women from a neighbourhood in their city. But in Southern Ontario, this story is often viewed (mistakenly) as relevant only to Vancouver, or possibly to Western Canada, but certainly not to the nation's centre. And yet, if I had been teaching in Southern Ontario in 2002, when Robert Pickton's arrest for the murders of several women began to garner national and even international media attention, no doubt many of my students would have been more familiar with the Downtown Eastside and the murders of so many women who lived there. But I have repeatedly learned that this background is simply not something I can safely assume any shared knowledge about today. Now, in 2014, a shockingly large number of my students at McMaster University have never even heard of the women who have been disappeared from the Downtown Eastside, or even of the Downtown Eastside neighbourhood itself.

As a result, I find it necessary to begin by recounting some of the details of these events, even though throughout this book I take issue with many of the ways that the story of "Vancouver's Missing Women" has been conveyed to a wider public. This book is not an investigation into *what really happened* to the many murdered or missing women from the Downtown Eastside, for there are – for better and for worse – many places where one can read recaps of the events that surround the disappearance and murder of so many women from this one neighbourhood (see, for example, Cameron 2010). While many such reports that aim to outline *what really happened* remain contentious – the BC Missing Women Inquiry has rightly been critiqued for its deeply flawed process by numerous writers, scholars, and non-profit organizations, for example – it is nonetheless not my project to attempt to recount all the details of these events in this book.[2] Instead, I aim to trace *what lives on* from the violent loss of so many women who called the Downtown Eastside home. Determining what really happened to murdered or missing people is an essential task, one that we cannot do without, and I don't mean to seem dismissive of such efforts. But in the drive to sort out all the details of what really happened (and to attempt to prove them beyond a reasonable doubt), it is my contention that some important questions tend to get pushed aside or lost, questions such as: How does what happened live on, or matter, in and for the present? What social conditions and arrangements, what widely shared understandings of what it means to be human, are implicated in what happened? In what ways can what happened be read as evidence of a past that continues to make claims on the present? And what might it mean, then, to come to see ourselves as inheriting *what lives on* from the violent loss of so many women, especially for those of us who did not know any of the women when they were living? These are the questions that I take up in this book, but before I can make a persuasive case for why these questions might be just as important as questions about what really happened, it *is* necessary for readers to know at least some of the details of these events, especially those readers who might not have heard much about them from the news or other sources.

By 2007, sixty-five women who for the most part lived or worked in Vancouver's Downtown Eastside neighbourhood were listed by a joint Vancouver Police Department and Royal Canadian Mounted Police (RCMP) Missing Women Task Force as "missing." I put the word "missing" in scare quotes here because it seems odd to me that a number of women whose remains were discovered by police before November 2003 were nonetheless still categorized as "Missing Women" on a reward poster redistributed in 2007.[3] To be sure, the poster does indicate that charges have been laid in connection with the disappearance of some of the women it lists, but since the evidence suggested that many of these women were no longer actually "missing" in 2007, it still seems curious to keep them listed this way – the descriptor becomes misleading, although the women certainly do remain missing from the lives of their friends, family, neighbours, and loved ones.[4] Sarah Hunt, Kwakwaka'wakw scholar, writer, and advocate, reminds us that our strategies of naming this violence can "become part of the problem, as the language of 'the missing women' masks the brutal reality of how they become 'missing'" (2014, 191).

According to the reward poster put out by the Missing Women Task Force, the first woman reported missing from Vancouver's Downtown Eastside was last seen in the late 1970s, but there are good reasons to believe that many, many women who remain unaccounted for were disappeared from this neighbourhood before then, too – reasons I explore later in this book. But since at least the late 1970s, more and more women from this community have been designated "missing" by police, with a sharp increase in the numbers of women listed as last seen in the late 1990s and very early years of the twenty-first century. For many of the women on the official list of the missing, those of us who did not know them personally can now, in some cases, learn little more than their names and the month in which police believe they were last seen:

Lillian O'Dare – September 1978

Rebecca Guno – June 1983

Sherry Rail – November 1983

Marlene Abigosis – January 1984

Sheryl Donahue – May 1985

Laura Mah – August 1985

Elaine Allenbach – March 1986

Taressa Williams – July 1988

Ingrid Soet – August 1989

Elaine Dumba – 1991

Nancy Clark – August 1991

Elsie Sebastian – June 1992

Kathleen Wattley – June 1992

Sherry Baker – January 1993

Gloria Fedyshyn – February 1993

Teresa Triff – April 1993

Leigh Miner – December 1993

Angela Arseneault – August 1994

Catherine Gonzalez – March 1995

Catherine Knight – April 1995

Dorothy Spence – August 1995

Diana Melnick – December 1995

Frances Young – April 1996

Tanya Holyk – October 1996

Olivia William – December 1996

Cara Ellis – January 1997

Marie Laliberte – January 1997

Stephanie Lane – January 1997

Jacqueline Murdock – January 1997

Sharon Ward – February 1997

Andrea Borhaven – March 1997

Kellie Little – April 1997

Sherry Irving – April 1997

Janet Henry – June 1997

Ruby Hardy – July 1997

Cindy Beck – September 1997

Marnie Frey – September 1997

Helen Hallmark – October 1997

Cynthia Feliks – December 1997

Kerri Koski – January 1998

Inga Hall – February 1998

Tania Petersen – February 1998

Sarah de Vries – April 1998

Sheila Egan – July 1998

Julie Young – October 1998

Angela Jardine – November 1998

Marcella Crieson – December 1998

Michelle Gurney – December 1998

Jacquelene McDonell – January 1999

Brenda Wolfe – February 1999

Georgina Papin – March 1999

Wendy Crawford – December 1999

Jennifer Furminger – December 1999

Tiffany Drew – March 2000

Dawn Crey – November 2000

Sharon Abraham – December 2000

Debra Jones – December 2000

Yvonne Boen – March 2001

Patricia Johnson – March 2001

Heather Bottomley – April 2001

Heather Chinnock – April 2001

Andrea Joesbury – June 2001

Sereena Abotsway – August 2001

Dianne Rock – October 2001

Mona Wilson – November 2001

It took quite a long time to carefully type out those names and dates, and it takes a long time to read them, too. Each time I read them I find that as my mind starts to grasp the length of the list my eye sometimes begins to skip past a name here and there, because I am not seeking or pausing upon a name or names of women that I knew. This is the trouble with listing the names of the missing or dead as a memorial practice: names themselves tell us so little, almost nothing, about the women they represent if we did not know them in life, such that even strung together in such a long list like this it is difficult, if not impossible, to take in the significance, the magnitude of the loss that the list represents. This particular list of names is also terribly incomplete, as it encompasses only the names of women designated by police as still "missing" in 2007 – a list of the names of *all* of the murdered or missing women from the Downtown Eastside over the last several decades would span many more pages still. Even more troublingly, some families might prefer that a loved one's name not be recounted in such a list; organizers of the annual Downtown Eastside Women's Memorial March note, for example, that the name of the woman whose murder compelled people to hold the first of these marches in 1991 is no longer mentioned on their website or spoken aloud out of respect for the wishes of the woman's family.[5] As Adrienne Burk recounts, "using a name, among some oral traditions, can disturb the spirit, already suffering, or prematurely still what should be animate" (2003, 330; see also Thrush 2011, 59).

For all these reasons I hesitate to list any names at all, and yet to proceed to describe the events surrounding the disappearance or murder of the women listed here, and in the next paragraph to name for a second time the man convicted or accused of murdering several of them, without having offered even space for their own names seems unethical. Philosopher Jacques Derrida argues that a personal name is of great significance to processes of loss and mourning: "A man's [*sic*] life, as unique as his death," he writes, "will always be more than a paradigm and something other than a symbol. And this is precisely what a proper name should always name" (1994, xiv). While I suspect that names do indeed mark such uniqueness after the loss of someone we know or love, I tend to agree with feminist theorists Judith Butler (1988) and Sharon Rosenberg (2003, 2004, 2005), who argue that names often register quite differently when one did not know the dead who are named in life. At the same time, the importance of naming the dead or disappeared as a practice of remembrance persists, and so I offer this list of names here with an awareness that it is far too small and too simple a gesture.

Where charges have been laid in relation to the disappearance of a woman named on this police list a bit more information about her life is available now to a wider public in the form of a brief, obituary-like personal profile compiled by members of the Canadian Press.[6] Through these profiles we can learn that many of the women had children, or that they had a love of horses or a fondness for singing or cooking or playing softball, or a quirky sense of humour. All the women have friends, families, and lovers or partners who care about them, and in several cases their absence was noticed almost immediately (in contrast to some initial suggestions otherwise). Many, perhaps most, of the women on the police list did outdoor sex work at the time they were last seen and were grappling with an addiction to criminalized drugs, and this is what most of us lacking a personal connection to the women first learned about them. A shockingly disproportionate number of them were also Indigenous women.[7] There remains some debate about how many of the murdered or missing women from the Downtown Eastside were Indigenous, but even conservative estimates suggest that around a third likely were, and this percentage could be as high as half. When one considers that Indigenous women make up just less than 2 per cent of the total population of adult females in Vancouver, it becomes glaringly obvious that their numbers here among the women from the Downtown Eastside who have been murdered or who remain unaccounted for are enormously out of line with their representation in the overall population of the city.[8]

By highlighting the fact that the women who concern me in this book were so disproportionately Indigenous women, I intend to signal that the disappearance of women from the Downtown Eastside in Vancouver is a project of racialized, sexualized, colonial violence, and therefore to follow the lead of organizations such as the Native Women's Association of Canada (NWAC) by situating their disappearances or murders in relation to NWAC's estimation that at least 582 Indigenous women were murdered or remain unaccounted for across the country. The oldest of these cases documented by NWAC is from 1944, but 56 per cent are from 1990 to 2010.[9] The organizers of Walk 4 Justice, an Indigenous non-profit organization co-founded in 2008 by Gladys Radek of the Gitxsan and Wet'suwet'en First Nations, whose niece Tamara Chipman was last seen in 2005 along what has been dubbed the "Highway of Tears" in Northern British Columbia, have long argued that there are over 3000 murdered or missing women in Canada.[10] For her doctoral research, Maryanne Pearce used publicly available information to compile a database of names and details of women murdered or reported missing in Canada between 1946 and 19 September 2013. She identifies 3329 murdered or missing women, including 824 Aboriginal women. And in 2014, just as I was completing final revisions on this book, the RCMP belatedly completed their own review of their files, reporting that the number of murdered or missing Indigenous women in Canada is actually higher still: they discovered 1181 police-recorded incidents of "Aboriginal female homicides and unresolved missing Aboriginal females."[11] Lubicon scholar and activist Robyn Bourgeois points out that although the RCMP report "gives us a good picture of the scope of the problem," the report also problematically "fails to address the role of dominant systems of oppression – colonialism, racism, heteropatriarchy – in this violence," which greatly limits its usefulness and differentiates it significantly from the important research and activism begun decades earlier by NWAC and other Indigenous women's organizations.[12] After more than a decade working on this research project it is now clear that the particular events I focus on in this book – the murders or disappearance of women from Vancouver's Downtown Eastside neighbourhood – *must* be understood as one aspect of a much larger national and international story about the murder or disappearance of Indigenous women rendered more vulnerable to violence by settler colonialism, by how they are constituted as subjects in settler colonialist contexts through racist discourses of disposability.[13] To begin by making these connections is therefore to write explicitly against a common sentiment that the women's violent deaths had less to do with race or colonialism than with gender-based violence, or simply with their own "poor choices" or "high-risk lifestyles." Instead, I agree wholeheartedly with Andrea Smith (2005) when she asserts that "the analysis of and strategies for addressing gender violence have failed to address the manner in which gender violence is not just a tool of patriarchal control, but also serves as a tool of racism and colonialism" (1). As a result, I begin by acknowledging how identity continues to matter and remains crucial to any analysis of these violent events. While necessary and important, it is also true that beginning this way risks framing my, and our, understanding of our relation to the murdered or missing women through the limited and limiting terms of identity categories. This is a tension that I return to over and over again in this book.

But for now, to continue with a version of key events: A much-belated police investigation into some of the many reported cases of missing women from the Downtown Eastside eventually resulted in a lone arrest: a man named Robert William Pickton was charged initially with two counts of first-degree murder in February 2002. By the summer of 2005, after a lengthy forensic investigation on his property in Port Coquitlam (a small city on the outskirts of Vancouver), Pickton was charged with murdering twenty-six of those sixty-five women on the task force's list of missing women and with one additional charge for the murder of an as yet unidentified woman known only as "Jane Doe" (a charge that was set aside by a judge in March 2006). The criminal legal proceedings against Pickton, which received massive media attention, finally came to an end in July 2010 when all avenues for appeal were exhausted; he was convicted of second-degree murder in six of the women's deaths at the conclusion of his trial in 2007, while another trial for the remaining twenty murder charges was at one time slated to begin in early 2008. The Crown opted not to proceed with the remaining charges after Pickton's initial convictions were upheld, however – a decision that brought much grief and anger to some of the family and friends of the women whose murders those twenty charges represent. The provincial inquiry – limited in scope to the police investigation and response of law enforcement and by geography to British Columbia alone – issued its final report in 2012; and now, in 2014, ongoing calls for a national inquiry on murdered or missing Indigenous women in Canada continue to be dismissed by the federal Conservative government. Meanwhile, Downtown Eastside activists and community organizers continue to point out that violence against women, particularly Indigenous women, has not abated since Pickton's arrest.[14] All these details serve as reminders that these are events that are very much ongoing and changing rapidly – I have rewritten this paragraph upwards of twenty times since I began this book, signalling that these events are certainly not *past*, but continue to bear heavily on the present.

Not surprisingly (at least, not to many Indigenous people, or to Downtown Eastside community organizers and activists), the "official" details I have just related only tell quite a small part of this story. Downtown Eastside residents, Indigenous women's groups, sex

workers, activists and advocates, service providers, and many friends
and family members of the women listed as "missing" were already
working to draw attention to the disappearance and violent deaths of
women from the Downtown Eastside long before the police or mainstream press were paying any noticeable attention. In fact, if we include
previously-accounted-for deaths (the deaths of women whose murders
were solved or who were determined to have died of drug overdoses),
then community organizers note that there are many, many more
women from this community who either remain unaccounted for or
died unjust, untimely deaths in the last thirty or so years. For example,
the program of the 15th Annual Vancouver Valentine's Day Memorial
March for women from the Downtown Eastside (held in 2006) lists 224
women's names *in addition* to the names of the women either presumed
murdered by Pickton or still unaccounted for at that time. Several of the
names in this list of 224 are recognizable as those of other women from
the area who were murdered, while many are likely those of women
who died from drug overdoses, for although the program itself states
only "in loving memory of the following women," a banner carried
during the march reads: "February 14th commemorates our sisters who
have died as a result of violence or substance abuse in the Downtown
Eastside and throughout Vancouver." As the Native Women's Association
of Canada (2010) argues:

> Although the immediate circumstances surrounding these deaths [of
> women who died as a result of drugs, alcohol, exposure or suicide] may
> not have been caused by a particular person, the root causes are often
> similar to cases of missing and murdered Aboriginal women and girls,
> such as increased vulnerability due to poor housing, poverty and other
> socio-economic inequalities. (35)

Since the same unjust conditions that increase Indigenous women's vulnerability to violence and murder are also heavily implicated in addiction
to criminalized drugs and death from overdose or suicide, these organizations make an important connection here through their insistence that the
actual number of deaths or disappearances demanding attention from a
wider public is significantly higher than official counts suggest. The fact
that there continues to be so much uncertainty and debate about how
many women are missing or murdered suggests that there is something
the matter with how these disappearances and violent or untimely deaths
have been framed, understood, and contextualized for and by a wider

public, and especially with how they are viewed by many of us who might lack a personal connection to any of the women in our own lives.

It is, I suspect, entirely possible to learn a great deal about the facts of these events, to take in, memorize, recount, and dedicate enormous amounts of time and resources to amassing all the details of what really happened, and yet still avoid grappling with *what lives on* from the violent loss of so many women. This is at least partly so because many of us imagine these events as distant from our own lives – because we did not know the women in life, or because the events are at a distance geographically, or time has passed, or maybe we don't recognize the women as "like us" because of differences that cut across gender, race, class, sexuality, neighbourhood, or something else entirely. And it is precisely this sense of distance that needs to be troubled but – crucially – not collapsed. To put it a bit differently, I argue in this book that a much wider public needs to grapple, individually and collectively, with how we are implicated in these events in order for things to actually change in a meaningful way for women who continue to live with such precarity and vulnerability to violence today. As a result, I try to demonstrate how different ways of representing or recounting these events can affect how implicated or how distanced we might feel. This sense of distance, where it exists, seems crucial to challenge, and yet it also remains important that we avoid erasing differences by imagining that the violent, unjust disappearances or murders of the women who concern me in this book could just as easily have happened to *any* woman. It *matters* in really significant ways that the women disappeared from the Downtown Eastside were disproportionately Indigenous, just as it matters that for the most part they lived in poverty, struggled with addictions, did outdoor sex work, and lived and worked in this particular neighbourhood. Disregarding these differences by imagining that their stories could just as easily be *my* story is another method for avoiding grappling with how I am implicated in the unjust social conditions and arrangements of ongoing settler colonialism, conditions and arrangements that leave some people more vulnerable to violence and disappearance than others. Stumbling towards this complicated balance between proximity and distance in relation to these events is what I aim to do in this book, in the interest of encouraging a much wider public to reckon with what lives on from the loss of so many women from the Downtown Eastside, with what their loss might mean for our own everyday lives.

As I write, the massive, ongoing search for five-year-old Nathan O'Brien and his grandparents, Alvin and Kathy Liknes, has just "gone high tech" with the additional use of a civilian helicopter equipped with aerial geo-referencing and high-resolution photographic capabilities.[15] This seemingly white (so far as I can tell from photographs, an unreliable source to be sure, but because their race did not receive comment in news coverage it seems likely that they are mostly *read* as white), middle-class couple and their grandson were taken from their Calgary home three weeks ago; murder charges have now been laid against a suspect, but the search for their bodies is currently ongoing. Over the past three weeks, I have watched the relentless media coverage of this story and considered how different the public response has been to these particular missing people. The story has remained in news headlines even when there was no new information to report. More than two hundred police officers have been searching "around the clock" for them, according to CBC reports. Hundreds of civilians also formed search parties, and one search organizer reported that volunteers had arrived in Calgary from as far away as Montana, British Columbia, and Saskatchewan.[16] Residents of the Liknes's community in Calgary also hung green ribbons on the outsides of their homes as a show of support for the O'Brien and Liknes families, while hundreds of people across Alberta released green balloons into the sky as a symbol of hope, love, and support after police announced their belief that the three had been murdered. After the murder charges were announced, Prime Minister Stephen Harper himself tweeted that his thoughts and prayers were with the O'Brien and Liknes families. This is a story about missing people that "has gripped the entire country," writes *Calgary Herald* journalist Valerie Fortney, and indeed at the time, given the coverage but also the casual conversations and the outpourings of public support and grief, it did feel as though this were true.[17] It would be a callous misreading of my argument to imagine that I draw attention to this massive outpouring of public attention and concern for Nathan O'Brien and his grandparents in order to question whether it was justified. Of course it was. Instead, in this book, I ask why a similar outpouring of widespread public attention and concern was *not* initially paid to the disappearance of so many women from Vancouver's Downtown Eastside. The answer may seem obvious to some, but it is this very obviousness that I think we must question and challenge if we hope to eliminate the disparities in our collective responses to lives cast as "grievable" or "ungrievable" that make such vast discrepancies in how we attend and respond to missing people possible in the first place.

REMEMBERING VANCOUVER'S DISAPPEARED WOMEN

Settler Colonialism and the Difficulty of Inheritance

Inheriting What Lives On

In January 2011, the Museum of Anthropology (MOA) at the University of British Columbia cancelled a scheduled exhibition of artist Pamela Masik's *The Forgotten* project, an exhibit consisting of enormous, eight-foot by ten-foot portraits of 69 women presumed murdered or missing from Vancouver's Downtown Eastside. The MOA cited a desire to avoid causing further distress to family or friends of the women as their main motivation for cancelling the show, along with serious concerns about whether the exhibit would spark the kinds of productive dialogue they had hoped for.[1] Controversy over Masik's portraits erupted at least the summer before her exhibit was cancelled, though, when she spoke on a conference panel at Simon Fraser University's downtown campus. There, Downtown Eastside activists and representatives of Indigenous women's groups raised critical questions about how Masik, a white artist from a nearby but significantly more prosperous neighbourhood, was publicly representing herself in relation to the women she painted and in relation to Indigenous women's long-standing organizing and activism in the neighbourhood. In response to such concerns, Masik repeatedly described herself as a *witness* to murdered or missing women from the Downtown Eastside; as she stated in the MOA's press release announcing the cancellation of her show: "I saw my role as an artist to bear witness to the 69 women who were marginalized." The controversy surrounding Masik and her exhibit offers an apt illustration of the central concerns of this book, in that it points to the limits of a particular approach to bearing witness to the suffering of others. In this more limited approach, the witness, despite good intentions, tends to collapse differences between themselves and those who suffered violence first-hand, erasing complex histories in ways that make it difficult to see how wider social contexts are related to the injustice or violence being witnessed. As a result, in this book I argue instead that coming to recognize ourselves as *inheritors of what lives on* from the disappearance and violent deaths of so many women might prompt more ethical encounters between the living and the dead than the more limited approach to bearing witness evident in the exhibit *The Forgotten*.

The cancellation of *The Forgotten* at the MOA received much national media attention, and although most reporters turned to Masik and the MOA's director to explain the reasons for the decision, a handful of mainstream news broadcasts or articles (as well as several pieces in the alternative press and the blogosphere) featured comments from women involved in organizing the annual Women's Memorial March for murdered or missing women from the Downtown Eastside. The *Vancouver Province*'s coverage, for example, includes the following statement from March organizer Corinthia Kelly: "'The Forgotten' does nothing to stop the violence against women in this community. It exoticizes them and turns them into commodities to promote the 'Masik brand.'" Gloria Larocque, another March organizer, is identified in the same article as the source of concerns that "the show would have made Masik the 'spokesperson' for aboriginal women's issues, denying the efforts and voice of aboriginal and Downtown Eastside women, as well as causing pain to family members of the murdered and disappeared."[2] Meg Pinto reports that in August 2010, members of the Women's Memorial March Committee sent an email to the MOA's director outlining similar concerns about Masik's exhibit. Part of that email included the following statement:

> First Nations women, the life givers, are best empowered by inviting them to be heard in a respectful and honourable way. We have, in our midst, many powerful and articulate First Nations women ... [who] would have been more appropriate choices since they have demonstrated their awareness and commitment to accurately and respectfully honour women living on the margins. (cited in Pinto 2013, 10)

These criticisms of *The Forgotten* (and of the MOA's decision to host the exhibit) suggest that many local Indigenous women – women with greater proximity and more shared markers of identity with the women who were murdered or missing – had not been consulted or included in the process of selecting *The Forgotten* for exhibition, and the twenty years of activism and remembrance exemplified by the annual Women's Memorial March was also at risk of being erased by the suggestion that the exhibit represented "forgotten" women.

As many commentators have noted, to suggest that these are "forgotten" women discounts the important work done for decades now by friends, lovers, families, and local community organizers to draw attention to the disappearances and murders of so many women and to publicly mourn and memorialize their loss. In her essay on Masik's exhibit, literary critic Laura Moss reminds us that "the underlying – and somewhat grotesque – assumption … is that the women were without a community that might mourn their losses un-obliviously, and they needed Masik's representational grief" (2012, 54). The families and friends of murdered or missing women were not all in favour of the cancellation; some expressed disappointment and frustration about the decision, as they had been hoping the exhibit would bring further attention to the issue and, like the MOA, that it could spark further dialogue throughout the city. But the salient arguments of the women who organize the annual Women's Memorial March raise a number of important questions about the many ways that differences – of history, race, and class in particular – structure and produce differing vulnerabilities to violence, as well as differing opportunities to speak and to be *heard* and *listened to* in dialogues about how best to remember or represent such violence in public places.

Drawing on the work of memory scholars such as Roger I. Simon (2005, 2006, 2013) and Sharon Rosenberg (2000, 2003, 2004, 2009, 2010), I argue in this book that coming to care, or trying to persuade others to care, about violence on the basis of an assumption that "this could have happened to me or someone I love" is insufficient as an ethical *or* political response to violence suffered by others, especially by others whose histories or identities are quite different from our own. A promotional video for *The Forgotten* cultivates such an assumption through a caption that reads: "There is no separation between 'us' and 'them.'" The inclusion of a self-portrait in *The Forgotten* would also have risked inviting viewers to make such assumptions when interpreting the exhibit, and Masik made several public statements linking herself to the women she painted through a shared history of gender-based violence. The MOA, too, planned to frame the exhibit as an opportunity to discuss "the larger issue of violence against women worldwide" (Pinto 2013, 9). Certainly, the violence that murdered or missing women from the Downtown Eastside experienced *is* gender-based, but in this instance, as Gloria Laroque and Corinthia Kelly made clear to the MOA, deploying a primary framework of gender-based violence de-races the histories of injustice and colonialism that contribute to the overrepresentation of Indigenous women in the Downtown Eastside and among those murdered (ibid., 7–8). Such a framework might risk inviting non-Indigenous settler-viewers in particular to imagine that the violence experienced by the women in Masik's portraits could just as easily be, to draw on Roger Simon, "a version of [our] own stories" (2006, 188). As feminist theorists Marianne Hirsch and Valerie Smith insist, ethical responses to trauma and violence may well require "empathy as well as distance – being able to say 'it could have been me' but at the same time asserting that 'it was not me'" (2002, 10). Perhaps in an effort to challenge the latter more distant response, *The Forgotten* would have relied too heavily on the former, imaginatively implying a proximity that risks erasing difference and the many reasons difference *matters* to our understanding of the violence this art represents. It seems extremely unlikely that viewers of *The Forgotten* would have come away with any sense of how or why the historical conflicts and ongoing injustices of settler colonialism are related to the disappearance of so many Indigenous women today – extremely unlikely, then, that pushing for better, more just relations between settler and Indigenous communities would come to mind for viewers as an important ethical and political response to the violent losses that the portraits represent.

The exhibit *The Forgotten* exposes us to the limits of an empathetic, well-intentioned approach to witnessing which aims to raise awareness about violence and suffering primarily through calling upon universalizing frameworks that collapse differences and erase complex histories. The controversy surrounding the exhibit caused me to reflect on how overdetermined the language of *bearing witness* has become, given how often it seems to get used today to describe an empathetic or compassionate response to violence, suffering, or loss that stops short of a reconsideration of how we are ourselves necessarily *implicated* in the violence or suffering experienced by others. Simon, a scholar whose work on practices of cultural memory in the aftermath of mass systemic violence has had a profound impact on my own thinking, argues that art or artefacts that testify to traumatic pasts and historical injustices often arrive

in the public realm making an unanticipated claim that may interrupt one's self-sufficiency, demanding attentiveness to another's life *without reducing that life to a version of one's own stories*. This attentiveness sets out the possibility of learning anew how to live in the present with each other, not only by opening the question to what and to whom I must be accountable, but also by considering what attention, learning, and actions such accountability requires. (2006, 188, emphasis added)

While *The Forgotten* might well have evoked the kind of empathetic affective response frequently associated today with bearing witness, it seems highly unlikely to make the sort of "unanticipated claim" on its viewers that Simon calls for because it risks both depoliticizing and universalizing the violence experienced by women who are so disproportionately Indigenous as violence that is potentially inflicted on *any* woman, divorcing this violence from its colonial underpinnings.

In this book I shift away from advocating that a wider public should bear witness to the disappearance of women from the Downtown Eastside and instead advocate that we adopt and develop "practices of inheritance" (Simon 2006, 187; see also Simon 2005 and Simon, Rosenberg, and Eppert 2000). What might it mean to inherit what lives on from the disappearance of so many women, and why should a wider public engage in such practices, even – or perhaps especially – when we did not know the women in life? Simon describes practices of inheritance as follows: "A practice whose outcome is not guaranteed in advance, the work of inheritance is an inescapable consequence of the actions of another who has sent you something ... that implicates you in the necessity of a response (even if that response is ultimately to ignore or destroy the bequest)" (2006, 194). In this book I expand on the tensions, qualities, and conditions of possibility for developing (more) ethical practices of inheriting what lives on from the violent loss of so many women, which I argue requires us to recognize and grapple with the wider social context of settler colonialism that underpins these events. Such practices of inheritance might then support and encourage more of us to take responsibility for the significant shifts in how we see ourselves in relation to others that are necessary for stopping the ongoing violence experienced by too many women from the Downtown Eastside neighbourhood. While political, economic, and cultural changes are also vitally important and necessary to end this violence, it is my contention that without significant shifts in how we see and understand ourselves as already in relation to others, changes in these other arenas are unlikely to be more than piecemeal at best. In the pages ahead, I reflect critically on my own evolving practice of inheriting what lives on from the violent loss of so many women, but I also attempt to hail a wider public into such practices in the interests of conceiving the conditions necessary for an everyday social life premised on more just relations between people who may be situated quite differently across categories of race, gender, sexuality, class, culture, and geography. I discern some of the textures and nuances of these practices of inheritance in the interests of contemplating the qualities of (more) ethical encounters between the living and the dead, but also between those who continue to struggle, with varying degrees of proximity, against similar forms of injustice and violence daily and those who are living lives quite distant from such forms of injustice and violence.

This is not to say that there is no value to the language or act of bearing witness, or that practices of witnessing and practices of inheritance are somehow entirely different. Indeed, while I draw upon Roger Simon's work to develop the practices of inheritance I outline in this book, Simon's last book argues for a *Pedagogy of Witnessing* (2014), which I imagine will be equally important to the sorts of practices of inheritance I advocate for here. There are certainly much more complex approaches to witnessing cultivated in memorials, art, and activism, approaches that consider "how ... art [can] be conceived as a vehicle for bearing witness that recognizes both the responsibilities that attend to such an engagement *and* the limits of empathy" (Lauzon 2010, 76). As trauma theorist Jill Bennett (2005) rightly insists, affective responses to art must be subjected to critical interrogation in order to "produce a form of empathy that is more complex and considered than a purely emotional or sentimental reaction" (24). A more "complex and considered" form of empathic engagement seems crucial for developing practices of inheritance, and so throughout this book I explore some of the ways that such engagements might be more widely evoked and sustained. But because the act of bearing witness is so often today conflated with the kinds of empathic over-identifications with the suffering of others that *The Forgotten* exemplifies, for this book I sought language that could distinguish the significant differences between that particular approach to bearing witness and the practices of inheritance I want to advocate.

These differences are crucial because I am even more of an outsider to the Downtown Eastside community than Masik – I have never lived in the neighbourhood or been involved with community groups or organizing in an ongoing way, nor have I even called the city of Vancouver home since 2005. Thus, from a geographical point of view I am quite removed from directly witnessing, in the more literal sense, many of the events that concern me in this book. Like Masik, I am also a woman racially marked as white, and I am working as a professor at a university (with all the financial and cultural capital such a position accrues), living a life quite protected from the forms of vulnerability and violence that many women living in the Downtown Eastside contend with daily. And I am also in a line of work that has a long history of exploiting marginalized communities in its own interests, one for which the old adage "publish or perish" remains true – thereby inviting similar questions about careerism to those that some critics raised about *The Forgotten*. Also like Masik, I have at times been pushed by some Downtown Eastside activists or family members of murdered or missing women to better explain my research and writing on this topic and to be more explicit about my own interests and my approaches to doing this work. As a result, I imagine that this book will – and should – inspire similar challenges, questions, and critiques.

All these factors might understandably cause readers to question whether I am the right person to write a book on this topic. Given my distance – racially, geographically, and socio-economically – from the events I write about, I at times wonder this myself. And yet, as the flip side to the troubling approach to bearing witness exemplified by *The Forgotten*, there also remains a pervasively widespread tendency among people with whom I share more markers of identity to emphasize our distance from such events and ignore our proximity, and this distancing is something that I aim to challenge as well. It is necessary, I argue, to avoid overstating one's proximity to the histories and events that underpin the disappearance of so many women (by collapsing significant differences of race and class, for example). And yet, at the same time, I aim to challenge the idea that *any of us* are actually so distant from these histories or events that we can legitimately dismiss them as none of our concern. Haudenosaunee scholar Susan M. Hill argues that proximity and distance matter a great deal to the question of who is in the best position to conduct certain forms of research, but that those who might not belong to a particular community may still have something to contribute. As she writes:

> While it is critical that Haudenosaunee people play a central role in the production and analysis of our history, there remains room for non-Haudenosaunee to also be involved, especially in ... research that examines the relationships between the Haudenosaunee and other nations, including both Indigenous and settler peoples. (2009, 488–9)

I contend that settler peoples are often less likely to recognize (or, perhaps more accurately, more likely to *mis*recognize) our proximity to the events that concern me in this book, and so unpacking and underscoring *our* relationships – the relations of settlers – to the ongoing colonialism that underpins the disappearance and murders of disproportionately Indigenous women from the Downtown Eastside is a central concern of this book.

My own practices of inheritance involve unpacking where and how I am *in* the story of the disappearance of so many women from the Downtown Eastside, and how that realization might change me, how it "refashions the social relations in which [I am] located" (Gordon 1997, 22). This is quite a different thing from suggesting that this story is, or could just as easily be, my own story. Such practices therefore require that we resist locating ourselves at such a distance from others' suffering that it appears to have little or nothing to do with who, where, and what we are in the present, but simultaneously that we resist claiming the suffering of others as (a version of) our own. I therefore take seriously the challenge of locating myself *in relation* to the events I write about in this book, disrupting overly simplistic self/other binaries, yet, crucially, not collapsing them.

A much richer, stronger understanding of our relations to other beings – both human and non-human – and our responsibilities for those relations exists in many Indigenous epistemologies, perhaps better described as cosmologies, as Mohawk and Anishnaabe scholar Vanessa Watts insists. Building on Haudenosaunee understandings of Place-Thought, which is "based upon the premise that land is alive and thinking and that humans and non-humans derive agency through the extensions of these thoughts" (2013, 21), Watts insists that a Euro-Western epistemological-ontological frame greatly limits the extent to which those of us who operate through such a frame can comprehend, appreciate, or take responsibility for our relations to all other beings, including the land we make our lives upon, because through such a frame we are encouraged to understand our ways of knowing the world as separable from our understanding of who/what we *are* in relation to this world. Such a frame always posits the ability to reason (presumed to exclusively reside in humans) as superior or at least as distinct from an awareness of how our agency and our sense of our relations and responsibilities to others derive from place. In Place-Though, by contrast, as Watts explains, human relations to each other, to other non-human beings, and to spirit are not hierarchical, nor can humans be understood as the only beings with thought, desire, or agency. Watts argues that the difference in these frameworks can help us understand why Indigenous women are disproportionately subjected to violence: "In an attempt to conquer such people, where would you start? Our land and our women, disabling communication with Place-Thought, and implementing a bounded agency where women are sub-human/non-human" (31). In order to understand the extremely high rates of violence against Indigenous women, then, we have to interrogate how Western frameworks for understanding what it means to be a "self," and in particularly liberal humanist assumptions about rational, freely choosing autonomous selfhood, are profoundly implicated in the continuation of such violence.

But as Watts cautions, it would be a mistake to interpret Indigenous cosmologies that insist on the indelible relations between beings and land as "examples of a *symbolic* interconnectedness – an abstraction of a moral code" (26, emphasis added). To do so would be to interpret them yet again through a Euro-Western framework. Instead, Watts insists that these cosmologies are "more than a lesson, a teaching, or even an historical account"; they are world views that "directly extend to our philosophies, thoughts and actions as Haudenosaunee peoples" (26). There is a risk, she insists, that when interpreted through the dominant, Euro-Western frame, Indigenous cosmologies and Indigenous peoples become merely "a gateway for non-Indigenous thinkers to re-imagine their world." As she continues: "In this, our stories are often distilled to simply that – words, principles, morals to imagine the world and imagine ourselves in the world. In reading stories this way, non-Indigenous people also keep control over what agency is and how it is dispersed in the hands of humans" (26). Bearing this significant risk in mind, my desire to insist that understandings of how we are related to and responsible for other beings (including non-human ones) are richer and more complex in much Indigenous thought than they are in Euro-Western thought should be interpreted not as a moral lesson or an opportunity to simply reimagine the present world through an Indigenous frame, but rather as an insistence that dominant Euro-Western understandings of agency and responsibility can be limited and limiting, and they are certainly not the only way of making sense of who we are and of how we are related to others or to the land on which we find ourselves. In fact, colonization makes it virtually impossible for us (all) to engage with the complex ideas about agency, responsibility, and relations to other beings and to land evident in Indigenous thought because, as Mohawk scholar Taiaiake Alfred insists, "colonization is a process of *disconnecting* us from our responsibilities to one another and our respect for one another, our responsibilities and our respect for the land, and our responsibilities and respect for the culture" (2009, 5, emphasis added). While he is addressing Indigenous readers, I believe that Alfred's point is also relevant for settlers: as a non-Indigenous person, colonization has also disconnected me from the responsibilities he outlines, although through vastly different processes that ascribe privilege to my white skin and to the so-called superiority of Western world views. According to Mi'kmaw scholar and educator Marie Battiste and Chickasaw scholar and lawyer James (Sa'ke'j) Youngblood Henderson, "meeting the responsibility of challenging these [Eurocentric, imperialist] frameworks is not just a task for the colonized and oppressed; it is the defining challenge and the path to a shared and sustainable future for all peoples" (Battiste and Henderson 2000, 12).

That so many of the murdered or missing women from the Downtown Eastside are Indigenous suggests that one cannot begin to understand or counter the social conditions and arrangements that left these particular women more vulnerable to such violence without contending with Canada's colonial histories and their legacies – with evidence of rampant, ongoing colonialism in the present. That so many of them were also doing outdoor sex work when they were last seen suggests that one must also contend with the social stigmas surrounding sex work and with widespread social anxieties about sexuality in general and Indigenous-settler sexual encounters in particular. That so many of the women lived in dire poverty and experienced numerous forms of criminalization, not just of their sex work but also of their addictions and many of their other mechanisms for survival suggests that vast socio-economic disparities also underpin this story, disparities that expose the lie of conventional renderings of Canada as a classless society with a wide social safety net and strong commitment to protecting human rights.

By suggesting that these forms of pervasive injustice are social *arrangements*, I mean to imply that there remains fairly widespread complicity in maintaining such unjust conditions, which are too often perceived as natural, normal, or simply "the way things are." That some deaths are quite clearly rendered in a national imaginary as mattering more than others conveys something crucial, I contend, about unspoken arrangements that tend to overdetermine who gets widely recognized as living what Judith Butler calls a "grievable life" (see Dean 2013 for an elaboration of this point). Building on Butler's work with the concept of "grievability" in *Precarious Life* (2004) and *Frames of War* (2009), in this book I aim to provide an illustration of how "grievability" works to produce some lives (and deaths) as mattering more than others. "Some lives are grievable," Butler writes, "and others are not": "The differential allocation of grievability that decides what kind of subject is and must be grieved, and which kind of subject must not, operates to produce and maintain certain exclusionary conceptions of who is normatively human: what counts as a livable life and a grievable death?" (2004, xiv–xv). As Downtown Eastside poet and activist Bud Osborn puts it, there exists "a social apartheid in our culture / the segregation of those who deserve to live / and those who are abandoned to die" (cited in Campbell, Boyd, and Culbert 2009, 109).

I aim to bring what remains too often unspoken in this arrangement into wider conversation and awareness: namely, that whether one's death is widely deemed to *matter* to others depends in large part, still, on whether one's life was marked by the privileges adhering to whiteness, by what Sunera Thobani calls the "exalted" status of the Canadian national subject, by adherence to conventional norms of gender and sexuality, as well as by whether one died rich or poor, or lived in a space that gets talked about as a "good" neighbourhood (an idea made possible only in contrast to spaces that come to be associated with crime, poverty, the visual signs of addiction and outdoor sex work, and frequently with immigrant, black, or Indigenous communities, or what is sometimes described as "racial mixing"). These are the sorts of social arrangements that are both further entrenched by and simultaneously used to rationalize a host of unjust social conditions, and these conditions and arrangements combine to make it possible that so many women could disappear over such a long stretch of time with so little widespread public outcry. They are therefore the kinds of social conditions and arrangements that I – and many others – feel compelled to contest.

When I suggest that there has been little widespread public outcry about the disappearance of women from the Downtown Eastside, it is not my intention to exclude the important activism done by Downtown Eastside residents, Indigenous women's groups, sex-worker organizations, and family and friends of some of the murdered or missing women, which has most certainly constituted a decades-old public outcry and began many years before the police or mainstream media started to pay any serious attention to the disappearances. Instead, I am endeavouring to argue that the lack of a much more widespread willingness to contend with the important claims of these mourners and activists conveys just how much unspoken agreements about what qualifies as a "grievable life" continue to prioritize widespread public attention for certain deaths and certain losses, and not for others.

Murdered or missing women from the Downtown Eastside were initially cast as ungrievable losses due to how their absence at first seemed to merit little media or police attention, and then subsequently because of how they were repeatedly marked in media reportage and by police officials and politicians as "prostitutes" or "hookers," as "drug addicts," and more subtly as impoverished and racialized "others": in other words, by how they were framed as simply not belonging to hegemonic conceptions of the normatively human. Driven by a desire to evoke a fuller, more complex, less stereotypical, and less stigmatized representation of their missing loved ones, friends and family of several murdered or missing women worked tirelessly to publicly and repeatedly insist instead upon their grievability. As a result of their advocacy there has been a noticeable shift in how murdered or missing women are represented in mainstream media and official discourse – from an utter lack of representation at all; to representations that, although often sympathetic, still relied on stereotypes about the Downtown Eastside and about sex work that were stigmatizing and dehumanizing; to an increasing number of representations that make a noticeable effort to "humanize" the women or portray them in a more conventionally "flattering" way.[3]

This shift has proved an important – perhaps essential – political strategy, one that helped persuade officials to finally begin to take seriously and attempt to account for the significant numbers of women missing from this neighbourhood. And yet, accepting the rhetorical terms and conceptual frameworks that necessitate *proving* the grievability and "human-ness" of the lives of murdered or missing women risks inadvertently reproducing the idea that some lives *are* actually grievable while others are not (or are somehow naturally or understandably less so). So, for example, some representations of murdered or missing women try to distance the women from sex work, addiction, and the Downtown Eastside, understandably but troublingly accepting as natural (and thereby reinforcing) the stigmatization of these facets of the women's lives and the ways they are deployed to support assumptions that some deaths do – and should – matter more than others to a wider public. As geographer David Hugill argues about some of the later media representations that focus on "humanizing" the women by distancing them from stigma, such stories

> represent a genuine effort to restore dignity to a group of relentlessly stigmatized women. Yet in another sense, they operate to entrench a binary between the presumed authenticity and innate humanness of traditional familial roles (mother, sister, daughter) on the one hand, and the sub-humanity of street-involvement on the other. (2010, 65)

As sociology and social-work scholars Caitlin Janzen, Susan Strega, Leslie Brown, Jeannie Morgan, and Jeannine Carrière similarly argue, "the *amount* of recent coverage has not opened up *what can be said* about sex work or sex workers in the public sphere" (2013, 144, emphasis added). This tension between frameworks for understanding what makes a life grievable, which variably humanize or dehumanize but with strikingly similar limitations, is one I come back to throughout this book. Although it is a tension that I cannot fully resolve, I do uncover some of the facets or qualities of representations of murdered or missing women that I believe negotiate this tension without either dismissing the risks of dehumanization or falling into the trap of "humanizing" at any cost.

There is a link, Butler argues, between ungrievability and violence, between being constituted as outside of the human, as outside of the "real," and our ability to recognize violence *as* violence. "If violence is done against those who are unreal," she writes, "then, from the perspective of violence, it fails to injure or negate those lives since those lives are already negated" (2004, 33). Because the lives of murdered or missing women were, at least initially, so often cast as ungrievable, cast as outside of a hegemonic frame for recognizing what makes us human, in part through how their disappearances were for a long time not considered newsworthy or described in any way as mattering to Canadians on a national scale, I argue that there is a link between that casting and the violence that ended the lives of so many women. The injustice they suffered is thus not only a matter of the violence they experienced at the end of their lives, but also a matter of a pre-existing, widespread non-response to everyday forms of misogynist, racist, colonialist, classist violence and erasure, which predicts the final act of violence, in a way, by negating that life as a life that matters, again and again. It is this wider social context of negation and indifference that can be usefully articulated through Butler's development of the concept of grievability.

I am not suggesting that the majority of people who did not know any of the murdered or missing women in life feel no compassion about their deaths, for one only need consult the guest books of websites like missingpeople.net or the comments posted to online news stories to find a wealth of evidence to the contrary. Instead, I note that it is very possible to feel compassion or even grief in response to the women's murders and still maintain that their deaths have nothing to do with wider social contexts like settler colonialism. So, for example, those who express compassion or grief over the loss of so many women are, at times, the same people who will argue that colonialism is "over and done with" or has "nothing to do with me," blaming instead one's settler-ancestors or history's political figureheads (such remarks are often made by white people, though not exclusively). Similarly, a compassionate view of murdered sex workers can apparently coexist quite comfortably with the repetition of what Gail Pheterson (1993) calls "whore stigma," as evidenced by comments along the lines of "it's a shame what happened to those women, but women who sell themselves like that and get into stranger's cars on some level must know what might happen," comments that forget how the criminalization of sex work combined with the effects of colonialism, poverty, and sexism leave many women without the ability to set the terms of their sexual labour, or with few other options. And a compassionate view towards murdered women from the Downtown Eastside has often been expressed by politicians, journalists, civic officials, and urban development boosters who simultaneously propose, sanction, or enact policies and practices that contribute to further displacing and marginalizing many people who live or work in the Downtown Eastside neighbourhood today. So it seems quite possible to come to recognize murdered or missing women's lives as grievable but still resist accepting responsibility for how we are all *implicated* – albeit very differently – in the social conditions and arrangements that made those deaths appear ungrievable to so many people in the first place.

The following provocative questions from Vancouver-based cultural theorist, artist, and activist Margot Leigh Butler (2003) are helpful, I find, for thinking about what it might mean to recognize ourselves as implicated in the social conditions and arrangements that shape and delimit the events that concern me in this book:

What is "implicatedness"? What if it was considered a practice, a method, a technology for noticing and engaging with what we're part of, within relations of power? And if "implicatedness" is ... an approach to felt, involved and involving, lived politics, can we, with it, reconstrue our political engagements and possibilities? (n.p.)

Similarly, art historian Charlotte Townsend-Gault (2004) argues that feeling implicated can move us beyond the role of spectator in relation to the suffering of others. This sense of implication can be evoked, she argues, by cultural productions that address us, but only if we acknowledge the address and are then "drawn into affective relations with" that which we previously held apart from or outside of our sense of ourselves or our everyday lives (53). In her research on Indigenous law and literature, literary scholar Cheryl Suzack argues that "affective listening is necessary to conceptualize the human situations represented by Aboriginal women's stories," as such listening "may generate a form of political intervention that is not enabled by legal contexts but is urgently needed by them" (2010, 136). These affective relations must be at once affective and critical, reflexive and political, then, in order to escape the empathetic traps that invite a collapsing of others' stories into our own. For, as Paulette Regan insists, empathy in response to Indigenous people's testimonies about suffering and trauma can in fact act as a barrier "to transformative socio-political change," and while it may be "well intentioned, it is still colonial in nature" (2010, 11–12). Deena Rymhs similarly contends that the political claims of Aboriginal people often produce little beyond "an affective response from the national community," which risks inviting settlers to wallow in affects like guilt, pity, or even compassion, resulting in "a discursive re-enactment of past roles that overlooks the distance that Aboriginal people are asserting as they redraw notions of governance, political identity, and nationhood" (2006, 109). Without attending to the necessity of widespread change, without "reconstru[ing] our political engagements and possibilities," as Margot Leigh Butler advocates above, empathy alone can (re)colonize the stories, lives, and even the suffering of others (see also Simon 2013). Implicatedness, by contrast, evokes forms of empathic or felt engagement that necessarily tie feeling to responsibility, leading us towards practices of inheritance.

In this book I aim to encourage an "us," a wider public, to recognize ourselves as implicated in acts of violence that we did not directly commit. Importantly, many people already feel this sense of implication, and I certainly do not wish to imply otherwise – in fact, I am hopeful that those who already recognize ourselves as part of this "we" might still find ways of staying in conversation through this book. At the same time, those of us who are routinely marked by whiteness and the privileges that accrue to that marking, who are likely to experience the "exaltation" that critical race, postcolonial, and feminist theorist Sunera Thobani notes is common among those easily recognized as "legitimate" national subjects in Canada, are, generally speaking, far less likely to recognize this sense of our own implication in this (ongoing) violence. This wider public is impossible to neatly pin down through reference to identity categories, and yet those who tend to see the colonial injustices of the past as thoroughly and only historical, and to view the evidence of those injustices in the present as mere signs of individual failings rather than as symptoms of how the past lives on, are perhaps less likely to feel implicated in the events contributing to the disappearance of so many women, and it is *this* sense of distance that this book also aims to question and challenge.

To suggest that the "we" I address and the "us" I aim to provoke are completely unmoored from identity, then, seems untenable, even though these pronouns also cannot be mapped neatly to particular identities in any absolute or totalizing way. As Irit Rogoff compellingly explains about her own use of the "we" pronoun:

> Well, the "we" I have in mind is not identity-based – it cannot be found in the named categories by which an identity is currently recognized in the world. Rather, it comes into being fleetingly as we negotiate a problem, a mood, a textual encounter, a moment of recognition ... Those who agree to a suspension of the purely critical, to momentarily shared imaginaries, to a bit of groundlessness, lost and regained – that's us, that's who I mean. (2005, 123–4)

Here, the use of "we" as a mode of address aims to actually create collectives across differences of identity, collectives that nonetheless share particular understandings, imaginings, or political commitments. I too intend my use of the pronouns "we" and "us" in this book to work politically to *form* such a collective rather than to mark a pre-existing one. This intentional and strategic creation of a collective through "momentarily shared imaginaries" is my hopeful way of trying to contribute to a more widespread sense of implication in the events this book examines. And because I suspect that cultural productions (including memorials) can at times be especially effective at evoking imaginaries of the sort that might encourage or support a wider public to recognize our implicatedness in these events, I examine a wide array of such productions and memorials in this book, reading them for how they might succeed or, on the other hand, how they seem unlikely to evoke such a sense of implication in those of us who encounter them.

The cultural productions or texts that I analyse in this book include police posters, documentary films, photography and news stories, life-writing and poetry, performance and visual art, and memorials that take the form of marches, murals, benches, and monuments.[4] Not all of these explicitly represent murdered or missing women from the Downtown Eastside, as sometimes it is the women's absence that strikes me as significant. I have chosen to focus my analysis on the particular cultural productions discussed in this book because they each reveal something significant about the potential for such artefacts or events to provoke this sense of implicatedness in readers or viewers, the kind of implicatedness that could encourage a wider public to begin to recognize ourselves as inheritors of what lives on from the disappearance and murder of so many women and to therefore engage in practices of inheritance as an aspect of our everyday living. Most of my analysis therefore focuses on cultural productions that I suspect hold great potential for evoking that much wider sense of implicatedness, but at times I also discuss a particular cultural production because I think it is especially *un*likely to evoke such a sense in order to explore and try to better understand how this notion of implication works.

Cultural productions that seem less likely to evoke a wider sense of implicatedness in these events tend to rely heavily on stereotypes about "the prostitute" or "the drug addict," about Indigenous women, or about the Downtown Eastside in order to figure or "fix" their subjects in very narrow ways, denying them a complex human-ness or, at times, any human-ness at all. Art critic Ernst Van Alphen insists that evocations of such fixity are "constitutive elements of colonial discourse" (1999, 269) and that the traumatic effects of colonialism are frequently (re)invoked by cultural productions that employ such fixity as a rhetorical or visual strategy. As he explains:

> The harmfulness of the stereotype resides in its function of maintaining an ideological construction of otherness ... But images can also do harm more directly, and in a really painful way. Such damage relates less to the constative content of the image than to its performative effect: what it does to the world, or more specifically, to viewers who look at it. (269–70)

Van Alphen offers an analysis of a series of representations that risk evoking both "a traumatised collective historical memory" for viewers from previously or still-colonized nations or communities and a "repetition of colonialism for the other – white – audience" (271, 273). He is concerned with the ways that such images might impact different viewers *differently*, with how "representations of racism perform differently according to the public they address" (272). His insights offer a method for distinguishing between the sorts of cultural productions likely to evoke a wider sense of implicatedness in traumatic colonial histories and their legacies, versus those that seem merely more likely to reproduce colonizer/colonized binaries. As a result of the potentially (and differentially) harmful effects of such representations, Van Alphen is critical of "the practice of lavishly reproducing objectionable images in the context of a critique of colonialism" (272). I take this precaution to heart; while I cannot help but point to some cultural productions that figure the subjects of my analysis in harmful ways, I do try to avoid unnecessarily or lavishly reproducing them throughout the book.

Van Alphen's insights also call attention to the sorts of ethical issues that arise when one sets out to critique often very well-intentioned but sometimes also potentially quite harmful representations, memorials, activism, or other forms of cultural production that aim to convey stories or memories of murdered or missing women to a wider public. There is a way in which *any* critique of these sorts of cultural productions might appear unethical by its very nature, since these productions are so often performed, created by, or at least hold special meaning for those with close proximity to the losses they mark. The Cultural Memory Group (2006) asserts a strong connection between critical analysis and betrayal when they write that in their own research on memorials dedicated to murdered women they "intend to be true to those who have given us access to [their memorial] processes, not betraying their trust by an unrealistically purist, overly critical or unrelentingly interrogative analysis" (23). And yet, I do tend to agree with the sentiment expressed by Wendy Brown (2005) when she writes that "critique is not equivalent to rejection or denunciation ... The call to rethink something is not inherently treasonous but can actually be a way of caring for and even renewing the object in question" (x). Cultural productions that convey the stories of the murdered or missing women from Vancouver's Downtown Eastside to a wider public have continued to abound and proliferate over the years, so it seems to me that critical analysis of the many potential readings, meanings, or material effects of such representations is necessary. Not to do so potentially does a disservice to those productions and their creators, for critique can be a way of taking their work seriously, of offering interpretations that might strengthen such work in the future.

So while I am certainly aware of the difficult ethical terrain crossed by critiques of well-intentioned cultural responses to violence, suffering, and loss, I am also uncomfortable with the often too-easy equation of critique with rejection or betrayal, for it seems to me that the question of whether a practice of critique can be ethical or not has much more to do with its *form* than with its capacity to be critical. For example, I find that conventional approaches to critique are sometimes limited by their tradition of remove or distance from their objects of investigation, as it is precisely a tendency to distance ourselves from the suffering or violence experienced by others that I want my practice of critique to work against. Traditionally, critique also tends to position the author as authoritative, foregoing uncertainty and tentativeness in pursuit of definitive knowledge, academic expertise, and mastery of a particular field or body of literature. Yet uncertainty and hesitation have become characteristic of my reaction to the material I write about in this book; in fact, too much certainty seems to do a kind of injustice to the stunning complexity that surrounds the events that concern me here. Also dissatisfied with critique as it is conventionally practiced, Irit Rogoff (2005) advocates for a shift towards a form of writing that she calls "criticality," which moves "from finding fault, to examining the underlying assumptions that might allow something to appear as a convincing logic ... to *operating from an uncertain ground*" (119, emphasis added). While critique remains important here (indeed, for Rogoff, criticality crucially builds on critique), Rogoff is looking for an approach to critical writing that does something more, a form that not only invites critical reflection but also invites readers to begin to imagine otherwise.[5]

To imagine otherwise as a form of knowledge-making is a bit risky, subject today perhaps more than ever to accusations of impracticality, of not caring about or contributing something that matters to the "real world." Social analyst Avery Gordon (1997) suggests that imagining otherwise has much to do with a theoretical insight put forth by Patricia Williams (1991) in her important book *The Alchemy of Race and Rights*. "That life is *complicated*," Williams writes, "is a fact of great analytic importance" (cited in Gordon 1997, 3, emphasis added). "That life is complicated," Gordon continues, "may seem a banal expression of the obvious, but it is nonetheless a profound theoretical statement – perhaps the most important theoretical statement of our time" (3). Remaining aware that life is complicated requires me to pay a particular kind of attention to those whose lives inform my research. It requires remembering, according to Gordon, that "even those who live in the most dire circumstances possess a complex and oftentimes contradictory humanity and subjectivity that is never adequately glimpsed by viewing them as victims or, on the other hand, as superhuman agents" (4). Striving to recognize and represent that complexity in all of its messiness is central to the very possibility of imagining otherwise.

Yet it is admittedly difficult for those of us with strong political commitments to continuously keep in mind this "complex and oftentimes contradictory humanity" that we all possess. Sometimes, for the purposes of advancing a political claim it becomes necessary to emphasize an individual or group's status as victims (or as autonomous, freely choosing agents, for that matter). And sometimes we get so caught up in advancing that claim that we forget that life is complicated, forget that people's lives are often much more complex and messy than how we are constrained into representing them. I have certainly found myself bound by such constraints in other times and places and no doubt I will again. But here in this book I hope to hold such constraints at bay in the interests of imagining possibilities for sociality and subjectivity that can more fully capture the complexities and contradictions that Gordon reminds us of.

Such complexities and contradictions become evident when one considers the frequent use of the term "missing" to describe the women who concern me in this book. "Missing" is, compellingly for my purposes, a thoroughly social term, as a minimum of two people are required for someone to be considered missing: one to have (been) disappeared, and another to take note of her absence. Margot Leigh Butler (2006) draws our attention to how the phrase "Missing Women" has become a problematic trope or stand-in for the women from the Downtown Eastside, in part because there has been much disagreement (between police and local women's groups, for example) about just how many women this categorization encompasses (172). Butler notes that in a commemorative pamphlet handed out at the annual memorial march, the women's names are followed by the phrase: "Our prayers remain with the women who are still unaccounted for." Like Butler, I appreciate how the phrase "unaccounted for" might imply an obligation on others to account for those whose whereabouts and circumstances remain unknown. I make use of this phrase occasionally in this book, but I am seeking other language that might help to communicate something more about those complex and at times contradictory dimensions of the events and people that concern me.

Phrases like "Vancouver's Missing Women" become especially problematic when they begin to figure or fix social imaginings of the lives such phrases are intended to represent. "What is at stake," writes Sara Ahmed, "is the 'cutting off' of figures from the social and material relations which over-determine their existence, and the consequent perception that such figures have a 'life of their own'" (5). Precisely where and how and for what purposes the individual lives of murdered or missing women are turned *into* figures under the banner of "Vancouver's Missing Women" concerns me – or, to borrow again from Ahmed, I am concerned with *"how that figure is put to work, and made to work, in particular times and places"* (15, emphasis in original). While one could never hope to specify all of what the phrase "Vancouver's Missing Women" might signify, depending on context, audience, and framing, I believe it is nonetheless important to consider how it is usually deployed as a stand-in for a set of things that are conventionally framed as "social problems." For example, when the particular lives of many diverse women come to be lumped together under a banner like "Vancouver's Missing Women," then this catchphrase is repeatedly made to stand in for a set of assumptions about a shared life narrative (troubled childhood, "broken" family, abuse, children's services, adolescent rebelliousness, and then a fall from innocence brought about by drug experimentation, prostitution, addiction, mental illness, criminality, etc.) – assumptions that are both true and not true, both overdetermined and vastly oversimplified (Jiwani and Young 2006, 897). This is the sort of cultural work the name "Vancouver's Missing Women" performs, and so I seek a different language, one less likely to fix the lives of so many different women through such a narrow set of assumptions. Some of the things I experienced while I lived in Vancouver challenged me to start thinking differently about what it means for someone to be missing, for example, and about why this language cannot fully capture all the complexities of "missing" as a social experience.

When I moved to Vancouver I began living with a fairly new lover, a woman whose struggles with an addiction to crack cocaine were about to become all consuming. Despite the turmoil that addiction brings to any home or relationship, we continued to live together off and on for several years, and during those years my lover went missing many times. Sometimes she was missing in the sense of being away from me and from our home for lengths of time (days, sometimes, or long hours at others) when I simply didn't know where she was. At these times, since I had been expecting her and she didn't materialize, I was left to my own terrible imaginings about what might have happened to her. Sometimes my nightmarish fantasies were far from the mark, as she was simply waylaid by the complicated labour involved in buying and consuming criminalized drugs. Still other times, though, the worst and hardest times, when she was missing longest, she had instead been held against her will by others and subjected to terrible violence. My lover often went missing *to* the Downtown Eastside to seek both the drugs she needed and the company of others who would not judge her for that need. These temporary disappearances became more and more anguishing for both of us as "Vancouver's Missing Women" started to receive some attention from news reporters and journalists. My lover is not among the women whose pictures appear on the official police poster of missing women; my experience of missing her is radically different from those of the families, friends, and lovers of the women who have been murdered or remain unaccounted for. Yet at its heart, this experience provided me with a number of insights into what it means for someone to be missing – or to experience someone *as* missing – that I might not have developed otherwise.

Sometimes, for example, a person who is designated as missing by police or reported missing by a loved one does not actually consider herself to be missing. This was certainly the case with my lover more often than not – *she* knew where she was and whether or not she was okay. *I* was the one who was missing that information, missing her. While contemplating the missing poster of a young girl, Vancouver author Anne Stone writes: "What is missing, then, what this poster marks the disappearance of, is her story from the minds of those who love her" (2004, 79; see also Stone 2009, 224). A missing person, Stone suggests, represents a "severed thread in a collective story" (2004, 79). That story, although changed, altered, rerouted, inevitably carries on. And the missing person may still be in *her* story, also carrying on within a new or different collective. Or she may not be. Not knowing which of these is true for her is precisely what is most anguishing when a loved one is missing. The not-knowing is what marks this form of missing, the adjective kind, as in "missing person," from the verb kind, as in "I miss you, let's get together, let's catch up." In the latter we usually assume that the other person's story has carried on and that our place in that story, in our collective story, also carries on, even across distance or absence. We hope this to be true about a missing person too, but not knowing whether it *is* true marks the former as distinct.

Perhaps what we most often fear when someone goes missing, then, is that they have *been disappeared*, or forced out of our collective story in some way, possibly permanently. And here I start to run aground on complicated questions about agency: could it really be the case that some people might *choose* to disappear, such that someone imagines them to be missing while they experience their lives as simply carrying on, perhaps taking a turn in a different direction but continuing nonetheless? This is what the police suggested, initially, about many of the women who were reported missing from the Downtown Eastside. They apparently implied or outright insisted that the women's lives were carrying on elsewhere, that their absences were temporary and that they would re-enter the collective stories of their loved ones in time, if they chose to. Now, of course, it is clear that for the most part they were terribly mistaken.[6] Yet when the police officer who came to our home to collect the details for a missing persons report about my lover suggested such a thing, I insisted, horrified, that it could not possibly be true, only to learn shortly after that in this instance it *was* true, that he had been right. It seems important that we distinguish this sense of being missing from a situation where someone has been forcibly disappeared. But how might we do so? Can we only make such a distinction in hindsight, when we learn the details of what has befallen someone who is missing? What if those details are never forthcoming? It seems unlikely to me that there can be any definitive answers to these questions, just as trying to distinguish between types of disappearance based on assumptions about agency or choice becomes, at times, a bit of a distraction from larger questions and concerns. I am seeking a language, a vocabulary that can capture the particular, anguishing complexity of that time between when friends or family of some of the women discovered that their loved one was missing and that time much later when they learned for certain that she had been murdered. For assistance, I turn to Avery Gordon's (1997) writings on *los desaparecido* (the disappeared) of Argentina to make a tentative case for the applicability of this term to murdered or missing women from Vancouver's Downtown Eastside.

There are compelling reasons for rephrasing "Vancouver's missing women" as "Vancouver's disappeared women," as I have chosen to do in this book, but there are also some compelling reasons against doing so. Disappearance as it was practised in Argentina (and many other places in the world), and as it is taken up by Gordon, refers to a state-sponsored, systematic array of practices, including "illegal abduction by the police, military and paramilitary squads, detention in secret centers, torture, usually death and improper burial, and denial by the authorities" (72). It is most commonly a method for quelling political dissent and as such has characteristics that distinguish it from the violence directed at women from Vancouver's Downtown Eastside. The United Nations, for example, defines "enforced disappearance" as

> the arrest, detention, abduction or any other form of deprivation of liberty by agents of the State or by persons or groups of persons acting with the authorization, support or acquiescence of the State, followed by a refusal to acknowledge the deprivation of liberty or by concealment of the fate or whereabouts of the disappeared person, which place such a person outside the protection of the law. (International Convention for the Protection of All Persons from Enforced Disappearance, article 2)

The evidence that is available to date suggests that the state and police are not explicitly authorizing or ordering the majority of violent acts against women from the Downtown Eastside, although it is important to note that some studies do implicate police as perpetrators of violence directed at women doing outdoor sex work in this neighbourhood.[7] But broadly this is not a state-*ordered* system of disappearance, then, and as such it seems essential to hold on to a distinction between the disappearance of women from Vancouver and elsewhere in Canada and the disappearance of people purportedly for their political views or activism in Argentina during the so-called dirty war.

That said, though, lengthy periods of government inaction invite one to argue that the disappearance of women from the Downtown Eastside is certainly state-*supported*. Not only were officials extremely slow to respond with any degree of seriousness or efficiency to missing persons reports about women from the area, but the Downtown Eastside itself has long suffered the state's neglect. Further, as a number of organizations of and for sex workers have argued, the criminalization of sex work in Canada is a very significant factor in the horrendous levels of violence experienced by women doing sex work, and outdoor sex work in particular, since it effectively prevents them from organizing and working in environments of increased safety and makes it almost impossible for them to seek any sort of protection or response from police when they are targeted for violence. I would thus argue that state *in*action functions as a tacit system of support – an acquiescence, one might say – underpinning the disappearance of women from the Downtown Eastside, since this inaction has fostered many of the social conditions that contribute to those disappearances. Such an argument implies that responsibility lies not only with the individual perpetrator(s) of the acts of violence that ended the women's lives but also with the broader social fabric of Canadian society, which is inextricable from its state formations in its tolerance for this inaction.

There are other reasons, too, why I think framing murdered or missing women from the Downtown Eastside as "disappeared women," with this terminology's associated resonances with *los desaparecidos*, is worthwhile and forges an important connection. In Argentina, for example, when people sought information about their disappeared loved ones, Gordon explains that they frequently received the following sorts of responses: "The state and its various representatives claim[ed] to know nothing. Or only that your child has gone abroad, or that your husband is having a secret affair, or that your guerrilla sister must be hiding out underground" (79). Similar excuses were apparently made to several of the families and friends of women from the Downtown Eastside, who were informed by police that their loved one had likely gone to work for a while in another city, or was hiding from the law, or in fact was not missing at all (as was the case with Angela Jardine, whose mother was told that Jardine had been spotted in the neighbourhood after she was reported missing. It turns out that Jardine was being confused with another Downtown Eastside resident, Sereena Abotsway, who was also disappeared a few years later).[8] The rhetoric used to explain the disappearance of so many women and to diminish the significance of the growing numbers of women being made to vanish – which became a kind of public secret of the kind identified by Michael Taussig (1999), since many in the city were aware of what was happening even as officials continued to deny its extent – is eerily similar, then, to rhetoric employed in state-sponsored systems of disappearance.

Finally, and I believe most compellingly, I also argue in this book that the state-orchestrated system of terror known as settler colonialism is indelibly tied to the present-day, ongoing disappearance, disproportionately, of Indigenous women from Vancouver and across the country. It is possible, then, to revisit Gordon's claims about the characteristics of "an organized system of repression known as disappearance" (72) with examples specific to this context: the abduction, detention, torture, death, and improper burial of many Indigenous children forced into residential schools between 1831 and 1996, for example, as well as a lengthy state denial of such practices, is now widely documented.[9] And while our Canadian governments and many Canadians themselves prefer to locate such examples of the violence of colonialism in our nation's distant past (or outright deny its role in Canada's history), there is much evidence to suggest that colonization is actively remade again and again in the present, belying its past-ness, and that the disappearances and murders of the women who concern me in this book are but one example of this remaking. This is perhaps the paramount reason to draw connections or point to similarities between the disappearance of women from the Downtown Eastside and *los desaparecidos* of Argentina, for state tactics for advancing and securing settler colonialism have produced genocidal violence against Indigenous people in Canada.

Many scholars and activists are forging these links between colonial histories and the extent of present-day violence against Indigenous women. Mohawk lawyer and scholar Beverley Jacobs and Andrea J. Williams of Sandy Lake First Nation (2008) argue, for example, that the ongoing crisis of missing and murdered Aboriginal women in Canada is a direct legacy of the residential school system and the discriminatory effects of the federal Indian Act. The Native Women's Association of Canada (2010) insists that "the overrepresentation of Aboriginal women in Canada as victims of violence must be understood in the context of a colonial strategy that sought to dehumanize Aboriginal women" (1). In her foundational book on this subject, Andrea Smith (2005) exposes how sexual violence has been deployed historically and in the present to further the colonial project of American Indian genocide. The Native Women's Association of Canada's Sisters in Spirit campaign was also based on research and strategies for action that link colonialism and racism to contemporary violence against Indigenous women, and in her National Film Board of Canada (NFB) documentary *Finding Dawn* (2006), Metis filmmaker Christine Welsh draws attention to the complex ways that colonial histories have shaped the many forms of violence inflicted on Indigenous women in the present. Sherene Razack (2000) demonstrates how the murder of Pamela George, a Saulteaux woman from Saskatchewan, is intertwined with Canada's colonial history. And, at a recent conference entitled "Missing Women: Decolonization, Third Wave Feminism, and Indigenous People of Canada and Mexico" (held at the University of Regina in 2008), connections between colonial histories and the disappearance or murder of large numbers of Indigenous women in Canada and Mexico were a central theme.[10]

The term "disappeared women," then, works to more clearly mark the wide array of social conditions and arrangements implicated in this present-day violence; its resonance with *los desaparecidos* is intended to convey that a much wider array of individuals and social forces are implicated in these events than initial perceptions might suggest.

In North America, though, the trope of the "disappearing Indian" has a long and troubling history that my shift to the language of "disappeared women" risks repeating. In the nineteenth and early twentieth centuries, Indigenous people were cast in numerous cultural productions as a "dying race," a fact that was often rationalized with reference to the social Darwinism popular at the time. Edward S. Curtis's attempt to photographically document the lives of many different Indigenous groups across North America before they purportedly vanished offers but one example of a representational practice premised on this "dying race" ideology. Many Euro-Canadian political leaders, cultural producers, and settler-colonizers publicly lamented the (according to this logic) apparently inevitable destruction of Indigenous communities while at the same time sanctioning or carrying out the genocidal policies and practices that aimed to transform this rhetoric into a self-evident truth. My decision to rely on wordings like "women who *were* disappeared" over either "disappear*ing* women" or "women who disappeared" is strategic in that it conveys my desire to draw attention to how these disappearances have been brought about by numerous complex social forces, and to mark this present-day story of disappearance as indelibly linked to the ideologies that (re)produce this too-familiar trope of the "disappearing Indian." Shifting from "disappearing Indian" to "Indigenous women who have been disappeared" might help to undermine the inevitability implied by the *–ing* suffix. Yet in her critique of the language of "missing women," Sarah Hunt (2014) reminds us that "girls and women don't simply disappear – they are beaten, murdered, kidnapped, violated and raped" (191). The language of "disappeared women" can diminish or forget this violence just as easily as the language of "missing women," and so I am cognizant that the language of disappearance does not solve all the problems associated with the language of "missing women" – it too can become a too-easy phrase.

To undermine further the inevitability implied by the trope of the disappearing Indian, in this book I also analyse how settler colonialism, and in particular the frontier mythology so popular and commonplace (still today) in Western Canada, are related to the contemporary violence experienced disproportionately by Indigenous women from the Downtown Eastside. In the next chapter, I examine the historical regulation of Indigenous women's lives in British Columbia and make connections between this history and the present-day violence against women in the Downtown Eastside. This chapter links contemporary processes of gentrification and displacement in the Downtown Eastside with the ongoing violence against women from this neighbourhood and examines how conventional understandings of history as linear, progressive, stable, and past (here meaning "over and done with") are intimately connected to the displacements and violence occurring in the present. While such an unsettled understanding of temporality has been elaborated profusely in the realms of both postcolonial and trauma theory, there nonetheless remains a widespread common-sense belief that past, present, and future are naturally linear and neatly separable. I argue that this conventional view of temporality has played a role in the more recent disappearance of women from the Downtown Eastside and therefore requires further troubling. Chapter 1 concludes with a story about my own encounter with the absent presence of Sereena Abotsway, who was, among other things, an activist in the Downtown Eastside before she was disappeared in 2001 and subsequently murdered. This encounter, I argue, aptly exposes how unsettling conventional understandings of place, temporality, and history can work to provoke a wider sense of implicatedness in the disappearance of Abotsway, which might in turn disrupt narrow arguments about who or what is responsible for the suffering and violence experienced by Abotsway and other women from the Downtown Eastside who have been disappeared.

Following this reflection on my encounter with Abotsway, in chapter 2 I explore how the spectral *presence* of women who have been disappeared can be mobilized in opposition to the racial logic underpinning colonial ideologies invested in the trope of the "disappearing Indian." Attending to traces of the life of Sarah de Vries, a woman who was disappeared from the Downtown Eastside in 1998, I argue that De Vries's spectral return in numerous cultural productions (a memoir, film footage, countless newspaper stories, but especially through her own poetry and journal writing) has the potential to evoke a much wider sense of implicatedness in her disappearance, thereby affirming the ways she *has been disappeared* rather than merely vanished. I take up a poem written by De Vries that offers an example of the sort of cultural production that invites a wider sense of implicatedness through which practices of inheritance might develop.

Next, in chapter 3, I investigate how and why disappeared women from the Downtown Eastside were initially cast, in a variety of representations, as living lives widely recognized as "ungrievable" (Butler 2004, 2009). After providing a closer analysis of the series of posters released by police seeking information about increasing numbers of "missing" women, posters that use images signifying criminality to represent victims of crime, I then turn to artistic representations which purport instead to "humanize" the women for a wider viewing public, contemplating how these well-intentioned practices might nevertheless risk reproducing assumptions that some lives are deservedly grievable and others "naturally" less so. The images most frequently used to represent the women, I argue, significantly shaped public sentiment in the wake of their loss, reducing the likelihood that a wider public might come to feel a sense of implicatedness in their disappearance. As a result, a radical reimagining of such representational practices seems urgent.

Chapter 4 turns to an analysis of figures I have located only in the shadows of the "Missing Women" story, namely, "squaw men" and "whores," figures that I argue are queer(ed) in part because of how profoundly sex has been equated in this story with "degeneracy" and "evil." Here I argue that the oft-repeated reclaiming of the women as "mothers, sisters and daughters," a politically strategic remembrance practice, also risks distancing the women from sex work – or, indeed, from any form of sexuality at all. When the women are made to appear largely devoid of sexuality in posthumous representations, sex gains traction in the story of their disappearance only through representations of Robert Pickton, whom I argue gets produced as a figure of a contemporary "squaw man." A term common in nineteenth-century parlance, "squaw man" was used to describe working-class European (white) settlers whose sexual and/or marital relationships with Indigenous women became an increasing irritant to more "genteel" white folks and a solidifying settler-colonial state. The shadowy reappearance of the figure of a "squaw man" can be read as yet another sign of colonialism's present-ness, I argue, and adds context to the widespread fascination with Pickton as a representative of "evil" and vessel of responsibility for the disappearance of so many women. Ultimately, I argue that analysing how the various queer(ed) figures explored in this chapter are shaped by and are in turn shaping the contemporary context of settler colonialism can help draw attention to broader questions about justice that get eclipsed or downplayed through sensationalist stories about a lone man on trial.

In order to better understand what might be needed to increase the possibility that a wider public might come to feel implicated in the disappearance of so many women, in chapter 5 I investigate the kinds of memorials that seem most capable of hailing such a public into practices of inheritance. In this chapter I analyse several memorials dedicated to Vancouver's murdered or missing women, including permanent memorials in CRAB Park in the Downtown Eastside, a memorial mural located in Montréal, the Women's Memorial March that happens annually on the fourteenth of February, and the memorial art of Janis Cole and Rebecca Belmore, looking for the ways that each of these memorializations might hail an "us" into everyday practices of inheriting what lives on from the loss of so many women.

I am concerned throughout this book with understanding what might be required to support a wider public – especially those of us with less material, geographical, or identity-based proximity to the women who have been disappeared – to grapple with how we are implicated in the social conditions and arrangements facilitating the disappearance of so many women, with how a wider sense of this implication is helped or hindered by particular cultural productions and the frameworks they mobilize for understanding what makes a life grievable, and finally, with what it might mean to inherit what lives on from the disappearance of so many women, to adopt everyday practices of inheritance that demand more than an empathetic or compassionate identification with murdered or missing women alone. I make no claim to address these concerns definitively, as though such finality were possible. Instead, I aim to address and contribute to the formation of an "us" committed to transforming the present, now, into a present entirely otherwise than the one in which we find ourselves, in which the violence experienced by the women who concern me in this book remains an ongoing crisis.

Chapter One

The Present Pasts of Vancouver's Downtown Eastside

The name "Downtown Eastside" is frequently made to do a certain kind of cultural work, signifying beyond the particular character of the neighbourhood that bears that name.[1] In the imaginations of many Canadians, the phrase "Downtown Eastside" has become a stand-in for urban poverty, drug use, disease, "degeneracy," and a host of social ills, not just among Vancouverites but across the country, even quite possibly the globe. What are the potential effects of such significations? How has the name "Downtown Eastside" become a kind of shorthand for so many different social issues in the imaginations of so many? And in what ways has this series of significations been challenged – in what ways can it be continually challenged through an attention to the work of local residents and activists, for whom the name "Downtown Eastside" usually signifies very differently? In this chapter, I analyse how the production of the "Downtown Eastside" and "Vancouver's Missing Women" as figures tends to dovetail, such that we can scarcely utter one without conjuring the other; as Sarah Hunt points out, "though today the dominant image of the Downtown Eastside is that of an Indigenous sex worker, current media and police attention has not translated into change" (2013, 97). If not meaningful change, then what *are* the potential effects of this slippage between figures?

Stan Douglas's composite photographic panorama, "Every Building on 100 West Hastings" (see figure 1.1), offers a striking image of a Downtown Eastside streetscape. The photograph was installed as part of a broader exhibition of Douglas's art at the Vancouver Contemporary Art Gallery in 2002. This sixteen-foot panorama seamlessly brings together twenty-one separate photographs of the various buildings on the south side of the 100-block of West Hastings Street in the heart of

1.1 Stan Douglas, *Every Building on 100 West Hastings.* Photo courtesy of the artist and David Zwirner, New York/London.

the Downtown Eastside. The first thing about Douglas's photographic composite that likely strikes anyone who has ever been on the 100 block of West Hastings is the curious absence of people: a street that is usually teeming with humanity is eerily deserted, with not a single person anywhere in sight. The only thing visible is a row of old buildings, many boarded shut and in need of repair, alongside a few remaining businesses – a convenience store, a pawn shop, the entrance to a single room occupancy (SRO) hotel. The sheer size and length of the photograph prevents the eye from fixing on a single point; as art critic Denise Blake Oleksijczuk suggests in an essay on Douglas's photograph, "there is no zero-point from which the image would spatially make sense *as a whole.* Instead, it has many viewpoints that compete for the observer's attention" (2002, 108, emphasis in original). Rather than fixing on one aspect of the panorama, then, the viewer scans the length of the street, looking, searching, for a spot on which to rest our gaze.

As my eyes scanned this photograph for the first time, searching for what was missing, for why I could not settle on any one point, I realized quite suddenly that of course what is missing from the Downtown Eastside today (and also from this photograph) are so many women who lived or worked there, most of whom were murdered, many who remain unaccounted for. For just a moment, as this realization dawned, I felt struck by the photograph's haunting absences. With reference to the women who have been disappeared from this neighbourhood, Oleksijczuk insists that the timing of Douglas's photograph cannot be considered accidental: "A picture of this block at this time ... has the

potential to indicate that a space of tragedy, and its long-term dismissal by those at a safe distance from it, lies at the core of Vancouver's social and psychic life" (99). Yet the absences in the photograph might also point us towards others whose unjust, untimely, and too often violent deaths are further in the past or even more recent than the disappearances and murders of the women named on the official police list, for also missing from the Downtown Eastside today are those who died from a drug overdose or from mostly preventable illnesses such as smallpox, tuberculosis, HIV, or hepatitis C. Then there are those who committed suicide in despair, or who died from some of the many other brutal effects of colonization, genocide, poverty, homelessness, displacement, starvation, isolation, loneliness. It could be any combination of these disappeared people that the viewer is invited to visually search for in Douglas's panorama, or all of them.

In the act of looking for what is missing from Douglas's photograph, Oleksijczuk argues, we may start to see ourselves as implicated in the losses it invokes: "The multiple perspectives of *100 West Hastings* demand that we as spectators adopt a staccato-like act of viewing that keeps our eyes moving as if we were engaged in a frantic search for something we have lost" (109). While photographs that contain single vanishing points, or points we can fix on easily, allow spectators to "obtain an illusion of mastery and control," Douglas's panorama, Oleksijczuk argues, avoids this trap (107). Similarly, rather than photographing the residents of the Downtown Eastside themselves, which most often provokes feelings of "pity, or worse, of being comforted by the fact that [we ourselves] are much better off," Douglas instead presents us with this conspicuously empty block, and in doing so perhaps shifts our focus to "broader social issues" (Oleksijczuk 104). Through this sense of being implicated, the self/other binary so common in popular representations of the Downtown Eastside starts to break down and a different relationship to the women disappeared from this neighbourhood is suggested – a relationship in which their disappearances cannot be held outside of or separate from what it means to be who we are and where we are standing in the moment of looking.

And yet, troublingly, Douglas's panorama (and Oleksijczuk's interpretation of it) also risks reifying assumptions that the Downtown Eastside is an *empty* space, when in fact it is a neighbourhood populated not just by ghosts but also by living residents and many activists, all very much alive and often actively involved in preventing the suffering, loss, and displacement of more of their neighbours. Vancouver writer Reg Johanson points out, for example, that in 2002, a year after Douglas shot "100 West Hastings," the same photographs would have been "impossible to take again," since the people "missing" from Douglas's photograph had returned to mount an enormous protest against homelessness and the loss of social housing (known as the Woodwards Squat) on that exact block – as Johanson compellingly reminds us, "Suddenly, and all too briefly, the streets were filled with people who refused to disappear" (Johanson 2007, 98). Indeed, I have since wondered how Douglas achieved his photograph at all, as it is hard to imagine ever clearing the 100 block of West Hastings of people, even in the middle of the night, without the aid of police or some sort of security presence. In his poem "Skid Road (Establishing Footage)," Downtown Eastside writer My Name Is Scot deftly and strikingly weaves together text from several "notices informing residents about the temporary colonization of streets and lots by film crews" (Asfour and Gardiner 2012, 13). As one line of the poem conveys, "Vancouver Police will be on hand to perform a temporary road closure when necessary during the filming of these scenes" (My Name Is Scot 2012, 137). In fact, most of the lines of Scot's poem point to some restriction or inconvenience to be forced on neighbourhood residents. The material conditions under which Douglas's photograph, and other films and photographs shot in the neighbourhood, are produced profoundly complicate their potential to evoke practices of inheritance; any representation of the neighbourhood that requires increased policing, surveillance, or even a general disregard for the mobility of its residents necessarily fails politically to provoke increased solidarity or (more) ethical relationships between locals and outsiders.

Douglas's photograph therefore raises a number of questions about both the generative possibilities and the serious risks of representing absence. Oleksijczuk develops a compelling psychoanalytic argument about the photograph's potential to invoke a sense of implication in viewers through its animation of haunting absences. But, drawing on Johanson's insights, it is also true that representing the space of the Downtown Eastside as an *empty* space risks reinforcing some contemporary desires to render this space vacant for the purposes of encouraging gentrification. As such, I value the photograph's potential for animating hauntings, and at the same time I want to contest its representation of the Downtown Eastside as empty space by turning in this chapter to an analysis of some of the activist work of Downtown Eastside residents, work that demonstrates how the Downtown Eastside is anything but empty.

Geographically speaking, the Downtown Eastside is actually a space that is difficult to define. A 2005/6 City of Vancouver publication indicates that the area encompasses the distance between Clark Drive in the east and the end of the 400 block of West Hastings (at Richards) in the west, and from the end of Thornton Park at Main and Terminal in the south to the outskirts of the industrial area that borders Burrard Inlet in the north. (See figure 1.2.) This same document also acknowledges, however, that "these areas do not, nor are they intended to, reflect neighbourhood boundaries which are perceived differently by the diverse communities that live and work in this part of the city" (City of Vancouver 2006, 4). John Mikhail Asfour and Elee Kraljii Gardiner, editors of *V6A: Writing from Vancouver's Downtown Eastside*, relate the following anecdote about their own process of trying to sort out the neighbourhood's boundaries: "One city hall employee explained the variance in maps to us by saying that some people 'feel the neighbourhood includes this area, some don't'" (2012, 9). Such disclaimers signal that among the "diverse communities" living and working in this neighbourhood, the boundaries of the Downtown Eastside are contested. For Asfour and Gardiner, "our sense is that by-law and zoning maps reflect a different reality than maps based on the organic flow of social exchange" (ibid.).

Unsurprisingly, then, another page on the City's website proclaims the space of the Downtown Eastside to be "bound by Burrard Inlet to

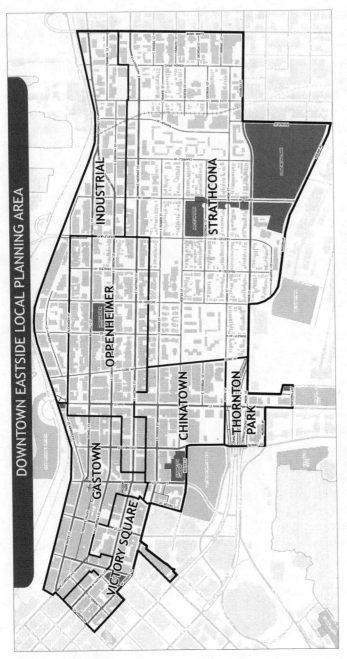

1.2 Map of the Downtown Eastside Local Planning Area. Variance in maps of the neighbourhood delimits contestation over the boundaries and ordering of space. Reproduced courtesy of the City of Vancouver.

the north, Clark Drive to the east, Hastings Street to the south, and Main Street to the west," a dramatically smaller area geographically than that described in the first document. More confusing still, the map accompanying this second statement indicates that the neighbourhood boundaries extend from Burrard Inlet to well past Terminal Avenue (much further south than Hastings Street). On some maps (such as the one designed for tourists that I was handed recently while attending a conference in Vancouver) the Downtown Eastside simply does not appear at all. Surrounding neighbourhoods like Gastown and Chinatown are mentioned but the name "Downtown Eastside" is conspicuously absent (even though its geographical area is included on the map): it is imagined away, perhaps because the city deems it a less-than-desirable neighbourhood for tourists to visit.

Although the geographical boundaries of the Downtown Eastside depend much on whom you ask and for what purpose you ask them, there is nonetheless a sense that this neighbourhood is marked by a "border that often differentiates Hastings Street, and its residents and habitués, from the rest of Vancouver" (Shier 2002, 10). Social anthropologist Jean McDonald (2003) aptly exposes how this sense of a border around the Downtown Eastside is both invoked and perpetuated by numerous mainstream media representations. "Characterization of the Eastside as a space of degeneracy and disease – a space clearly in need of containment, if not eradication" is a "predominant theme" of such representations, McDonald finds (117). Geographer Beverley A. Pitman (2002) similarly identifies a "'bad neighbourhood' stereotype of the Downtown Eastside in dominant representations of Vancouver" (175), and sociologist Andrew Woolford (2001) argues that Vancouver-based print newspapers often represent the Downtown Eastside as a "tainted space" that requires "distance or cleansing" (49). Each of these researchers documents numerous examples of such stigmatizing representations of the Downtown Eastside, and because I am keenly aware that these sorts of representations not only reflect but also constitute and, when reiterated, potentially performatively produce this sense of the neighbourhood, I see no reason to repeat them here. Suffice it to say that most mainstream media representations of the Downtown Eastside, and in particular mainstream news and documentary media, contribute significantly to this sense of the neighbourhood as a bordered, "degenerate" space.

Geographers Jeff Sommers and Nicholas Blomley (2002) argue that this stigmatization of the Downtown Eastside "can be traced for most of the twentieth century" (29). The Downtown Eastside is Vancouver's oldest neighbourhood and as such has a long, varied, and often contentious history.[2] In the early part of the twentieth century it was primarily the neighbourhood's reputation for social activism that established it as a trouble spot for police and local governments. As early as 1904 the management of the Woodward's department store, which had at that time just recently opened at the corner of Hastings and Abbott, wrote an angry letter to city council complaining that "its customers were prevented from entering the store by the crowds of people congregating on the streets outside, selling and buying labour newspapers, listening to radical speakers, or simply enjoying the ambience" (in Sommers and Blomley 2002, 29). In the 1930s the area was a "hotbed of political mobilization" on labour and anti-poverty issues, and unemployed workers or strikers occupied several Downtown Eastside buildings and parks, resulting in numerous confrontations between protestors and police (Hasson and Ley 1994, 174; see also Sommers and Blomley 2002). It seems likely that this early sense of the Downtown Eastside as a space of radicalism and resistance contributed to its later representation as a space of degeneracy and social deviance, since these social protests were too often described simply as "riots."

An early reputation for supposed social deviance was also likely tied to the Downtown Eastside's proximity to Chinatown and Japantown. Sometimes described as neighbourhoods of the Downtown Eastside and sometimes as bordering it, Chinatown and Japantown have not always been viewed as welcome developments within the city of Vancouver. In 1907, for example, a protest incited by racist anti-Asian ideologies damaged or destroyed several Chinese and Japanese businesses in the area, further entrenching its reputation as a so-called trouble spot. Constructions of immigrants, particularly immigrants racialized as other, as "outsiders" to the nation, are instrumental to what Sunera Thobani (2007) calls the "exaltation" of the national citizen/subject, an exaltation also bolstered by representations that posit Indigenous subjects as national "outsiders," and so the struggles of these groups are in many ways intertwined even when they are not perceived as such. Thobani argues that "the national, the Indian, and the immigrant" are "fundamental categories of Canadian nationhood, born in the violence of the colonial encounter ... It is the relationality among them," she insists, "that gives these categories their concrete – sometimes explosive, but always political – meanings" (28). Thobani's work challenges us to reconsider the connections between the people and spaces of Chinatown, Japantown, and the Downtown Eastside, for the stereotypical representations of a predominantly discordant relationship between residents and business owners in these neighbourhoods certainly cannot do justice to the complexity of the coalitions and relationships that exist between residents who recognize themselves as part of these (often overlapping) communities.[3]

After the Second World War, as a result of significant economic changes throughout the province, a neighbourhood that had for years been populated largely by men working in various resource-based industries slowly began to change. In the early 1950s newspaper articles began to describe the Downtown Eastside in very similar terms to how it is often construed by the press today. Jeffrey Sommers and Nicholas Blomley argue that the more recent stigmatization of the neighbourhood stems in large part from what they describe as the "moral panic over drugs and HIV," which became conflated in the 1990s with increasing "signs of growing poverty and marginality such as homelessness, begging, and 'squeegee kids'" – along with outdoor sex work, I would add – resulting in "the pathologization of the entire neighbourhood" (2002, 21). This is without doubt a neighbourhood where the unjust and uneven effects of urban poverty are deeply felt, but these more common perceptions or imaginings of the Downtown Eastside fail to do justice to the area's fierce sense of community and activist spirit.

Long recognized as one of the few neighbourhoods in Vancouver offering anything close to affordable housing, the Downtown Eastside nonetheless saw a significant loss of low-income housing in the lead-up to the 2010 Vancouver Olympics. This displacement of local residents did not escape the notice of neighbourhood activists, and was documented in the interests of challenging the City's repeated claims that displacements due to a city-sponsored "revitalization" of the area would not occur. According to a report published by the Carnegie Community Action Project (C-CAP) (2008), 174 rooms in SROs closed in the first few months of 2008, while another 225 rooms were in immanent danger of closing.[4] While C-CAP certainly acknowledges that SROs mostly provide less-than-ideal accommodations to local residents, they also argue that the rooms they do make available are some of the only affordable housing in the city and can provide "stopgap" housing while more social housing is, ideally, developed.

Meanwhile, new condominium projects with limited commitments to social or low-income housing have been given a green light by the

City despite tremendous resistance from local activists and residents.[5] Clearly, the City's "zero displacement" commitment is not being met, as the thrust of "development" forces low- or no-income residents either out of the neighbourhood or onto the streets. Likely at the insistence of residents and activists, the City was careful not to imagine away the existing Downtown Eastside community through the design of its revitalization project, repeatedly emphasizing that the revitalization was intended for the benefit of the existing community, not a community of new middle-class "pioneers" yet to come. Nonetheless, residents of the Downtown Eastside are today struggling against displacement; their absence is imagined as a way to make room for a new wave of "settlers" who will stake claims on this space, claims that many seem to imagine as more legitimate or desirable.

It is hardly coincidental that the language and metaphors frequently invoked to describe or represent the space of the Downtown Eastside today very closely resemble those used to describe the land now known as British Columbia (or Canada more broadly) around the time of initial contact between European colonizers and First Nations. As Sommers and Blomley (2002) argue, the Downtown Eastside is frequently cast in contemporary representations as a "mythical frontier" that is "wild, dangerous, and, ultimately, [an] empty space, ripe for (re)settlement" (45). This repetition or recycling of language and metaphor can be read as a sign that colonization is not a finished, "settled," or past project, but instead is ongoing and continually remade in the present. With reference to the Downtown Eastside, Dara Culhane (2003) argues that "recognition of the burden of social suffering carried by Aboriginal people in this neighborhood ... elicits profound discomfort within ... Canada, evidencing as it does the *continuing* effects of settler colonialism, its ideological and material foundations and its ongoing reproduction" (595). The Downtown Eastside is rife with evidence of the ongoing-ness of settler colonialism, which helps explain why the neighbourhood is so stigmatized and shunned by many settlers in particular.

The place now represented by the name "Downtown Eastside" was of course not always demarcated this way. In fact it did not become known as the Downtown Eastside until around 1973, when the Downtown Eastside Residents' Association was founded to try to change negative public and civic perceptions of the area, then most commonly referred to simply as "Skid Road" (see Hasson and Ley 1994). But before the City of Vancouver was incorporated as such in 1886, before the province now known as British Columbia entered into the

Canadian confederation in 1871, before Vancouver Island was established as a British colony in 1849, and before the establishment of Fort Langley in 1827 brought about more regular contact between Europeans and Indigenous people on the west coast, the space now known as the Downtown Eastside was travelled across, lived on, and occupied primarily by Coast Salish First Nations (who of course were not known as, and did not come to know themselves as, "Coast Salish" or as "First Nations" until the violent imposition of a colonial settler society on what is now known as the west coast of British Columbia). Mid-nineteenth- and early-twentieth-century representations of this place as a vast, empty, rugged wilderness have contributed to a social imaginary that frequently eclipses those with prior claims and ties to the area, claims and ties that were not dealt with justly but instead were outright denied or suppressed, in part through efforts to decimate the people who stood to make them.

Such is the weight of those discourses that posit the colonization of British Columbia as the discovery of a vast, empty wilderness that they continue to influence the way histories of colonization are written and understood today. In his book *The Resettlement of British Columbia*, geographer Cole Harris reflects on the impact of such discourses on the historical research he published in a reputable academic journal as recently as 1985. As he explains:

> When I wrote that there was no evidence of Native settlement near Idaho Peak [in the British Columbia interior], I did not know about the smallpox epidemics of 1782 and 1862, or about the measles epidemic of 1848, or about influenza in 1849 ... Mine is another example, from one who should have known better, of the substitution of wilderness for an erased Native world. (1997, xvi)

Harris also points out that by 1877 much of the Indigenous population of the lower mainland was sequestered on reserves. Colonial acts that resulted in the decimation or displacement of Indigenous peoples and communities shape the organization of space and social life in contemporary British Columbia and continue to have a significant impact on how the place known as the Downtown Eastside is imagined today.

Around the time of its entry into confederation in 1871, British Columbia, according to historian Adele Perry (2001), "hung precariously at the edge of Britain's literal and symbolic empire" (3). Colonialists were routinely frustrated or outraged that this outpost of empire "bore little resemblance to the orderly, respectable, white settler colony that imperial observers hoped it would become" (ibid.). At a time when Indigenous people still outnumbered Europeans, when white women were scarce and mixed-race relationships (between white men and Indigenous women, primarily) commonplace, considerable effort was required to try to bring this colony in line with colonial ideals and imaginings. Such efforts constituted and sanctioned a particular understanding of Indigenous womanhood, one that is indelibly bound to the violence directed at Indigenous women in the Downtown Eastside (and across Canada more broadly) today.

Anxieties over sexual and domestic relationships between white men and Indigenous women were part of the reasoning behind official policies aimed at evacuating Indigenous people from the burgeoning urban spaces of the new colony. There were many debates among governors and clergymen about the merits of officially wedding such couples. Some argued that "white men's morality would inevitably be imperiled by connections with Aboriginal women," while others argued that Aboriginal women should be protected from the debasement of extramarital relationships with European men (Perry 2001, 107; see also Van Kirk 2006). Regardless of their reasoning, Perry writes, "all shared the motivating conviction that relationships forged between white men and Aboriginal women were indicative of the failure of respectable gender and racial organization to develop" (97). Significant efforts were thus made by colonial governors and by the church to prevent or disrupt such relationships.

Calls from across the colony to restrict the presence of Indigenous peoples in the developing cities of Victoria and New Westminster led to official and unofficial policies intended to produce this effect. In April 1861, for example:

> Police issued orders "to drive all Indians found in town after 6 o'clock p.m. across the bridge" that separated settler-Victoria from the Lekwammen (Songhees) reserve. Aboriginal people found on the wrong side of the racial divide after 10 p.m. were to be searched and prevented from returning until morning unless they could produce documentation of a clear and subservient relationship to the colonial community, namely "passes from white persons by whom they are employed." (Perry 2001, 113)

While anxieties over mixed-race relationships were not the only cause of such policies (Perry suggests that smallpox was another convenient and perhaps coincidental excuse for them), they were certainly one cause. Such determined efforts to rid urban spaces of the presence of Indigenous peoples, and of Indigenous women in particular, hauntingly (and alarmingly) foreshadow contemporary examples of similarly violent expulsions of Indigenous people from urban centres.

Another technique for discouraging mixed-race relationships in the colony involved employing language and imagery that would eventually secure a near-synonymous symbolic conflation of "Indigenous woman" with "prostitute." As Perry explains, "A convenient shorthand for signifying the immorality of First Nations womanhood was the suggestion that Aboriginal women were, by definition, prostitutes" (2001, 54). This mapping became so pervasive that at the time it took "little to 'prove' [Aboriginal women's] participation in the sex trade" (110), which was in turn used as both a tool and a justification for ejecting Indigenous people, and Indigenous women in particular, from urban centres. As historian Sarah Carter (2006) asserts, "The Canadian state adopted increasingly segregationist policies toward the Aboriginal people of the West, and central to these policies were images of Aboriginal women as dissolute, dangerous and sinister" (147). In December 1862, for example, a Victoria city councillor "proposed a by-law 'declaring it to be unlawful for any person to Harbor Indian women within the City limits'" (Perry 2001, 119). To legitimize this proposal he insisted, "'the squaws might all be considered as prostitutes, and that was sufficient grounds for their rejection'" (cited ibid.). While his proposal was not successful, it suggests a generalized tendency towards this conflation of Indigenous womanhood and prostitution in colonial British Columbia (see also Barman 2006, 273; and Carter 2006, 155 on this point). While I am reluctant to reiterate these assumptions here by reproducing such representational practices, an understanding of the colonial impetus behind these problematic constructions of Indigenous womanhood works to challenge a belief in their naturalness or truthfulness, and is also essential, I believe, for understanding the contemporary violence against disproportionately Indigenous women from the Downtown Eastside and across the country. In her doctoral research, Maryanne Pearce (2013) discovered, for example, that only 20 per cent of the Aboriginal, First Nations, or Metis women she identified as murdered or still unaccounted for were involved in sex work, although it should be noted that for 34 per cent of the women in her database who did sex work, ethnicity is unknown (50). Still, her finding challenges the common assumption that participation in sex work is always a strong factor in the disappearance or murder of Indigenous women, suggesting that the historical conflation of Indigenous womanhood with prostitution still bears heavily on how Indigenous women are widely perceived today.

Whether or not someone is widely recognized as human (or as grievable, to return for a moment to Butler's language) has much to do with the spaces they occupy in their everyday lives, then, and one could also argue that such spaces do not remain static across time, that different spaces are constituted on similar terms during different epochs. For example, the reservation became the space of containment for Indigenous communities in the late nineteenth century, while the Downtown Eastside is frequently framed through similar terms – as a space of containment – today. That the population of the Downtown Eastside today is disproportionately Indigenous should therefore come as little surprise, for during initial contact the lands now known as British Columbia were described on very similar terms (as empty space awaiting "improvement") as those used to describe the Downtown Eastside today. The mythologies used to define particular spaces and bodies are thus trans-temporal, and the conflations of the land with "emptyness" or of Indigenous womanhood with "prostitute," although historical, are nonetheless certainly not *past* (when the past is construed as settled, finished, over-and-done-with), but instead shape the contours of present-day British Columbia. In fact, very similar symbolic and material practices are evident in the Downtown Eastside today.

The contemporary Downtown Eastside has become notorious for drug use, prostitution, and extreme poverty not just through news reportage but also in part through the immense popularity of a National Film Board of Canada (NFB) documentary, *Through a Blue Lens* (1999). This film documents the lives of several people who at the time of filming were addicted to criminalized drugs and living for the most part on the streets in the Downtown Eastside, as filmed (and framed) through the gaze of a group of Vancouver police officers (who contribute much of the footage). *Through a Blue Lens* is frequently used in drug education and awareness programs in Canada and beyond; according to the police-turned-filmmakers, it is "the NFB's most successful video in their history" and has been viewed by "tens of millions of viewers worldwide."[6] The documentary purposefully constructs the Downtown Eastside along the lines of the "mythical frontier" that Sommers and Blomley describe above: opening shots of drug deals and people smoking and injecting drugs are accompanied by steel guitar music intended, according to geographer Jennifer England (based on an interview with the film's director, Victoria Mannix), to "give the inner city a purposeful wild-west groove" (2004, 301). In an interview with England, Mannix explained that her aim was to represent the Downtown Eastside as "an untamed frontier: a place of good guys and bad guys, cowboy cops and outlaw addicts" (ibid.), a polarization she imagines might begin to crumble as the film continues, but that I would argue remains firmly entrenched.

Through a Blue Lens is rife with scenes evocative of the Wild West. In one scene, for example, with the steel guitar again twanging in the background, a police officer encounters a man in an alleyway, makes him dump his heroin on the ground and then says, "Turn your pocket inside out there, *partner*." When he is satisfied that the man has no additional drugs, the officer instructs him to "move along, *partner*." The music and language here are right out of a typical Western. The scene concludes with the officer's statement that Downtown Eastside residents addicted to drugs have "really tragic, pathetic, wasted lives." This construction of Downtown Eastside residents as "pathetic" and as living "wasted lives" legitimates claims that the neighbourhood ought to be "cleaned up" in the interests of (good) citizens who desire to resettle the area (perhaps not so coincidentally, the film was released just shortly after the neighbourhood began undergoing its city-sponsored "revitalization").[7] The reference to waste (i.e. "wasted lives") echoes nineteenth-century rationales for colonizing the space that has become Vancouver; as Nicholas Blomley (2004) explains, "Native lands ... were deemed unimproved, and could thus be justly expropriated by those who were capable of reclaiming the 'waste'" (116; see also Perry 2001, 126).

As Blomley (2004) further argues, "To characterize a dense, inner-city neighbourhood – containing several thousand people – as 'empty' seems a striking claim" (91). Initially, I found myself confused by the tendency to conflate "degeneracy" with emptiness in descriptions of the Downtown Eastside – after all, a space requires contents, people and places and events, in order to be rendered "degenerate." Yet I have come to see that there is a definite connection between images of the Downtown Eastside that emphasize "degeneracy" and "waste" and those that render it empty. The logic goes something like this: because "waste" is non-productive, in economic terms, it is easily rendered as nothing, and therefore as nothing *there*. This kind of (indisputably capitalist) logic is thoroughly bound up with the Enlightenment principles of "progress," those taken-for-granted markers of triumph and success that are in turn thoroughly immersed in the logics of imperialism and colonization. So the characterization of life in the Downtown Eastside as "degenerate" and as "waste" is essentially an old frontier trick remade for a contemporary moment.

What are the potential effects of these representations that invite us to imagine the space of the Downtown Eastside through the language and metaphors of the Wild West? What sorts of encounters between people might such imaginings invite? Geographer Neil Smith (1996) argues that in the late twentieth century, frontier mythology became characteristic of urban revitalization projects aiming to "clean up" and transform the character(s) of inner-city spaces across North America. "In the end," he writes, "the frontier discourse serves to rationalize and legitimate a process of conquest, whether in the eighteenth- and nineteenth-century West, or in the late-twentieth-century inner city" (xv). The use of frontier mythology to describe the space of the Downtown Eastside serves to (re)define it as in need of taming and resettlement by (presumably white and wealthy) "pioneers," although the class and race dynamics of such urban projects are often ignored or outright denied. As Smith explains:

> The term "urban pioneer" [often used to describe those imagined as the desirable new occupants of a "revitalized" inner city] is therefore as arrogant as the original notion of "pioneers" in that it suggests a city not yet socially inhabited; like Native Americans, the urban working class is seen as less than social, a part of the physical environment. (xiv)

The urban working class is posited by such mythology as outside of, or not belonging to, the social world – a dangerous presupposition that portends a dehumanization that rationalizes and naturalizes violence and the displacement of people positioned to be "of" this class. Because Vancouver's Downtown Eastside is a neighbourhood with a disproportionate number of people frequently categorized as urban poor / low-income / working class *and* Indigenous, the frontier mythology evoked to describe this neighbourhood today becomes all the more salient: the visible presence of "real Indians" lends legitimacy to the idea that struggles over the Downtown Eastside are aptly captured by this mythology.

The echo of early descriptions of Indigenous people in contemporary descriptions of residents of inner-city neighbourhoods should make us curious about what kinds of encounters such descriptions might authorize. As Blomley (2004) explains:

> Characterizations of the residents of the inner city as mobile and unfixed bear a striking resemblance to many representations of native people. In both cases, the effect is to force a separation between a population and the space it occupies, rendering a collective claim to this space void, even invisible. (xx)

Blomley makes a compelling connection between private property and citizenship, underscoring that the characterization of groups of people as "mobile and unfixed" places them outside of the category of property-owner (often equated with citizen) and, by extension, outside of the realm of the human. Such descriptions are used not only to rationalize a resettlement of urban spaces but also to explain away the displacement or even disappearance of people belonging to spaces like the Downtown Eastside, and also to legitimate an official strategy of non-response. Those who followed early media coverage of the belated realization that dozens of women were "missing" from the Downtown Eastside in the late 1990s will recall that the women were frequently described as "transient" and "mobile," and thus, officials insisted, there was no reason to look for them (or else it was deemed impossible to look for them). These two claims – that a space slated for resettlement is "empty" and that the people who occupy it are "transient" and "mobile" – work together to rationalize not only displacement but also a sense that those supposedly transient and mobile lives are less valuable, less grievable, and therefore less worthy of attention or concern if they are disappeared.

Sherene Razack's (2000) delineation of how colonialist legacies naturalize violence against certain bodies occupying certain spaces becomes particularly instructive when considered alongside the predominant use of frontier mythology to describe and rationalize contemporary efforts to "clean up" and resettle inner-city spaces like the Downtown Eastside. In an earlier article, Razack (1998) analyses how and why the urban spaces where prostitution happens are produced as racialized spaces, asking, "How is prostitution always about race, class, and gender, even when the prostitutes are white?" (345). Her analysis of the racialization of such spaces is essential to understanding the connections between British Columbia's colonial past and the disappearance of women from the Downtown Eastside today. For it is not as though all the women who have been disappeared from the Downtown Eastside are Indigenous, but I would argue that a kind of metonymic slippage is at work here. In the racialized spaces of the contemporary Canadian inner city, spaces that are often described much as the frontier was described during early contact between Europeans and First Nations, histories of colonization, and in particular that aspect of those histories that produced a conflation of Indigenous womanhood with prostitution, work to render "the prostitute" in such spaces as symbolically Indigenous, such that she is in effect racialized as "other" even when her skin may be read as white. Similarly, in his historical analysis of the settlement of Seattle and its outskirts, Coll Thrush notes that "prostitutes visiting the [Hooverville] encampment were 'squaws,' whether they were Indigenous or not" (2011, 67). A spatial analysis reveals how racialization is produced concomitantly through the histories which also (re)produce particular understandings of a place, such that "race" signifies quite differently in different places and different epochs. This insight can help us to understand how colonial histories are implicated in the contemporary violence directed at women in the Downtown Eastside, even though not all of the women are Indigenous.

Sara Ahmed (2000) similarly argues that "contemporary modes of proximity *reopen prior histories of encounter*" (13, emphasis in original). She is interested in investigating "how colonial encounters are both determining, and yet not fully determining, of social and material existence" (11). Read alongside the "histories of encounter" between Indigenous women and white men in colonial British Columbia, it becomes imperative to consider the violence experienced by Indigenous women in the Downtown Eastside (and in neighbourhoods cast as "new frontiers" in Canada more broadly) today as encounters that are fully enmeshed with that history, belying its past-ness. Yet, although a history of colonization delimits the encounter, it is important to note that history cannot *fully* determine it; that because history *produces* the categorizations rather than the other way around, other outcomes were and are possible. As Ahmed reminds us, "rethinking the primacy of the encounter over ontology is ... a means by which we can introduce historicity, as the very absence of any totality that governs the encounter" (10). It would be a mistake, then, to represent these contemporary acts of violence as the *inevitable* result of an unjust past.

Building on comments by the Native Council of Canada, Razack (2000) notes that the rearrangement of space during the colonial period continues to sustain a "'perception that being Aboriginal and being urban are mutually exclusive'" (Native Council of Canada in Razack, 102; see also Pratt 2005, Peters 1998). This perception, though, is largely false, as Indigenous people have lived in Canadian cities since their founding (in fact were instrumental *to* their founding in many instances, as is true of Vancouver; see, for example, Robert McDonald's *Making Vancouver*). Historian Jean Barman's book *Stanley Park's Secret* offers a compelling history of the presence of several Indigenous families on the land now known as Vancouver's Stanley Park during the city's founding, for example. The common perception that the onset of the reservation system emptied urban centres of Indigenous people is untenable, then. But although an urban Indigenous presence has been constant in many Canadian cities, the *numbers* of Indigenous people living in urban centres grew substantially in the last half of the twentieth century. As Evelyn Peters notes (drawing on census data and the findings of the 1996 report of the Royal Commission on Aboriginal Peoples), in 1951 only 6.7 per cent of those identifying as "Indians and Eskimos" (the colonial terminology of the time) lived in urban areas, whereas by 1991, a full 41 per cent of those identifying as "North American Indians" were living in cities. Further, due to the extensive sex discrimination of the Indian Act, which made it more likely that Indigenous women would have little choice but to leave their reserve communities (upon the dissolution of a marriage, for example, or if they married a non-Indigenous man), Peters notes that "First Nations women have been overrepresented in urban areas since at least the 1960s" (674).

This significant increase in the numbers of Indigenous people – and Indigenous women in particular – in urban centres has somehow continued to coexist with the mistaken perception that Indigeneity and the city are mutually exclusive, which shapes how Indigenous people occupying city spaces are perceived by many non-Indigenous residents. In her analysis of the murder of Pamela George, a woman of the Saulteaux (Ojibway) nation, Razack (2000) draws our attention to the fact that George's murderers first drove her to the outskirts of Regina, where they killed her and abandoned her body. She locates this violent act on a continuum of similar contemporary efforts to violently expel the bodies of Indigenous people from cities in western Canada, such as the horrifically common police practice of driving Indigenous people out of the city and abandoning them there, which has been linked to the freezing deaths of several Indigenous men in recent years.[8]

Many of the women who have been disappeared from Vancouver's Downtown Eastside were of course also removed from the inner city, their remains discovered on a rural property in the suburban outskirts. The pattern has been similar in Edmonton, where the bodies of women doing outdoor sex work in the inner city have, over a period of several years, been found in fields just beyond the city limits. It is the same pattern documented by journalist Warren Goulding (2001), who writes about the murders of at least three Indigenous women whose bodies were discovered on the outskirts of Saskatoon, and the pattern is also evident in Winnipeg, where several women's bodies have been found near the city's northern outskirts. How can we explain that, of the 582 cases of Indigenous women identified as murdered or missing by the Native Women's Association of Canada, a shocking 68 per cent resided in one of the four western provinces, where frontier mythology remains such a salient "origin story"?[9] And might the intensification of such violence in a city like Vancouver have at least some small amount to do with how "Vancouver stands apart from many other North American cities of the period in the degree to which it retained elements of its 'frontier' past" (McDonald 1996, xii)? These contemporary acts of colonial violence against Indigenous women are *precisely* the sorts of encounters that are authorized by the ongoing use of frontier mythology to describe the inner-city spaces from which women are being disappeared – a deeply unsettling illustration of the social and psychic legacies of a colonialism that is anything but past.

The resurfacing of such frontier rhetoric in recent efforts to resettle the Downtown Eastside (and other neighbourhoods like it) indicates that these efforts are haunted by the city's colonial past, a past with claims on the present that are frequently disavowed and are yet to be reckoned with. Frontier mythology slips into these efforts and makes this colonial past "there and not there at the same time" (Gordon 1997, 6): "there" because the mythology evokes this past, but "not there" because the past's significance to the present is so frequently disavowed or disregarded. Instead, efforts to effect a present-day displacement of Downtown Eastside residents rely on a taken-for-granted assumption that the past is "settled," so to speak, and therefore irrelevant to the present. But frontier mythology allows the presence of the past to seep in, haunting the present by calling attention to the ways that the relationship *between* past and present is much messier, much more enmeshed, than conventionally conveyed.

What, then, might it mean to recognize and reckon with the haunting aspects of the frontier mythology frequently evoked to describe this place today? Wendy Brown (2001) acknowledges that even "when avowed, [a haunting] does not make perfectly clear what its meanings and effects are" (153). The outcome of encountering a haunting, any path it might suggest towards greater justice for Downtown Eastside residents, is not neatly laid out for us. Anything it might signal is necessarily partial, contestable, situational. So what good can come from recognizing hauntings, one might ask, when to do so does not guarantee a different approach or a different outcome? To offer a partial answer to this question, I need to convey a story about my own recent encounter with the haunting presence of Sereena Abotsway, an Indigenous woman who was disappeared from the Downtown Eastside in 2001.

Nettie Wild's documentary *Fix: The Story of an Addicted City* (2002) is haunted by absent presences and by a presence now made absent – a presence that has since been violently disappeared from the Downtown Eastside. The first haunting is intentional, the other accidental, but both draw attention to contemporary injustices and together show how hauntings are multilayered, how "even those who haunt our dominant institutions and their systems of value are haunted too" (Gordon 5). *Fix* documents the struggle of the Vancouver Area Network of Drug Users (VANDU) to secure funding for a safe injection site in the Downtown Eastside.[10] Filming of the documentary began just after the release of *Through a Blue Lens*; VANDU, though, was formed in 1998, while *Through a Blue Lens* was still being filmed, yet the fledgling organization is curiously elided in this documentary about drug use in the Downtown Eastside. This oversight contradicts the filmmakers' professed desire to make *Through a Blue Lens* an "apolitical" film: by drawing attention to the social and historical causes of poverty and addiction, the work of VANDU undermines the desire of *Through a Blue Lens*'s police-turned-filmmakers to paint a picture of addiction as simply a matter of individualized "bad choices"; if VANDU were given representation in the film, *Through a Blue Lens*'s ideological stakes might well be exposed or questioned. By contrast, through its focus on the activism of VANDU, *Fix* draws out the social dimensions of addiction, providing an opening for contemplating the relationship between past and present injustices that might work to evoke in viewers a wider sense of implication in the difficult, at times horrendous, social conditions depicted on screen.

The members of VANDU seem aware of the power of hauntings to provoke recognition of injustice among a wider public. They attempt to deliberately animate ghostly presences in their protests against funding cuts to Downtown Eastside services or refusals to fund social housing and harm reduction programs, programs that might reduce some of the vulnerability to unjust, untimely death that many people from the Downtown Eastside contend with daily. Repeatedly, they establish rows of wooden crosses in parks, in front of city hall, and on the grounds of the provincial legislature in Victoria. They also take coffins to city council meetings, cloaked in spectre masks. In doing so, they insist that public officials reckon with the dead of the Downtown Eastside, drawing important connections between public policy, the uneven distribution of social resources, and the untimely, unjust deaths of many of the people who share their neighbourhood. A laudable effort to animate hauntings for the purposes of creating immediate, and urgently needed, change, there is nonetheless something about the intentionality of VANDU's work here, about their strategic deployment of the dead, that seems less likely to evoke a more widespread sense of implication in the losses their protests mark, despite this work's incredible importance as a form of political activism.

But for me, *Fix* provoked an encounter with another, less obvious haunting presence, one captured on film entirely by accident. The second time I watched the film, I was suddenly struck by a face I thought I recognized among those filmed in Oppenheimer Park installing row upon row of crosses for a demonstration (see figure 1.3). I puzzled over where I knew this face from, backed up the DVD, and suddenly felt quite stunned as I realized why I recognized the woman: she is Sereena Abotsway, and I recognized her from her photograph on the Missing Women Task Force poster and others I have seen of her on websites and in newspapers. In life, Abotsway was, among other things, an activist in the Downtown Eastside. She participated in VANDU protests as well as in the annual Valentine's Day Memorial March, where she once remembered murdered and missing women from the neighbourhood and is now one of the women whom marchers remember and mourn. Today, marchers pause to remember Abotsway and perform a smudge to honour and release her spirit in front of the Portland Hotel on Hastings Street, where she was last seen.

It is of course not surprising that a documentary made in this neighbourhood at this time would capture the images of some of the women who have since been disappeared: Wild began filming *Fix* in 2000 and Abotsway was disappeared in 2001. Yet Abotsway's presence in the film, because it is unexpected, is unsettling, all the more so because it is a moving image of a woman whom I have only ever seen in still photographs. In the film Abotsway is alive, and in the few seconds in which

1.3 Sereena Abotsway hammering a wooden cross into the ground for a protest organized by the Vancouver Area Network of Drug Users (VANDU). Frame from the documentary film *Fix: The Story of an Addicted City*, dir. Nettie Wild. Reproduced courtesy of Canada Wild Productions.

she appears on screen she pounds a wooden cross into the ground, her hammer hitting the top of the cross four times before the camera pans away to other activists doing the same thing. Here, Abotsway is protesting the social conditions that make her and others from the Downtown Eastside more vulnerable to unjust, untimely, and too often violent deaths. Her presence here among those whose deaths she protests and mourns indicates a double haunting: Abotsway, haunted by the deaths of friends and neighbours, likely also lovers, acquaintances, and strangers, has herself come to haunt, her presence (now made violently absent from the Downtown Eastside) a warning to pay attention to hauntings, to heed what they can tell us about the complicated enmeshments of past and present.

After I noticed Abotsway's presence in *Fix* I could not watch the rest of the film in the same way. Recognizing Abotsway in the film and knowing of her (coming) death is disorienting because it collapses time: here in the film I can see the living presence of a woman now murdered, whose death is today considered to be in the past, yet in the present captured by the film it is still in the future, still to come – in other words, still preventable. Knowing of her (coming) death and seeing her alive in this film seems to implicate me, the viewer, in her murder, particularly when considered alongside the other hauntings that the film intentionally animates. In other words, Abotsway's presence has the potential to provoke a sense of urgency about the ways that injustice and vulnerability are so unevenly distributed and lived.

For me, what lives on from Abotsway's violent death is the necessity of maintaining a continuous awareness that everything about who I believe myself to be and how I live my life today is indelibly bound up in the myriad injustices that are everywhere evident in the neighbourhood she called home. This does not mean that I can, or want to, collapse the vast differences between myself and Abotsway or myself and many of the people who today call the Downtown Eastside home, even though those differences, rather than reflecting some inherent or biological truth, are instead a complicated legacy of history. But to collapse them would be to erase the evidence of settler colonialism in the present, the evidence of the many ways that the past's presence *in* the present left Abotsway so much more vulnerable to the violence she experienced and living with so much more exposure to precarity in her daily life. Unravelling the complicated binding of our existence is what I inherit from Abotsway and others from the Downtown Eastside whose absent presences continue to haunt our social world. An attention to the haunting presences of Abotsway and others like her provokes me to begin to imagine a present (and future) that might be otherwise; or, to try to stage "interventions" instead of "repetitions" (Van Alphen 1999, 279), in the interests of a (future) present in which the presence of the past is a provocation for reckonings instead of disavowals.

What might such an intervention look like? The search for interventions requires that we attend not only to how such injustices remain evident but also to what can and is being done in a daily way to confront them. For Abotsway also lives on through the political activism that is documented by the film in which she appeared, activism that carries on today in the Downtown Eastside in forms too many and too varied to give a full account: anti-poverty activism; activism and coalition-building among sex-worker organizations; media activism that tells alternative stories and presents alternative visions of the Downtown Eastside, such as the annual PIVOT photo contest, "Hope in Shadows," or the Downtown Eastside Power of Women Group's "In Our Own Voices" project; activism by Indigenous groups and their allies, some of which forcefully proclaimed "No Olympics on Stolen Native Land"; activism by the Carnegie Community Action Project and the Save Low Income Housing Coalition that aims to stem the tide of homelessness brought about by gentrification; activism by the Vancouver Area Network of Drug Users and their allies who founded and battled to keep Insite, the safe-injection site; activism by the coalitional forces that maintained the Woodward's squat in 2002; the activist and memorializing projects of the Women's Memorial March Committee; activism that is taking aim at the laws that so greatly increase the vulnerability of women doing sex work ... I could go on and on.

Most of this activism is performed by residents of the Downtown Eastside who are tired of watching their friends and loved ones die violently or suffer, as Abotsway was. Taking our cue from such activism, advocating that it lead and structure any form of "change" that is imagined as desirable in the Downtown Eastside, would be one way to offer Abotsway "a hospitable memory *out of a concern for justice*" (Derrida in Gordon 64, emphasis Gordon's). If justice is to make itself known in the Downtown Eastside, it will be through contending with the work and claims of these many local activists. This activism, work that Abotsway participated in, lives on just as powerfully as the injustices which shaped and constrained Abotsway's life, and, as Brown suggests, it can and should "inspirit our imaginations and visions for the future" (150), not just for those who live in the Downtown Eastside, but for all of us who inherit what lives on from Vancouver's disappeared women.

Chapter Two

Following Ghosts: Different Knowings, Knowing Differently

Vancouver writer Maggie de Vries published *Missing Sarah*, a memoir about the life and disappearance of her sister, Sarah de Vries, in the summer of 2003. Members of the De Vries family – a middle-class white family from one of Vancouver's more prestigious neighbourhoods – were influential in the struggle during the late 1990s and early years of the new century to get officials to finally respond with any seriousness to the disappearance of so many women from the Downtown Eastside neighbourhood. *Missing Sarah* is therefore an important and timely book. It offers readers a vivid description of what it is like to witness a loved one struggling with an addiction to criminalized drugs, and eloquently captures the sensations of living with the anguishing uncertainty and ongoing, penetrating grief that arises when a loved one has been disappeared. *Missing Sarah* also compellingly introduces readers to some of Sarah de Vries's own journal writing and poetry.

It would be fair to say that I find myself haunted by Sarah de Vries, in the sense that Avery Gordon (1997) makes of haunting: "Haunting is a constituent element of modern social life. It is neither premodern superstition nor individual psychosis; it is a generalizable social phenomenon of great import" (7). And: "Being haunted draws us affectively, sometimes against our will and always a bit magically, into the structure of feeling of a reality we come to experience, not as cold knowledge, but as a transformative recognition" (8). Through the metaphor of haunting, I am attempting to convey how Sarah de Vries's words and various representations of her life pull me affectively, as Gordon describes, sometimes against my will, into a transformative recognition of my own implication in the social conditions and arrangements that underpin De Vries's disappearance and murder. Traces of her life, found in media, art, her sister's memoir, and selections of her own writing, compel me to investigate what it might have meant for De Vries to repeatedly encounter how lives so similar to her own were cast, in a variety of representations, as suffering deaths that are frequently (and sometimes casually) deemed unworthy of widespread grief, or even concern or acknowledgment.

Following ghosts is a practice of inheritance that requires a different approach to doing academic research. As Gordon explains, such a practice could "be conceived as entering through a different door, the door of the uncanny, the door of the fragment, the door of the shocking parallel" (66). It is a practice postulated by Jacques Derrida in his seminal work *Specters of Marx* (1994), developed further and transformed into something more like a methodological approach (or, perhaps more accurately, something more like a critique of methodology) by Gordon in *Ghostly Matters* (1997, reissued in 2008), and deployed since then in an explosion of texts by numerous other critics in the humanities and social sciences. For Gordon, recognizing that a haunting is taking place involves noticing "how that which appears to be not there is often a seething presence, acting on and often meddling with taken-for-granted realities" (8). Hauntings draw our attention to the social and psychic remainders of injustice, violence, disappearance, trauma, and loss – in other words, to the past's ongoing claims on the present. Following ghosts, then, is in part about a different way of understanding what knowledge *is* and how we might recognize it, since those of us engaging in this practice are tasked with looking not for what *is* there but instead for the "seething presence" of what "appears to be *not* there" (8, emphasis added). It is a critical practice that aims to rethink or challenge dominant Western or Euro-American ways of knowing, to challenge the forms of knowledge that get produced or recognized *as* knowledge through the logics of imperialism and colonialism, potentially opening spaces for different knowings and for knowing differently.

I am deeply apprehensive, however, about how framing my encounters with the spectral traces of some of the women disappeared from the Downtown Eastside through a metaphor of haunting risks reiterating the problematic trope of the "disappearing Indian." Literary critic Renée Bergland raises this problem in her book *The National Uncanny: Indian Ghosts and American Subjects*, in which she traces representations of the "ghostly Indian" through three hundred years of American literature. As she insists: "The image [of the Indian ghost] ... draws ideological power from the sense of *fait accompli* (the Indians are already gone), and from reinforcing the intractable otherness of Indians (they are so other that they are otherworldly)" (2000, 5). Sarah Kavanagh similarly argues that the erasure of "documented histories and corporeal evidence of actual Native peoples" is "paired with an insistent memorializing of 'the Indian' ... a replacement of actual people with imagined constructions" (2011, 167). When a critic like myself, who comes to be in Canada today as the descendent of Europeans, racially marked by whiteness, evokes the spectral traces of women who are repeatedly racially marked in numerous representations as Indigenous "others," I undoubtedly risk reinscribing the ideological power of this trope. I do try to speak *to* and not *for* the ghosts I encounter in this book, though, which might be a practice that "respects the ghost and the *intersubjective* nature of a haunting" (Van Wagenen 2004, 292, emphasis added). Focusing on the intersubjective relations involved in following ghosts seems to me to have the potential to draw attention to colonization as a *shared* history in ways that presuming to speak *for* those ghosts perhaps cannot.

Still, as Emilie Cameron compellingly argues, "confining the Indigenous to the ghostly also has the potential to re-inscribe the interests of the powerful upon the meanings and memories of places" (2008, 390). Cameron is astutely critical of settler-critics' fascination with the metaphor of haunting, insisting that Indigenous ghost stories often "manage to 'write out' the bodies and voices of living, politically active Indigenous peoples" (388). Warren Cariou also argues that a renewed interest in "spectral Native figures" might simply reflect "a widespread and perhaps growing anxiety suffered by settlers regarding the legitimacy of their claims to belonging on what they call 'their' land ... a sense that their current legitimacy as owners or renters in a capitalist land market might well be predicated upon theft, fraud, violence, and other injustices in the past" (2006, 727–8). It appears that an interest in Indigenous ghosts might tell us more about settler cultures and anxieties and risk drawing more attention to settler guilt than to decolonizing practices.

These concerns about how a fixation with Indigenous ghosts can eclipse the significant political claims of Indigenous peoples and communities are crucial, and I have learned much by engaging with the important scholarship, writing, and activism of many of the Indigenous scholars and activists who are working to draw attention and demand a just political response to the disappearance or murder of so many Indigenous women. While too many Indigenous women have been subjected to the violent forms of disappearance I write about in this book, countless others are at the forefront of a movement to end and redress this violence and are calling for political reforms directed at changing the social conditions and arrangements that facilitate such violence, as well as the many other forms of injustice, discrimination, and violence that provide evidence of ongoing settler colonialism in the present. Many Indigenous writers and scholars also work with theory arising from Indigenous knowledge that presents important and serious challenges to colonial logics and the Euro-Western philosophies and epistemologies that underpin imperialist and colonialist mindsets. As Cree-Metis scholar Deanna Reder argues:

> What is needed is a space that is not thought of as haunted but rather one where the existence of the spiritual alongside physical dimensions can do the work of reclamation using our epistemologies as sources – to build a place in which Indigenous history, interpretation, academic voices and perspectives can be *present*. (2010, 413, emphasis added)

Through my efforts to read, write, and think with contemporary Indigenous scholars, writers, and activists, I hope to further expose the trope of the "disappearing Indian" for the fiction that it is. As Colleen Boyd and Coll Thrush argue in their introduction to *Phantom Past, Indigenous Presence*, "the survival of both ghosts and native peoples suggests that for all their power, colonial accounts of progress – whether triumphal or lamenting – are in themselves just another kind of fiction" (2011, xxi). My encounters with the spectral traces of disappeared women, *in addition* to engaging with theory, writing, and activism produced by Indigenous scholars, writers, and activists, have in fact all been quite pivotal to my own ability and desire to expose these colonial accounts of "progress" as purely fictional.

Both Indigenous and non-Indigenous scholars appear somewhat divided on the significance, effects, or political potential of following ghosts, then, and this division does not map neatly onto particular identity categories. Many note that ghosts and spirits are crucially important to several Indigenous world views and spiritualities. In the introduction to his important book *God Is Red*, prominent Lakota scholar Vine Deloria Jr writes: "I conclude that our ancestors lived in a strange condition in which they were in touch with the spirits constantly, and I see that as a goal for our present activities" (2003, xvii). James (Sa'ke'j) Youngblood Henderson argues that the ghost dance, which he insists has been widely misunderstood in Eurocentric studies, offered Indigenous people "a sustained vision of how to resist colonization" because it passed on insights about "how to release all the spirits contained in the old ceremonies and rites" to multiple generations (2000, 57–8). Warren Cariou argues that the spirits identified by Indigenous communities (and often written into Indigenous literature) "do seem to address the transgressions of the colonial past, [but] they usually do so as part of a call for some kind of redress or change in the present" (2006, 730). To follow ghosts in the interests of trying to track their claims on the present, then, rather than as mere symbols of an unjust past, seems to mark a crucial difference in understandings about what ghosts are, as well as about their political potential and effects. Bergland argues that "metaphors of Native spectrality *can* work to empower Native people and to challenge United States [or in my case, Canadian] hegemony" (169, emphasis added), while Boyd and Thrush insist that "taking Indigenous hauntings and ghosts seriously involves taking Indigenous peoples and their histories seriously, with ramifications for the present and future of Native and settler societies alike" (xxxiii). These authors seem to be suggesting that the interpretive possibilities of hauntings might depend more on the context and purpose for which a haunting is taken up than on the fact of its analysis. For example, I contextualize my evocation of the ghostly presences of some Indigenous women who have been disappeared within a narrative that aims to expose how settler colonialism and its ongoing effects are at the root of such ghostly-ness, rather than some naturalized, inherent predilection for disappearance. I am cautiously optimistic that this difference in framework matters in an important way.

If it were not for the fact of my settler roots, though, it is unlikely I would experience these encounters with spectral traces of Vancouver's disappeared women as haunting. This is not necessarily a bad thing: "In a settler-colonial context, the experience of unsettlement [arising from encounters with hauntings] is a potentially decolonizing force, where 'what is "ours" as settlers is also recognized as potentially, or even always already "theirs"'" (Gelder and Jacobs in Freeman 2011, 212). Hauntings might, for settlers, "unsettle" our previous assumptions and senses of entitlement in a settler-colonial context. I do worry, though, that in the effort to confront and challenge the hegemonies of colonialism, hauntings also inevitably reproduce these hegemonies in some way; as Derrida (1994) writes, "Hegemony still organizes the repression and thus the confirmation of a haunting. Haunting belongs to the structure of every hegemony" (46). The trick, I believe, is to follow ghosts in the interest of exposing these hegemonic assumptions, such as the trope of the "disappearing Indian," for the fictions that they are, but to do so does mean attempting to include within one's mode of address people for whom hegemony maintains the unquestioned status of "just the way things are," the same people for whom the metaphor of contemporary colonial Canada as "haunted" might register, literally as well as figuratively, as unsettling.

Margot Francis's auto-ethnographic story about her own encounter with hauntings also gestures to the productive way that hauntings might spur us to begin "sketching out a politics of 'locatedness'" (2011, 6). Francis's project contributes to "mapping the affective processes through which spectres are both remembered and refused within the [Canadian] national consciousness" (5), and she importantly reimagines spectrality as a possible fate for a wider Canadian public that might refuse to reckon with the nation's unjust past. Building on Metis writer Maria Campbell's observation that her elders often describe white people in Canada as "Ghosts trying to find their clothes" (cited in Francis, 1), Francis argues that when Canada "forgets its own complicity in a deeply racialized legacy, we ourselves become ghostly" (14). Here, the potential for ghostliness arises from a refusal to grapple with how the unresolved injustices of the past might leave one out of place, which risks transforming one's claims to a particular place into something apparitional. Compellingly, Francis insists that we must reckon with the widespread refusal to recognize our racist history and its ongoing presence in the present if we hope to build and support different approaches to memory work that might provide "an antidote to the continuing lure of ghostliness" (163).

For those of us who came to know something about Vancouver's disappeared women only after they were disappeared, what we can know of them is necessarily apparitional, composed of traces appearing in stories or images that are mediated mainly by those who knew them in life. My encounters with some of these traces during the decade I have been working on this book dramatically transformed my sense of my own place in this story and on the land on which I currently reside. These encounters also led me to the work of Indigenous scholars and activists and prompted me to rethink some of my own taken-for-granted assumptions inherited from Euro-Western thought. For these reasons, although I have become sceptical and cautious about the risks of eclipsing the ongoing political claims and work of Indigenous people through the metaphor of haunting, I am nonetheless aware that were it not for the impetus provided by some of the haunted encounters I take up in this book, I would not likely have come to appreciate the importance of those claims and this work myself.

I am not so much interested in haunting as a metaphor for settler–Indigenous relations or for contemporary colonial Canada, then; what interests me about the practice of following ghosts is its implicit critique of the disciplining effects of conventional methods for the production of knowledge in the academy. The value of a haunting lies at least partly in its ability to unsettle us *through how it exposes us to the limits of what we believe ourselves to know*. This view of haunting is consistent with Henderson's description of "*postcolonial* ghost dancing," which he describes as a process of overcoming the myriad effects of the hegemonic Eurocentric world views and values imposed through colonization (2000, 73, emphasis added). Being exposed to the limits of what we assume ourselves to know might just produce the kind of unsettlement that could challenge or provoke more non-Indigenous peoples to learn from Indigenous knowledges and join decolonizing struggles, and it is for these reasons that I continue to hold onto the unsettling potential of some haunting encounters.

Taking a cue from Gordon, then, and in particular from where her theorizing converges with Butler's work on grievability (2004, 2009), I have come to see that an analysis of representations of disappeared women alone would not do justice to either the complexity of those representations or to their broader social implications. Nor would it tell us much about how those representations work to (re)produce hegemonic conceptions of what makes for a grievable life. "Coupling problems with representation to an ongoing and aggressive concern with representability," Gordon writes, "in the political sense, is what enables epistemology to be properly situated in the ensemble of social relations of power" (1997, 11–12; see also Butler 2009, 73). Following ghosts demands not only a different way of recognizing knowledge, then, but also a different approach to knowledge *production*, and in that sense it is a quasi-methodological approach that incorporates a staunch critique of the methods common to several of the paramount disciplines of the humanities and social sciences. It is therefore a practice that demands both a different way of knowing and a different way of (re)producing or animating that knowledge, one that attempts to account for significant theoretical shifts in the humanities and social sciences over the past several decades, but that also aims to do so in a way that situates such knowledge in relation to everyday social life. The practice of following ghosts is therefore twofold: first, it involves exposing a haunting's significance, and second, it involves animating that haunting for a wider public, which requires writing about my "own reckoning with how [I am] in these stories, with how they change [me], with [my] own ghosts" (Gordon 22).

So just how might one track "that which makes its mark by being there and not there at the same time" (Gordon 6)? And what might it mean to take such a practice seriously as a valid and important form of knowledge production? In my case, it has meant that while I was writing interpretations and analyses of representations of Vancouver's disappeared women I began to notice how certain unexpected things would emerge and demand my attention, leading me down pathways of thought or further research that I originally had no intention to follow (or else it had not occurred to me to follow them). Such disruptions significantly shaped both the content and the form of this book, and Gordon argues that they can be read as signs that a haunting is taking place. I came to see that while the women who have been disappeared are no longer physically "there" in the Downtown Eastside, they do indeed maintain a "seething presence" in Vancouver and, I would argue, in Canada more broadly. Learning to attend to their absent presence allows us to know something different(ly) from knowing the facts that make up this story. In fact, when we fail to make note of the ways that the ghostly traces of disappeared women remain a seething *presence* in everyday life, our ability to know how those disappearances matter in (and for) the present become quite circumscribed, as does our ability to imagine how things might be otherwise. So following ghosts, as a practice of inheriting what lives on from the disappearance of so many women, might work to provoke a more widespread grappling with the ways we are all differently implicated in those disappearances. Or at least, it has done so for me.

Let me try to explain in more concrete terms by returning to how I find myself haunted by Sarah de Vries. De Vries was last seen in the Downtown Eastside on 14 April 1998, and in 2008 she remained one of the women listed on the Missing Women Task Force official list of missing women, even though, as Maggie de Vries explains in the prologue to her memoir, "[Sarah] isn't missing any more" (xi).[1] Adopted by the De Vries family as an infant, Sarah's biological parents were "of mixed race – black, Aboriginal and Mexican Indian as well as white" (De Vries 2003, 1). Her placement in a white family in 1970 is consistent with the pattern of the "sixties scoop," a determined government effort to use child welfare practices to remove Indigenous children from their birth families and place them mainly in white households under the auspices of assimilation and integration into Euro-Canadian cultures and communities.[2] Like Indigenous children, black children are also overrepresented in child protection case files in Canada, although there is significantly less research about this (Pon, Gosine, and Phillips 2011).

The information available suggests that Sarah de Vries was not apprehended by child protection authorities, but her sister Maggie notes that Sarah's adoption fits the pattern of its time: her racial and cultural background were deemed irrelevant to her placement, as was any ongoing contact with her birth family, her extended biological kin, or her racial or cultural heritage. Sarah de Vries wrote about how this affected her in a journal entry later in life:

> Man, I don't understand how the adoption agency could let a couple that are both of the opposite colour as the child become this child's legal guardians. I understand that they were not as strict as they are today on things of race, gender and traditions. But, come on, did they honestly think that it would have absolutely no effect on my way of thinking or in the way I present my persona? I'm not accepted into the Caucasian social circle nor am I accepted in the black social circle, for I am neither white nor black ... I'm stuck in the middle and outside both. I have no people. I have no nation and I am alone.[3]

Despite her Indigenous as well as black heritage, Sarah recognized herself (and I suspect was mainly recognized by others, based on her photographs) as black, and the convergence of these identities – black, Indigenous, white – in her claim, "I have no nation and I am alone," signals something of the complex and intertwining oppressions and violence of white supremacy, Western imperialism, the global expansion of capitalism, and the colonization of North America. By linking her adoption to the sixties scoop or discussing her as one of many murdered or missing Indigenous women, it is not my intention to eclipse De Vries's identification as a black woman, for as Wayde Compton reminds us, "blacks ... so often get minimized out of existence when people comment on the demographics of Vancouver. There are none, people often say" (2012, 114). Instead, I hope to draw attention to the complexity of the processes by which De Vries is identified (and identifies herself) as "of" a particular racial category, to the exclusion of other possibilities. In many publications aiming to draw explicit attention to murdered or missing Indigenous women, De Vries's story is prominently profiled.

For example, in Amnesty International's report *Stolen Sisters*, De Vries's birth parents are described with a somewhat different emphasis: her mother is described as "an Indigenous woman from the West Coast of Canada, who was also of European and African Canadian ancestry. Her father was an Indigenous man from Mexico" (51). An emphasis on De Vries's Indigeneity need not eclipse her blackness, but in places she gets figured strategically in ways that risk just such an eclipsing. It seems important, then, to stress the complexity of De Vries's racial identifications in order to challenge how she is sometimes figured in ways that invite us to imagine that race is a matter of clear and distinct biological markers rather than a system of categorization that is constituted discursively and serves particular political purposes.

De Vries's journal entry echoes the words of many trans-racial adoptees, including many Indigenous people adopted outside of their communities (Sinclair 2007). The singular, personal event of Sarah de Vries's adoption is swept up in the complex and multifaceted histories of colonialism and capital, then, enacted in part through the histories of black slavery in North America and through Indian residential schools, as well as through racist child-welfare policies that are wielded against black and Indigenous communities with particular force. In fact, we learn in *Missing Sarah* that Sarah's biological father was himself adopted, suggesting again that this personal narrative is bound to wider histories of racial injustice with very long legacies indeed.

Focusing too much on the life of Sarah de Vries risks making her appear representative of the lives of many diverse women, turning her into a figure of "Vancouver's Missing Women" (see Dean 2010a, 2010d). And yet it remains true that despite the best efforts of hosts of investigative journalists, there is simply more information available to the public about De Vries's life than is available about other women who have been disappeared from the Downtown Eastside. Dirk Meissner of the Canadian Press reports, for example, that information about Diana Melnick, another woman on the official police list of missing women, is "scarce." "Where's her family?" he asks, "Where did she grow up? How did she end up on the streets? The answers aren't easily found. What's left are the … bare facts provided by police and court documents."[4] By contrast, countless newspaper stories have been published about the life of Sarah de Vries (as recounted by various family members and friends), her disappearance was featured in an episode of the television program *America's Most Wanted*, and, as mentioned, an entire memoir has been published about her life. I do not want to frame Sarah de Vries as though she is in some way representative of Vancouver's disappeared women (thereby risking turning her into a figure myself), and yet the striking differences in the availability of information about the women's lives make it possible to write about some of their lives with more attention to detail and particularity than is possible for others. This remains at present an irresolvable dilemma and points to the ongoing necessity of investigating the facts surrounding the women's lives and disappearances – the details of what happened – *as well as* of contemplating what lives on from that happening.

De Vries has often been produced as the kind of social figure that I am cautious about, in that the particulars of her individual life have been deployed as stand-ins for "Vancouver's Missing Women," signifying beyond the specific details of her life narrative in ways that both oversimplify that narrative and overdetermine how that narrative is likely to be received. Her sister writes, for example, about her own dismay at witnessing an image of Sarah caught on film by a CBC news crew, an image she knew the CBC was going to use in a documentary about the "Missing Women" story. Maggie de Vries clearly articulates the problem with representations that fix their subjects in ways that reduce the complexity of their lives and reduce them to a stereotype:

> Ironically, that last moving image [of Sarah] freezes her. CBC will include it in their documentary. They will call it the last image of Sarah de Vries, and viewers will think, oh, that's how she was before she died. She was out of it. They won't see the time she spent preparing that day – bathing, selecting an outfit that stood out and worked together, getting her makeup just right. They won't hear the conversations she had that day, animated, connected ... (258)

Although in the end Maggie expresses satisfaction with the way her sister is represented in the documentary, her concerns about how this image fixes her sister Sarah in a very narrow and particular way deserve attention.

When following the traces of Sarah de Vries's spectral presence, I try to strike a balance between acknowledging that I am talking about a complex, unique human life and, at the same time, exploring how that life has come to signify beyond its particularity. This is no easy task. Conveying a deep respect for the individual woman's life mixed with awareness that what most of us can learn about that life now is already constrained and mediated by an array of forces, frameworks, and representations may well be the best that I can offer. Faltering, stumbling, indeed failing in the attempt to represent a life in all of its complexity is likely an important ethical strategy in response to such overdetermining representational practices (see Butler 2004). But one way to give voice to the complexity of Sarah de Vries's life is to turn to her own writing.

The poetry written by Sarah de Vries and published in *Missing Sarah* functions as a form of testamentary material, and it has the potential to call an "us" into an awareness of how we exist in relation to De Vries even if we did not know her in life, a relation that involves the inheritance of what Roger Simon describes as "a terrible gift" (2006, 187). Such a gift is "terrible" because it is difficult. It makes claims on us that are frequently "onerous" (197). In one particular poem, De Vries addresses her readers directly by issuing a challenge to what she describes as a bystander's indifference to the murder of another woman from Vancouver's Downtown Eastside:

> *Woman's body found beaten beyond recognition.*
> *You sip your coffee*
> *Taking a drag of your smoke*
> *Turning the page*
> *Taking a bite of your toast*
> *Just another day*
> *Just another death*
> *Just one more thing you so easily forget*
> *You and your soft, sheltered life*
> *Just go on and on*
> *For nobody special from your world is gone*

(in Maggie De Vries 2003, 233)[5]

De Vries's lines "Just another day / Just another death," repeated throughout the stanzas of this poem, reflect the impact of her clear sense that her own death might pass as anonymously and unremarkably as just another day gone by. It is precisely this too-easy connection between "just another day" and "just another death," as well as the many ways that vulnerability to such a connection is so very unjustly and unevenly distributed and lived, that must be exposed and ultimately contested in order to end the sort of violence that ended De Vries's life. An attention to the haunting presence of De Vries and others like her has the potential to evoke a wider sense of implication in this violence, then, by hailing the "you" she addresses in the poem into practices of inheritance.

De Vries herself bore witness, during her life, to the unjust and violent deaths of many women from her neighbourhood. The poem that I cite above testifies not only to the murder of a woman who had touched De Vries's life, but also to a sentiment of disinterest or indifference to the woman's death among some whose lives are less susceptible to such precarity and violence: *"You and your soft, sheltered life | Just go on and on | For nobody special from your world is gone"* (in Maggie De Vries 2003, 233). It is clear in this poem that De Vries was well acquainted with the consequences of living a life that often gets cast as ungrievable. In her own reading of De Vries's poem, one that draws on Shoshana Felman's work on witnessing, Geraldine Pratt makes the following compelling argument: "The terrible burden of Sarah de Vries' poem comes from the fact that she is testifying (before the fact) about an event (murder) that she cannot witness. She speaks in proxy for herself, and her authority undoubtedly comes from her very own death" (2005, 1072). The poem is thus both an indictment of how another woman's death gets cast as ungrievable and a compelling testament to the absolute and unquestionable grievability of the life of the murdered woman (and, by extension, to the grievability of De Vries's own life). But the indictment De Vries makes is not of a generalized or anonymous "society": it is directed to a "you," and it is my argument that this mode of address is important because it challenges readers to take up the witness role that De Vries enacts in the poem. If readers accept her mode of address as a challenge directed towards us personally, then it seems likely that the poem is an example of the "terrible gift" of those materials that testify to historical traumas and injustices.

Some may well be tempted to turn away from the challenge posed by the poem, for it demands nothing less than "a reconsideration of the terms of our lives now as well as in the future" (Simon 2006, 189). Yet despite whatever individual decisions we might make about how to respond to such testaments, their challenge persists. Gordon would likely refer to the kinds of testamentary materials Simon designates a "terrible gift" as clear evidence of a "ghostly matter," and a "ghostly matter," Gordon writes, "will not go away": "It is waiting for you and it will shadow you and it will outwit all your smart moves ... until you too stage a shared word, a something to be done in time and for another worlding" (190). Our best efforts to shirk or forget the challenge posed by the poem's mode of address, although "it must be said that they can be sustained for quite some time," will nonetheless continue to haunt us until such time as we are ready to take up the difficult gift that is our inheritance (ibid.).

What, then, do such practices of inheritance require of us? First, and perhaps most importantly, they require that we begin to identify "how we are in this story, even now, even if we do not want to be" (Gordon 190). Even if the stories of the disappeared women from Vancouver are not "our" story because we did not know the women in life, and even though it remains necessary to *acknowledge* that these are not our stories and that proximity to the women in life does change our relationship to the women and their stories in significant ways, it is nonetheless still important to come to see that we are *in* this wider story, too. This does not mean that we are responsible for the disappearance of women like De Vries in the same way that those who directly committed violence against them are responsible. But it does mean that we are all *in* the story, in differing ways, and it is part of our inheritance to figure out just how.

To enter into a relation of inheritance with De Vries and other disappeared women therefore requires nothing more and nothing less than "altering one's ways of being with others" (Simon 2006, 198). This seems at once a tiny and an overwhelming request: tiny in that it is impossible to know how such a potentially small and personal shift could contribute much of anything to a significantly altered world; overwhelming in the enormous overhaul of one's everyday life that such a shift potentially demands. Accepting the challenge of De Vries's address means refusing an easy identification with the "you" in the poem who remains indifferent to the murder of a woman whose life has so frequently been cast as less valuable, her dying less grievable. To take up the challenge of refusing the point of view of the "you" in the poem requires an "us" willing to relinquish the hold that the common story that situates people as rational, free-willed and freely choosing individuals has on our relations to others – in other words, it requires giving up the idea that what "I" am is possible independently of a "you." It means realizing and accepting that what we are left with, then, in Judith Butler's words, is *"the tie* by which those terms ["I" and "you"] are differentiated and related" (Butler 2004, 22, emphasis in original). It is helpful, I think, to realize that in many languages, particularly in many Indigenous languages, there is often no word for "I" or "me," only "we" or "us," signalling the ways that we are bound to other beings in relations of responsibility. Altering one's ways of being with others involves realizing that what I thought "I" was may in fact be a very significant factor in why some lives are left so much more exposed to suffering and violence than others.

Simon describes the inheritance of testamentary materials like De Vries's poem as a terrible *gift* for a reason. Aside from binding us to an onerous combination of "thoughts and actions," challenges like those posed by her poem can also be read as a form of gift, not in the sense that they offer some sort of consolation for what has been lost, but because in their claiming of us they offer the possibility of hope (2006, 198). Gifts like these are addressed to whomever might take on the responsibilities involved with their acceptance, and although they are accepted (or not) by individuals, they possess a social dimension. That De Vries's poem is addressed to a "you" suggests that it could be a terrible gift for any one of "us," and so a "we" who might accept her bequest is constituted. The "we" in this instance becomes those of us inclined to dedicate "an attentiveness and shared reference" to the testimony offered in the poem (ibid., 195). The creation of this "we" is important, for "no single beneficiary can be said to be capable of rendering the full meaning and significance of this testament" (ibid.). Instead, a *"we"* must accept this gift, taking it up in different ways, in order for its hopeful potential to be realized.

Altering one's ways of being with others in the interests of forming relations of inheritance also requires a reconceptualization of the oft-assumed-linear relationship between past, present, and future. Again, a different way of understanding temporality is (and has always already been) present in many Indigenous world views. Being open to inheriting what lives on from the disappeared women from the Downtown Eastside means beginning to account for how past injustices are everywhere evident in the present and are therefore not "past" in the way this term is conventionally thought when time is understood as a linear progression, as it so often is in Western thought and practice. As Vine Deloria Jr insists:

> The very essence of Western European identity involves the assumption that time proceeds in a linear fashion; further it assumes that at a particular point in the unraveling of this sequence, the peoples of Western Europe became the guardians of the world. The same ideology that sparked the Crusades, the Age of Exploration, the Age of Imperialism, and the recent crusade against Communism all involve the affirmation that time is peculiarly related to the destiny of the people of Western Europe. And later, of course, the United States. (2003, 62)

Linear conceptions of time are embedded in (and used to rationalize) notions of "progress" that pretend to be neutral and objectively-measurable, but fail to ask *progress for whom?* and *at what costs to others' lives?*

Such Eurocentric concepts of time also create "the illusion of a time-less Indigenous culture" (Battiste and Henderson 2000, 33), which in turn supports violent presuppositions about "disappearing Indians." By contrast, many conceptions of time in Indigenous world views, in my admittedly limited understanding, recognize time as of secondary importance to space, such that what is happening in the present in the particular ecological and social space in which I find myself is more crucial to attend to than stories about the past or visions for the future.[6] As Deloria writes, in this conception, "value judgments involve present community realities and not a reliance on … future golden ages toward which the community is moving or from which the community has veered" (2003, 67). This should not be interpreted to mean that the past or the future don't matter in Indigenous world views, for attention to one's relations with those who came before us and with future generations (both human and non-human) are also crucial in much Indigenous thought. Instead, it means that one is aware that those relations don't exist solely *in* the past or future, but are present *now*, which in turn has the potential to alter one's sense of one's responsibilities to and for those relations.

What terrible gifts like De Vries's poem and the relations of inheritance they provoke gesture hopefully towards, then, is a more just present, for while we are frequently encouraged through conventional conceptions of a linear relationship between past, present, and future to imagine that the future is always ahead, always open, always full of unrestrained opportunity, and always just over the horizon, a reconceptualization of the relations between present and past suggests that there actually *is* no future without reckoning with the past-as-present. Without such a reckoning, we are left with what Simon describes as "the endless repetition of a violent past" (2006, 203). The "hope" offered by such terrible gifts exists precisely in and through the relations of inheritance they hale us into. Such relations require us to begin to imagine our connections to others otherwise, to begin to contemplate "something to be done in time and for another worlding" (Gordon 190). By imagining us – indeed, by calling an "us" into being as inheritors of what lives on from her violent death, Sarah de Vries's address challenges us to consider how these injustices continue to inflect all of our lives, differently, daily, and to find ways to live, differently, with difficulty, based on this knowing, in the aftermath of her murder and in a present still consumed by the disappearance and violent deaths of those who continue to live and die as a result of similarly unjust social conditions and arrangements.

Chapter Three

Looking at Images of Vancouver's Disappeared Women: Troubling Desires to "Humanize"

Many of the women who have been disappeared from the Downtown Eastside came to be categorized and routinely referred to as "Vancouver's Missing Women" in part due to a controversy arising from how they were labelled on the first police poster advertising their disappearances, which was published by the British Columbia Ministry of the Attorney General and the Vancouver Police Department in 1999.[1] In this early version of a poster that would be redesigned and reissued by police several times in the following decade, a heading that reads "Missing Downtown Eastside Women" sprawls horizontally in bright yellow across the top of the women's photographs. This particular way of labelling the women was dropped from subsequent versions of the poster, I suspect because the stigmatization and stereotypical assumptions about the Downtown Eastside (discussed in chapter 1) cause its insertion between "Missing" and "Women" to work as a qualifier, an adjective that troublingly diminishes, in the imaginations of too many, the seriousness of this report that thirty-one women were at that time designated by police as "missing" from a single neighbourhood. As *Vancouver Province* journalist Bob Stall reported earlier that same year, the women "aren't from Kerrisdale" (a neighbourhood of mostly wealthy Vancouverites), and if they were, a wider public might have found the news more shocking or been more motivated to do something about it. "If 20 UBC [University of British Columbia] students went missing over the same period of time," Maggie de Vries told a reporter earlier in 1999, "there would be mayhem."[2]

A later version of the police poster contains sixty-nine photographs of disappeared women, a list much expanded from the original thirty-one names. In this version, released in 2004 (see figure 3.1), the yellow banner

MISSING WOMEN TASK FORCE

Lillian O'DARE — Last Seen: Sep 1978
Wendy ALLEN — Last Seen: 1979
Rebecca GUNO — Last Seen: Jun 1983
Sherry RAIL — Last Seen: Nov 1983
Yvonne ABIGOSIS — Last Seen: Jan 1984
Linda GRANT — Last Seen: Oct 1984
Sheryl DONAHUE — Last Seen: May 1985
Laura MAH — Last Seen: Aug 1985
Elaine ALLENBACH — Last Seen: Mar 1986

Taressa WILLIAMS — Last Seen: Jul 1988
Ingrid SOET — Last Seen: Aug 1989
Elaine DUMBA — Last Seen: 1991
Mary LANDS — Last Seen: Apr 1991
Nancy CLARK — Last Seen: Aug 1991
Elsie SEBASTIAN — Last Seen: Jun 1992
Kathleen WATTLEY — Last Seen: Jun 1992
Sherry BAKER — Last Seen: Jan 1993
Gloria FEDYSHYN — Last Seen: Feb 1993

Teresa TRIFF — Last Seen: Apr 1993
Leigh MINER — Last Seen: Dec 1993
Angela ARSENEAULT — Last Seen: Aug 1994
Catherine GONZALEZ — Last Seen: Mar 1995
Catherine KNIGHT — Last Seen: Apr 1995
Dorothy SPENCE — Last Seen: Aug 1995
Diana MELNICK — Last Seen: Dec 1995
Frances YOUNG — Last Seen: Apr 1996
Tanya HOLYK — Last Seen: Oct 1996

Olivia WILLIAM — Last Seen: Dec 1996
Cara ELLIS — Last Seen: Jan 1997
Marie LALIBERTE — Last Seen: Jan 1997
Stephanie LANE — Last Seen: Jan 1997
Jacqueline MURDOCK — Last Seen: Jan 1997
Sharon WARD — Last Seen: Feb 1997
Andrea BORHAVEN — Last Seen: Mar 1997
Richard 'Kellie' LITTLE — Last Seen: Apr 1997
Sherry IRVING — Last Seen: Apr 1997

Janet HENRY — Last Seen: Jun 1997
Ruby HARDY — Last Seen: Jul 1997
Cindy BECK — Last Seen: Sep 1997
Marnie FREY — Last Seen: Sep 1997
Helen HALLMARK — Last Seen: Oct 1997
Cynthia FELIKS — Last Seen: Dec 1997
Kerry KOSKI — Last Seen: Jan 1998
Inga HALL — Last Seen: Feb 1998
Tania PETERSEN — Last Seen: Feb 1998

Sarah DEVRIES — Last Seen: Apr 1998
Sheila EGAN — Last Seen: Jul 1998
Tammy FAIRBAIRN — Last Seen: Jul 1998
Julie YOUNG — Last Seen: Oct 1998
Angela JARDINE — Last Seen: Nov 1998
Marcella CREISON — Last Seen: Dec 1998
Michelle GURNEY — Last Seen: Dec 1998
Jacquelene McDONELL — Last Seen: Jan 1999
Brenda WOLFE — Last Seen: Feb 1999

Georgina PAPIN — Last Seen: Mar 1999
Wendy CRAWFORD — Last Seen: Dec 1999
Jennifer FURMINGER — Last Seen: Dec 1999
Tiffany DREW — Last Seen: Mar 2000
Dawn CREY — Last Seen: Nov 2000
Sharon ABRAHAM — Last Seen: Dec 2000
Debra JONES — Last Seen: Dec 2000
Yvonne BOEN — Last Seen: Mar 2001
Patricia JOHNSON — Last Seen: Mar 2001

Heather BOTTOMLEY — Last Seen: Apr 2001
Heather CHINNOCK — Last Seen: Apr 2001
Andrea JOESBURY — Last Seen: Jun 2001
Sereena ABOTSWAY — Last Seen: Aug 2001
Dianne ROCK — Last Seen: Oct 2001
Mona WILSON — Last Seen: Nov 2001

NB: All dates are approximate and are subject to change as new information becomes available.

IF YOU HAVE ANY INFORMATION ON ANY OF THE ABOVE WOMEN AND HAVE NOT YET SPOKEN TO POLICE, PLEASE CALL:

1 877 687 3377

3.1 Missing Women Task Force poster (2004 version).

that once read "Missing Downtown Eastside Women" is replaced simply with a header that reads "Missing Women Task Force." The photographs of women that make up this poster are thumbnail-sized and organized into a 9-by-7 image grid with a remaining six images occupying the bottom row. Some of the "last seen" dates that accompany each woman's name are followed by dates that apparently signal "charges laid," and for these the text is highlighted in blue. In the 2004 version there are several photographs that *ought* to have this blue highlighting, but it is still conspicuously absent, a circumstance arising from the fact that the poster was released after the arrest of Robert Pickton in 2002, but before the Crown finished laying all charges against him. As a result, in this version only fifteen photographs are marked by the blue highlighting, while in a version of the poster released in 2007 that number rises to twenty-six.[3] The addition of the "charges laid" dates on these two later versions of the poster communicates next to nothing about what happened to each individual woman pictured, suggesting that the charges are perhaps themselves of greater consequence than the violence the women experienced.

The photographs on this poster have been replicated so exhaustively now, in media reports about the story of "Vancouver's Missing Women," that they have come to stand in for the entire series of events, as well as for the lives of the women pictured. As David Hugill's analysis of extensive media coverage of the "Missing Women" story uncovered, the poster photographs "saturate the coverage ... They are unflattering, close cropped and conjure associations with familiar prisoner processing photographs" (2010, 61). These images have thus become all too familiar to readers of newspapers or viewers of television news, and frequently the photographs are reproduced in these media in grid patterns similar to that found on the poster.[4] Seldom are they reprinted alone. More recently, these same photographs have been reimagined by a number of artists who, like Pamela Masik, have used them as models for portraits. Projects such as these have further disseminated images of the women framed as they are in the poster images, albeit in somewhat different form. How are these images and reimaginings of the women enmeshed with particular frameworks for viewing a face that are, as Judith Butler argues, "variably humanizing and dehumanizing" (2005, 29), and what does this suggest about the frames of reference that underpin how and why some lives are widely understood as more grievable than others? What do these images communicate, what frames of reference are available for viewing them, and how might these frames shape various meanings and interpretations of the photographs? I contend that these poster images significantly impacted public sentiments about the women whose disappearances they mark, and that in their present form they are unlikely to evoke a more widespread sense of implication in those disappearances. As a result, practices of representation need to be challenged and rethought, as some of the artists I discuss in this chapter aim to do – and yet, the impulse to use representation to "humanize" requires just as much interrogation as those representational practices that *de*humanize.

The 2007 version of the police poster is composed of sixty-five photographs rearranged in a grid alphabetically (in contrast to their ordering by "last seen" date in the 2004 version).[5] While in the 2004 version most of the images with the blue highlighting indicating "charges laid" are clustered around the bottom of the poster, in the newer version the reorganization by last name spreads the blue highlighting more evenly across the page, making it less obvious that many of the women now known to have been murdered were disappeared within the time frame and scope of the Missing Women Task Force's official investigation. The reorganization also diminishes the importance of the dates of disappearances in favour of a new emphasis on the charges laid, since the alphabetical ordering draws our focus away from the chronology of the disappearances, making it much more difficult to recognize that women have been disappeared from this neighbourhood not just in recent years, but for decades. The 2007 version of the poster also reaffirms the offer of a $100,000 reward, first issued in 1999, for "information leading to the arrest and conviction of the person or persons responsible for the unlawful confinement, kidnapping, or murder of any or all of the listed women, missing from the streets of Vancouver." The insertion of the phrase "the streets" not-so-subtly evokes images of criminality, outdoor sex work, addiction, and homelessness, conjuring quite a different understanding of who these women might be (or why they might be missing) than if the statement simply read "missing from Vancouver."

The photographs used in the different versions of the poster have changed little over the years – only one or two women are represented by a different photograph in a later version. A handful of the images look like conventional family snapshots or school portraits, but many of the photographs resemble or are obvious reprints of police mug shots, marking the women pictured with criminality and deviance.[6] This functional use of mug-shot photographs makes the poster seem more like one seeking *wanted* rather than missing persons, at least at a first glance. In their analysis of coverage of the "Missing Women" story in Canadian mainstream newspapers, Caitlin Janzen, Susan Strega, Leslie Brown, Jeannie Morgan, and Jeannine Carrière found that "the street sex worker exists as not quite: not quite a victim, not quite an agent, not quite a woman, and often, not quite a person" (2013, 143). Similarly, in her critique of the media response to murdered or missing Indigenous women in Canada, Carol Schick argues: "Whether an Indigenous or racial minority person is the victim or perpetrator of a crime, the person will be depicted in a surprisingly similar way," as ultimately responsible for his or her own fate (2010, 139). David Hugill develops this argument further, insisting that "these mug-shot collages collapse distinctions between individuals, producing the collective as a common caste, those who experience a shared destiny borne of a shared lifestyle" (2010, 61). The mug-shot photographs risk being read, then, as sealing the women's fate – as confirmation of their own role in somehow bringing about the violence they experienced. In fact, the inclusion of text that merely reads "Charges Laid" and a date could just as easily be read as an indication that some form of charge has been laid *against the woman pictured herself*, since nowhere on either the 2004 or 2007 versions of the poster is there any indication of *who* has been charged or *what* they have been charged with.

The most obvious of these mug-shot photographs are those of Cindy Beck, Andrea Borhaven, and Inga Hall, in which the top portion of the board held up by suspects when being photographed by police is evident just above the bottom frame of the photograph, but several others are similar enough to these to suggest that this board might be just below the frame. A mug shot, after all, "typically uses – to disclose an individual's unique and distinguishing features – even and consistent lighting, a neutral background, and a fixed distance between camera and sitter" (Duganne 2007, 71; see also Sekula 1986, 30). Given this description, it seems likely that at *least* a third of the photographs in the poster are mug shots. The inclusion of these photographs risks constituting a hierarchy of grievability among the women, such that viewers are invited to imagine that some came from "good families" who were willing or able to supply recent and in many instances happy, smiling photographs of their missing loved ones, while others could be represented only through their recent contact with police. This hint of a hierarchy is itself challenged, though, by how the arrangement of the photographs into a grid invites the mug shots to spill out of their frames to the other, more familial photographs, linking them with visible markers of criminality, poverty, and addiction (already broadly associated in many imaginings with the neighbourhood of the Downtown Eastside or with "the streets") – in essence, with the sorts of markings that contribute to rendering certain lives less grievable to many, and perhaps particularly to those whose only encounter with the women is through these photographs.

Using photography to identify, categorize, and thereby produce certain subjects as deviant is a practice that has a long history, almost as long as the history of photography itself. As Allan Sekula (1986) explains in his groundbreaking work on photography: "The potential for new juridical photographic realism was widely recognized in the 1840s, in the general context of … systematic efforts to regulate the growing urban presence of the 'dangerous classes,' of a chronically unemployed sub-proletariat" (5). The practice of using photographs to document and classify prisoners was commonplace by the 1860s, and Sekula argues that through the proliferation of this practice, "a new object is defined – the criminal body" (6), against which a novel framework for what would qualify as a normative body was invoked and, over time, naturalized: "Photography came to establish and delimit the terrain of the *other*, to define both the *generalized look* – the typology – and the *contingent instance* of deviance and social pathology" (7, emphasis in original). Interpretations of the police posters today are inseparable from this lengthy, entrenched pattern of using particular visual signifiers to identify a "criminal body" and thus cement its "otherness." Indeed, this is one of the common techniques, Sekula argues, by which one might reaffirm that one's own body is normative, which may signal that the proliferation and widespread interest in viewing these particular images of the disappeared women involves a complex process of (dis)identification that is not fully explained by mere curiosity or fascination with violent crime.

Sekula tracks the development of the notion that there exists a "criminal type" whom the trained eye can identify strictly by his or her appearance. This notion was also applied in the nineteenth and early twentieth century to a number of other "social types" considered deviant, which, Sander Gilman (1985) suggests, also included the "prostitute" (94–101). Both Sekula and Gilman reproduce selections of nineteenth-century images that were deployed in an effort to catalogue and "prove" the existence of a standard appearance of "the criminal" or "the prostitute" as social types. These images show photographs organized into grid patterns alarmingly similar to the one offered in the police "missing" posters analysed here.[7] Arranging the photographs into a grid enhances the sense that one is looking at a list of wanted, rather than missing, women – at people who have been criminalized rather than subjected to violence, since this arrangement has long been used in efforts to catalogue supposed deviance. Although each woman is pictured alone, the grid arrangement groups the women such that they are barely separable – individual identities are stripped away as the images are swept into a figuration of "Vancouver's Missing Women." Further, the similarity of many of the photographs lends credence to those historical assumptions, still very much present, that "deviance" has a particular *look*. As a result, it is easy to mistake the uniformity of style and arrangement as communicating a truth about the inherent criminality or deviance of the women themselves. By unpacking the framing of the images and the lengthy history of such framing devices in photographic documentation of presumed deviance, it becomes easier to recognize that the images are indeed *framed* and, through that framing, communicate much more about the lives of the women represented than one might initially think.

In the introduction to her book *Framing the West: Race, Gender, and the Photographic Frontier in the Pacific Northwest*, feminist historian Carol Williams notes that in the late nineteenth century, a series of guides that included "step-by-step instructions for taking photographs and collecting anthropometric measurements" were published and distributed by the British Association for the Advancement of Science (BAAS) to colonial travellers, officials, and missionaries visiting "exotic" locales (including British Columbia) (17–18). Like the standardization evident in mug-shot photography, the BAAS "provided travelers with explicit instructions on how to standardize their photographic depiction of 'exotic' peoples." As Williams elaborates:

> Consequently, the visual conventions employed to portray non-Euro-American individuals, most notably Indians and Asians, diverged from those applied to the portraits of settlers. Thus certain racially or culturally distinct residents were isolated by a collective, and unquestioned, adherence to these pictorial and descriptive conventions. (18)

These standardized photographs of Indigenous subjects were frequently "'stolen,' or taken without permission, as bluntly admitted in the third (1899) edition of the BAAS guidebook" (26). There was, of course, resistance among Indigenous people to these practices, which Williams asserts was motivated "not so much [by] fear as an assertion of rights over the representation of self and territory," and some Indigenous people also commissioned their own photographs "of self and kin" (26–7). But the colonialist efforts to standardize such photographs to mark the distinctive "otherness" of Indigenous people and to gather such photographs in the interests of preserving evidence of a "disappearing" race echo unsettlingly with the development (and contemporary use) of the mug-shot photographs. When we look at the standardized mug-shot images of disproportionately Indigenous women on the police poster today, the complex history of these colonial photographs also necessarily informs how we *see* them – and risks reinforcing those troubling assumptions about an inherent predilection for disappearance discussed in the previous chapter.

As Shawna Ferris (2007) argues, the repeated grouping of the women's photographs into a grid also risks implying that "their disappearances only become remarkable when grouped together" (20). And yet, as Ferris elaborates, because each woman is contained alone within the frame of her photograph, captured in a reductive headshot that allows no possibility of a backdrop or wider context for her life, the grid also has the effect of suggesting isolation and vulnerability, reinforcing the trope of "the lone streetwalker." As a trope, Ferris argues, "the lone streetwalker" has become so common in mainstream media reportage on sex work that it heightens the vulnerability of outdoor sex workers by implying that they live and work in total isolation from each other, despite the fact that many have reported they seldom, if ever, work alone. Grouped as they are together and yet entirely framed off from each other, the grid has the effect both of erasing the women as individuals and, at the same time, of heightening a sense of each woman's isolation and vulnerability through its use of these reductive headshots.

The poster's purported intent is of course to solicit information about the disappearances, which is much more likely to be forthcoming if viewers can visually recognize the women. Yet I suspect that a poster for missing persons has at least a double task: not only must it offer a venue for viewers to try to identify those whose disappearance it advertises, but it must also try to get viewers to care, to feel a sense of compassion about (or at least interest in) the disappearance of its subjects. Only by evoking the latter response (and thereby sustaining viewers' attention) is the former response likely to be forthcoming – in other words, I suspect that people need to care something about a missing person in order to keep an eye out for her or be motivated to come forward with any information they might have about her disappearance. Yet these particularly reductive photographs seem unlikely to produce the latter response, mainly because, as Roland Barthes (1981) insists in his seminal work on the function of the photograph, *Camera Lucida*, "a photograph is always invisible: it is not it that we see" (6). Instead, what we *see* is often what we imagine to be beyond the photograph's frame – the context or narrative that we imagine to have occasioned the photograph, which we in turn believe tells us something about the life of the person in the image.

The individual photographs that make up these posters, whether mug shots or not, appear to have been chosen and arranged to imply very little variation: each one pictures a woman alone, without so much as a hint of someone else in the frame, someone (or even something) that would necessarily have been cropped to focus our attention on the missing woman but might have maintained an elusive presence that could have signalled the wider social context of the women's lives. It seems likely that what has been cropped from some of the photographs to allow such a narrow focus on individual faces might have functioned like one of Barthes's *punctums*, an "element which rises from the scene, shoots out of it like an arrow, and pierces me" (26). Although, as Barthes insists, the perception of a *punctum* in any photograph is radically subjective, the photographs that make up the police poster likely lack a *punctum* for most viewers: they belong to the realm of the *studium*, composed of those photographs in which we might "take a kind of general interest," but for which anything we might feel arrives "almost from a certain training" (26).

The "training" Barthes mentions relates to the frames of reference through which we view an image of a face and find it either humanizing or dehumanizing. This "training" evokes those ephemeral understandings with which we view an image and make meaning from it. Often we cannot pinpoint directly what form this training has taken or when it occurred. I could not tell you with much specificity, for example, where I picked up my understanding of what it means to be from "the streets," or where I learned to identify a photograph as a mug shot. Nonetheless, we are immersed in frames of reference that evoke and frequently over-determine such interpretations. For many people, such frameworks tend to appear not as frames but as "realities" or taken-for-granted assumptions about the way things are. It helps that such frameworks inform or underpin many of the representations (visual and textual) one is likely to encounter in the course of a day, whether they be in the morning newspaper, prime-time television, billboard advertisements, or broadcast or Internet news (and here I have only begun to touch on the many ways our sense of reality is mediated). We are trained to recognize chains of signification that, for the photographs in the missing poster, might for many viewers signify something like: mug shot = criminal = inherently bad or deviant person = unworthy of concern (while those images that are *not* mug shots might be imagined as "guilty by association"). Unless this prior training is disrupted, challenging us to consider other frameworks for interpreting the poster, then it seems likely that most readings of these photographs will remain within the realm of, in Barthes's coinage, the *studium*.

Barthes argues that news photographs are especially likely to reflect the characteristics of the *studium*: "In these images," he writes, there is "no *punctum*"; "a certain shock – the literal can traumatize – but no disturbance; the photograph can 'shout,' not wound. These journalistic photographs are received (all at once), perceived. I glance through them, I don't recall them; no detail (in some corner) ever interrupts my reading" (41). The photographs of disappeared women reproduced on the poster (and then over and over again in the news) function much as Barthes has described here: they may shock, but are unlikely to "puncture" us; they may seem to "shout" the suffering of some of the women pictured, but they seem unlikely to "wound" most viewers in the way that Barthes describes, and thus it remains doubtful that they will evoke a wider sense of implication in the disappearances they mark. The "detail (in some corner)" that might have shaken a viewer's complacency by functioning as a *punctum* has been cut from the frame, eliminated in the interests of the poster's purported functional purpose of helping viewers to identify the women pictured.

To make this argument more vivid, it is worth juxtaposing Helen Hallmark's poster photograph with a handful of images of her easily located online.[8] Hallmark's poster photograph looks like a mug shot, and although I cannot say for certain that it *is* a mug shot I think it is quite safe to say it could easily be read as one: it fits the typical standardization and framing of its type. The mug-shot photographs, being already reductive and taken before an empty, neutral background, are in fact *designed* in a way that makes observation of a *punctum* unlikely. The photograph of Hallmark is entirely composed of her face and a bit of her upper torso, while the backdrop is a whitish-grey – similar in many of the images that look like they could be mug shots – and in this photograph Hallmark faces the camera squarely. Her hair would be described by many as "unkempt" (although such a description is itself reductive, already reliant on norms for femininity and class). She appears to me to be staring out with something of a smirk on her face, and her eyes are ringed with dark circles. Her clothes, from what we can see of them, do not appear to be particularly "stylish" or "feminine"; at the risk of perpetuating the troubling notion that there is one stylish or feminine way to dress, taking note of Hallmark's hair and clothes potentially points to visual signs that will signal many viewers to categorize her as "of" a particular class of women (one that cannot afford to purchase clothes or have one's hair cut in the latest styles and is subsequently judged by many to be of a "lower" class, possibly belonging to "the streets," for example).

So, in Hallmark's poster photograph I see no *punctum*; because it is so generic, it bears the characteristics of the *studium*. When this photograph is juxtaposed with one that accompanies another missing-person poster of Hallmark I found online, this one likely created by a member of Hallmark's family, the differences between *studium* and *punctum* come into sharper focus.[9] In this photograph, Hallmark appears more conventionally stylish and she is smiling openly, directly facing the camera. For me, the *punctum* in the photograph is not Hallmark's face or appearance, however, but a can of Pepsi and two white china teacups and saucers visible in the background. The backdrop of this photograph is clearly some sort of social gathering, likely at a banquet hall of some sort (perhaps a wedding or family reunion?), and the everydayness of the backdrop invites me to imagine how Hallmark, at times, lived a life that many of us might describe as quite ordinary, one composed of the usual (often familial or kin-based) relationships which cause us to attend an event like the one pictured.

Another picture of Hallmark posing with her siblings at what appears to be a wedding (perhaps her own?) affects me similarly: the *punctum* is found in the ordinariness of the family snapshot, in which I can observe what might be a slight tension in the face and stance of her sister, inviting me to imagine that perhaps some everyday family disagreement has just taken place.[10] The *punctums* in these photographs invite me to imagine Hallmark and the narrative of her life on very different terms from the photograph on the police poster. In contrast to the one-dimensional representation in the mug-shot photograph, these images communicate a sense of Hallmark's relationships to others. They also illustrate how much a *punctum* is both subjective and contextual: it is because I know of Hallmark from this other context in which she is repeatedly framed very narrowly as a woman from "the streets" that these signifiers of everyday ordinariness leap out from the other photographs as *punctums* and "wound" me. My ability to see *punctums* in these more conventional family photographs of Hallmark and not in the mug-shot-like one says as much about me, the viewer, as it does about the photographs: it is because the family snapshots seem so *familiar* to me, so ordinary, that they speak to me in this way. But why do I need *these* images in order to feel the woundedness of the *punctum* that Barthes describes? Why does the mug shot of Hallmark's face not evoke a similar reaction? And what might this signal about the frames of reference that form the backdrop for my ability to recognize a face as a human face, as Butler asks (2005, 29)?

These other images of Hallmark both humanize and familiarize her for many viewers, and it is necessary to reflect critically on why such images of the women seem preferable to many of us. But it is not the fact that Hallmark herself looks more conventionally stylish or less like what someone from "the streets" purportedly looks like in the online photographs that provides the *punctum* in my reading: instead, it is what the background of these photographs, including those seemingly inconsequential "detail[s] (in some corner)" are able to communicate about the broader social context of Hallmark's life that matters (Barthes 41), given how she has been figured in that other narrative as someone whose life is primarily marked by addiction, sex work, violence, "the streets," isolation, and criminality. Imagine, then, what the police poster might look like if it were not one poster at all but a book of posters, made up of a series of different photographs for each of the women; imagine how such photographs, so different from the ones used in the poster now, photographs that each capture a unique "detail (in some corner)," something that communicates the broader social context of the life of each woman pictured, might get us thinking differently not only about the women's lives but also about how we imagine ourselves in relation to them.

Certainly the present poster photographs may evoke responses of compassion, sympathy, or pity, but for most viewers I doubt that they cultivate the kind of implicated-ness that might lead to practices of inheritance, because in their reductiveness they cannot communicate anything about the broader contexts of the women's lives beyond that narrow, widespread framework for imagining a life lived on "the streets." For some viewers this might lead to sustained attention or compassion of a charitable sort, but this reductiveness seems more likely to reaffirm those conventional frameworks that position the women's "poor choices" or "lifestyle" at the root of their vulnerabilities, rather than the whole of how our sociality is organized and lived. What the photographs cannot communicate, then, is how the relative freedom from precarity of some viewers is in fact bound up in the increased vulnerability to suffering and violence that the images document.

Frequently people assume that a lack or refusal of representation is dehumanizing, while those who "gain representation ... have a better chance of being humanized" (Butler 2004, 141). We might therefore read the circulation of the poster photographs in the media as a positive, humanizing project, for certainly the lack of representation of the disappeared women in the media or official parlance in the early 1990s contributed greatly to their dehumanization by implying that their disappearances weren't newsworthy or worth investigating. It may be true that some representation is always preferable to no representation at all, and certainly the publication of the poster drew an attention to the disappearances that was sparse before its release. But it is also true that "personification does not *always* humanize," that it can repeat the dehumanization caused by a lack of representation (Butler 2004, 141, emphasis added). The poster photographs are framed in a way that implies criminality (that ultimate category of human deviance), they are cast as belonging to "the streets" (but not to homes or communities), and they are frequently surrounded in the media by headlines and text that label the women pictured as "hookers," "prostitutes," "sex workers," or "drug addicts," as though these are the whole sum of their lives rather than just one aspect of them. As a result, it is perhaps *not* surprising that this framing undoes the potentially humanizing effects arising from the fact of gaining representation where previously there had been little or none.

Although the poster photographs individually seem to lack the sort of *punctum* Barthes describes, that detail or "unexpected flash" (96) that has the potential to "wound" us, in the more recent versions of the poster the presence of the photographs with blue highlighting might have the potential to act as the second form of *punctum* that Barthes identifies near the end of his investigation of photography. This second version of a *punctum*, "which is no longer of form but of intensity, is Time, the lacerating emphasis of the *noeme* ('*that-has-been*'), its pure representation" (Barthes 1981, 96, emphasis in original). Looking at a photograph of a young man who is about to be hanged, Barthes tells us that "the *punctum* is: *he is going to die.* I read at the same time: *This will be* and *this has been*; I observe with horror an anterior future of which death is the stake" (96, emphasis in original). So when considered as a whole, as its own text, Barthes' insight offers us another possible reading of the later versions of the poster. Looking at the images of the twenty-six women pictured with blue highlighting over their names in the 2007 version, the high-lighting indicating that they have been murdered and that charges have been laid in connection with these murders, one might get this sense of observing, in the same instance, something that *will be* and yet *has been.* For at the moment those photographs were taken the women were not yet murdered; they may not even have suspected that they would die violently in the future, although some of them certainly did. They were not yet linked with each other, either – although they may have had some things in common, they were not, in life, routinely produced as figures of "Vancouver's Missing Women."

When we look at these photographs now, many viewers will be aware that these twenty-six women, at least, have been murdered. In the last while, as a result of the massive media coverage of the trial of the man accused of their murders, we have even come to know some of the terrible details of how they were likely killed. Looking at the photographs, now, these deaths are in the past, most likely at different points in the past for each individual woman. Yet in the moment that each photograph was taken their deaths were still ahead, a prevent-able future. This realization has the haunting potential to implicate the viewer in this story in much the same way as my sighting of the pres-ence of the now-absent Sereena Abotsway (in chapter 1): viewing the images of the women (taken when they were still alive) and knowing of their (coming) deaths (Barthes's future anterior) might just provoke a sense of urgency about the injustices that heightened the women's vulnerability to violence in the first place. I offer this insight hesitantly because I am far from certain that this sense of implication is likely to be forthcoming for all viewers of the poster. Whether or not we feel this sense of implicated-ness probably has a lot to do with our frames of reference for understanding and interpreting the images, and possibly even with how we conceive of ourselves in relation to the women pic-tured. Frames of reference, and in this instance frameworks for think-ing and identifying the human, have an enormous impact on how or whether we understand some lives as grievable and others as less so, such that if we are influenced by a frame of reference that suggests that the women pictured in the poster lived ungrievable lives, then we are perhaps less likely to feel the poster's haunting potential or recognize "the lacerating emphasis of the *noeme ('that-has-been')*" that it captures too well (Barthes 1981, 96, emphasis in original).

Still, the collapse of time invoked by the juxtaposition of the photographs (representing life) with the blue highlighting (representing death) does seem indicative of a haunting. The poster is haunted by what its frames cannot contain, or by its *own* implication in the disappearances and murders it advertises. For certainly one framework for interpreting the poster would view it as a straightforward law-enforcement document, the purpose of which is solely to solicit information about missing persons. In this framework the mug-shot photographs, while perhaps out of place on a poster for missing persons, nonetheless serve a functional purpose. But there are other frameworks for interpreting the purpose of such photographs, and here I am particularly interested in a framework advanced by cultural critic Susan Sontag in her book *On Photography* (1990), in which she describes photography as "an act of non-intervention" (11). Sontag argues that taking a photograph can be a way of,

> at least tacitly, often explicitly, encouraging whatever is going on to keep on happening. To take a picture is to have an interest in things as they are, in the status quo remaining unchanged (at least for as long as it takes to get a "good" picture), to be in complicity with whatever makes a subject interesting, worth photographing – including, when that is the interest, another person's pain or misfortune. (12)

Although she is referring to the photographic practices of war journalists and not to the specifically bureaucratic uses of photography like the collection of mug shots, this still seems an apt description of the practice of photographing women arrested for acts deemed criminal but often performed in the interests of survival, such as outdoor sex work or the use of criminalized drugs. If we can see suffering or heightened vulnerability in the faces of the women as captured in the poster photographs, then it seems important to reflect on the fact that *someone took those photographs*.[11] Such a reframing of the function of photography draws our attention to the time and space in which the poster photographs were taken, the time and space in which intervention in the injustices and vulnerabilities that led to so many violent, untimely deaths was still possible. But this time is both past and *present*, since the disappearance and violent deaths of women from the Downtown Eastside are an ongoing concern, and so intervention remains possible, now.

This second form of *punctum* might work to provoke recognition in viewers of our own implication in the practice of merely documenting vulnerability and suffering (rather than intervening in it). Such a recognition, however, offers only a very initial starting place for contemplating practices of inheritance; it indicates an opening or an opportunity to move us beyond empathy or compassion as adequate responses to the suffering and loss that the poster documents. Such a move is important because, as Sontag offers in her more recent treatise on photography, *Regarding the Pain of Others*:

> So far as we feel sympathy, we feel we are not accomplices to what caused the suffering. Our sympathy proclaims our innocence as well as our impotence ... To set aside the sympathy we extend to others ... for a reflection on how our privileges are located on the same map as their suffering, and may – in ways we might prefer not to imagine – be linked to their suffering, as the wealth of some may imply the destitution of others, is a task for which the painful, stirring images supply only an initial spark. (2003, 102–3)

It would be easy, I think, to argue that the photographers who captured these images should have done more to intervene in the suffering that so many of the photographs document – that the police should have *done something* instead of merely documenting the women for their bureaucratic purposes. Yet such admonishments, while important and necessary, are also another technique for deflecting the necessity of considering how we are ourselves implicated in the suffering and violent deaths that these photographs predict. Barthes's second form of *punctum*, time, is enacted by these images through their *collapse* of time, through how each captures an "anterior future of which death is the stake" (1981, 96). And I suspect it may be at least in part through their enactment of this second form of *punctum* that the poster photographs have inspired several artists to use them as models for the creation of portraits of many of the women who have been disappeared from the Downtown Eastside.

In addition to Pamela Masik's *The Forgotten* project, a number of artists have created collections of sketches or portraits of women who have been disappeared from the Downtown Eastside.[12] While these projects vary greatly in medium, size, scope, and arrangement, they have at least one thing in common: they reframe and reimagine the poster photographs. A group of artists from Project EDAN (Everybody Deserves a Name), an organization of forensic sketch artists whose usual work involves volunteering to sketch unidentified murder victims for police forces that lack the budget to keep such artists on staff, are particularly insistent about their desire to "humanize" the women by re-envisioning and refashioning the poster photographs. In 2005, artists from EDAN created individual portraits of the twenty-six women Pickton is accused of having murdered and of two other women whose DNA was found on his property.

The portraits of the women created by the EDAN team were first published in the *Vancouver Sun* under the headline "Sketches express softer side of missing women."[13] (See figure 3.2.) Todd Matthews, founder of EDAN and initiator of the portrait project, claimed that the mug-shot-like photographs of the women in the media compelled him to gather together a group of artists to create the individual portraits: "'I think people were seeing a criminal rather than a victim,'" Matthews told *Vancouver Sun* reporter Lori Culbert. To counter this negative image and allow the women to "be viewed in a more positive light," Culbert reports that Matthews "wanted [the women's] hair styled nicely and a 'Mona Lisa' smile on their lips – to reflect a happier time." Another artist who worked on the project, Wesley Neville, reported to Culbert that his technique involved "imagin[ing] how the women would have looked when they were happy, healthy and safe." As Neville elaborates: "I saw through the damage that had been done physically to them. It's obvious their diets were bad, and drugs had taken their toll on some of them. I pretty much take that out – it's like an age-regression ... I wanted to try to make them look as lifelike as possible, in a more innocent time." EDAN artist Charlaine Michaelis also reported a similar approach: she tried to imagine how Georgina Papin's photograph would be different if she were smiling, then sketched Papin accordingly. Michaelis told Culbert she hoped Papin's family would see the sketch and think, "Yeah that's the girl we remember before she got into her situation." The efforts of the EDAN team resulted in a series of sketched portraits that do indeed represent the women very differently from the police photographs.

It is revealing that artist Wesley Neville compares his work creating these portraits to the creation of age-progression sketches. In a detailed reading of an age progression, one created from an image of a missing girl "from Point St-Charles, a working class neighbourhood in Montreal," Anne Stone (2004) argues that the changes evident in the age progression are "telling of what qualities define the ideal child victim and what class markers need correction in order for this ideal to be met" (81).

3.2 *Vancouver Sun*, Observer section front page (C1), 17 December 2005, featuring sketches by Project EDAN. Courtesy *Vancouver Sun*. Sketches reproduced courtesy Project EDAN.

Stone notes that in this girl's age-progressed image her head is angled slightly away from the camera rather than gazing at it directly, as in the original picture, and her clothes and hairstyle are more typical of a "middle-class suburb" than of her urban, working-class neighbour-hood (80). The age-progression is edited, Stone writes, "with an eye to satisfying ideals of the feminine, of the ideal victim" (81). We can certainly hear echoes of such an approach in the language that the Project EDAN team uses to describe their work. And similar kinds of changes, changes that are very much about what markers "need correction" for a wider public to more readily identify the disappeared women as "victims" who lived grievable lives, are abundantly evident in the EDAN portraits.

The EDAN portrait of Mona Wilson is particularly instructive about the kinds of changes imagined to be necessary for enhancing griev-ability, I find, and as the first and one of the largest sketches published in the *Vancouver Sun* article, it is also framed there as representative of the series. In Wilson's poster photograph, I see an Indigenous woman (Wilson was from the O'Chiese First Nation in Alberta) who faces the camera squarely, maybe somewhat defiantly I think, although I hesitate to make this claim because it fits rather too neatly with those stereotypes that posit Indigenous women as always already angry or defiant. Still, Wilson's mouth is slightly downturned and appears to be rather determinedly set or locked in place, enhancing the effect of a defiant countenance. Given the likelihood that this image is a mug shot, defiance here can be read as resistance to criminalization, as an expression of strength. In the photograph, Wilson has what appears to be amblyopia (more conventionally known as a lazy eye) and her eyes appear shadowed by dark make-up. Her hair is shorn roughly around the bangs and a few strands stand up from her head. There is a small dark dot on her left earlobe that could be a single stud earring, or perhaps just a shadow. She wears a red knit sweater that could have been designed for men, although it is impossible to say for sure, but it certainly does not resemble clothing that is conventionally read as especially feminine. Although the backdrop of the photograph is a different colour than many of the photographs that appear to be mug shots (blue, while many of the others have a greyish-white background), the emptiness of the background, focus on Wilson's face and torso, and similar distance between herself and the camera are at a minimum evocative of the mug-shot photographs, even if hers might not actually be one of them.[14]

At a first glance, the EDAN sketch of Wilson seems quite similar to her poster photograph. Wilson's head faces the same way, and it is still tipped slightly to the right. It is no longer what I would call *cocked* to the right, though, and her chin is decidedly lower in the portrait; her mouth is also slightly upturned, the hint of defiance I saw in the poster photograph erased with the hint of a smile. The effect of these changes does indeed present what might conventionally be called a "softer" version of Wilson. The amblyopia is corrected and Wilson's gaze points downward, no longer squared directly at the viewer as it is in the photograph. Her hair has been smoothed and she now has neatly cut bangs; there are no disorderly wisps here. The collar-line of her sweater also seems to me to have been softened by enlarging the ridges around the neck and erasing the texture of the sweater, such that the appearance seems much more conventionally feminine. The hint of a lone earring, which could signal rebelliousness or perhaps just inattentiveness to achieving a putatively polished look, is not reproduced in the portrait. And because of the shift from a colour photograph to a black and white sketch along with some subtle changes to her facial structure, I think Wilson's EDAN portrait is more likely to be mistakenly interpreted by some viewers as an image of a white woman. I hesitate here because I do not want to suggest that there is one particular way that an Indigenous or white woman *looks*. Certainly that is not the case – race cannot be reduced to phenotype, and I have no desire to give credence to any such reduction. Yet even if it is only an effect of the shift in medium (from a colour photograph to a black and white sketch), it does seem important that Wilson is perhaps more likely to be read, by some viewers at least, as white in the "softer" version of her created for the portrait; this may imply a framework through which it would be considered advantageous to downplay any racial markers associated with Indigeneity in order to encourage some viewers to recognize a "victim" instead of a "criminal."[15]

With a few subtle changes, Wilson's image has been transformed to fit within conventional frameworks for an idealized, innocent victim.[16] Several of the other portraits offer very similar transformations. One could certainly read the EDAN portraits as succeeding at their goal of humanizing the women, since the reimagining of the women evident in the portraits presents versions (or visions) of them that are indeed much more likely to be read as grievable by a wider audience, particularly an audience influenced by predominant frameworks for what it means to be normatively human. The "softer" versions of the women represented in the EDAN sketches much more closely resemble the "twenty-something soccer moms" (presumed white, middle-class, and conventionally feminine, although these markers are usually not explicitly mentioned) whose disappearances Matthews, among others, insists would have elicited a much stronger and swifter public response.

Such a reading is certainly possible, and yet there is something very troubling about the frameworks for interpreting a life as grievable that the EDAN sketches rely upon. Their efforts to humanize the women through aesthetic changes to their appearances seem to risk further entrenching a *de*humanization of the women as represented in the photographs (and, by extension, of women who continue to live in similar social conditions, women similarly physically marked as living outside of conventional frameworks for grievable lives). The drive to "soften" the women's appearances in the interests of making them seem grievable to a wider audience risks reinforcing the notion that there *is* indeed a universal framework for what makes a life grievable, and that the women as pictured in the photographs simply do not fall within that framework. Altering the women's appearances to make them look more conventionally middle-class and feminine in this instance implies that there is something wrong with the women *themselves* that must be altered in order to justify a more widespread public grief or even attention to their loss – in order to *make them fit the frame* that delimits hegemonic conceptions of grievable life. This notion that the problem lies with the women themselves is reinforced by some of the accompanying text of the *Vancouver Sun* article: for example, by artist Michaelis's hope that her sketch would remind Georgina Papin's family of what she looked like "before she got into her situation." The women are imagined here as the agents of their own suffering, the authors of a set of circumstances that are theirs individually, not ours collectively.

The transformation of the individual women's faces in the EDAN sketches risks downplaying any consideration of whether there is instead something the matter with a social order that prioritizes such a narrow frame of reference for a grievable life. The sketches not only acknowledge but also risk vehemently reiterating the assumption that normative humanness maps on to markers that signal white, middle-class, conventional femininity (through the focus on creating "stylish," well-kept hair, "Mona Lisa" smiles, and "innocent," "softer" appearances). They risk implying that one's image must conform to these norms in order to matter, in order to fit inside the frame through which someone's life is intelligible as grievable. Even though the artists were inspired to create the sketches because they actually strongly object to a social prioritizing of "twenty-something soccer moms," their recuperative renderings of the women's faces expose, but also reiterate a belief that those who *look like* what many people think a "twenty-something soccer mom" looks like are more worthy of our care and concern than those who might be physically marked as having lived what many troublingly view as a less grievable life; namely, a life that is racialized as "other" than white, and a face that may show physical markers that are often interpreted as signs of poverty, addiction, criminalization, and a life lived on "the streets."

I recognize that my argument might seem somewhat contradictory, since earlier in this chapter I myself advocated for the replacement of the poster photographs with different, less mug-shot-like images of the women. Yet I would argue that to simply replace the mug-shot images with more conventionally flattering images *still narrowly focused on the individual women themselves* repeats the same mistake: such images in their reductiveness still fail to either signal a wider social context for the lives of the women pictured or redirect our attention to the social conditions and normative frameworks that facilitated their disappearances and greatly delayed an official response. For example, I found that of the changes made in Wilson's EDAN portrait, the erasure of that hint of a lone earring continued to irritate me. Going back through some earlier press coverage I discovered why: Wilson's sister has a few times been quoted in the press relating a story about how she regularly gave Wilson jewellery as a Christmas gift.[17] Because she did not make it home for Christmas in 2001 (Wilson was reportedly last seen in November of that year), her sister still has the earring and pendant set that she planned to give to her. Erasing that hint of an earring from Wilson's portrait in the interests of "softening" or "cleaning up" her appearance erases the possibility for that earring to function like one of Barthes's *punctums*, signalling something of the wider social context of Wilson's life. The reductive effect of these "softer" images remains much the same as that of the poster images themselves. And it is only that broader social context for the women's lives, I believe, that might have the potential to invoke some wider sense of implication in viewers about how precarity and vulnerability to violence are so unevenly distributed and lived.

The EDAN portrait project seems premised on an assumption that if a wider public could only *recognize* the women as "like us," then we might feel badly about, or at least pay more attention to, the deaths or disappearances of the women whose images they represent. Here the deployment of the pronouns "us" and "we" starts to reveal some of its most troubling aspects, for their use in this instance signals much about the insidiousness of the assumptions that underpin just *who* it is that presumably needs to recognize the women as "like us" in order to generate broader public concern about their disappearances. Those who knew the women in life, for example, do not tend to require "softer," "nicer" versions of the women or reminders about their innocence in order to care about, take note of, or attempt to intervene in the violence they experienced. Nor do many of the residents who share their neighbourhood, who were already advocating for changes that would reduce the women's vulnerability to disappearance and violence long before officials began paying any attention. The EDAN portraits seek recognition instead from individuals assumed to be members of that broader public who live lives that are frequently categorized as "normal" or "ordinary": that group of persons for whom hegemonic conceptions of grievable life are frequently interpreted as "just the way things are."

If these portraits aim to have an "us" recognize the women differently, then they must be assumed to work, like Masik's *The Forgotten* project, by trying to provoke an identification that invites (some) viewers to see something of ourselves or our loved ones in the women's faces. In her book *Witnessing: Beyond Recognition,* social theorist Kelly Oliver (2001) insists that this is a problem inherent to the politics of recognition itself: "Recognition seeks only itself and not the other. Recognition is not open to otherness, but only to confirmations of itself" (206). If we must recognize something of ourselves in another in order to care about her or feel a sense of responsibility towards her, then it makes sense to try to evoke such recognition from a wider public. But several scholars have questioned the value of recognition alone as a tool for provoking relations of responsibility or changes leading towards greater justice.[18] Oliver argues that trying to reverse dehumanization through securing recognition "reinforces the dominance of the oppressor and the subordination of the oppressed. For it is the dominant culture and its representatives who have the power to confer or withhold recognition" (26). So, although "dehumanization creates the desire and need for recognition from the dominant culture" (26), the act of recognition necessarily reiterates relations of dominance and subordination. Reacting against the dehumanization they observe in the poster photographs (and in that initial lack of attention to the women's disappearances among a wider public), these portraits, for example, attempt to provoke in viewers a recognition of shared humanness that the women, now murdered, are unable to pursue for themselves. But in the act of doing so, the portraits reconfirm the validity of a framework through which there *is* a dominant culture that maintains its power very much through its willingness to confer recognition on the women as imagined in the EDAN portraits, and by extension through its ability to *withhold* a similar recognition of shared humanness from the women as represented by the photographs, and therefore from women who continue to be visibly marked by the vulnerabilities with which they contended. As Butler (2004) insists: "It is not a matter of a simple entry of the excluded into an established ontology, but an insurrection at the level of ontology" that is necessary (33). Those of us compelled to incite such an insurrection may well need to critique the drive to humanize, then, even as we continue to recognize the laudable intentions behind such practices and the important political purposes that they sometimes serve.

Turning to a politics of recognition in an explicitly Canadian context, Glen Coulthard persuasively argues that the approach to recognition politics exemplified by the work of scholars like Charles Taylor will do little to address the ongoing injustices evident in our colonial context, because "the logic undergirding this dimension – where 'recognition' is conceived as something that is ultimately 'granted' or 'accorded' to a subaltern group or entity by a dominant group or entity – prefigures its failure to significantly modify, let alone transcend, the breadth of power at play in colonial relationships" (2011, 36). Instead, following Franz Fanon, Coulthard suggests that "those struggling against colonialism must 'turn away' from the colonial state and society and find in their own *transformative praxis* the source of their liberation" (50, emphasis in original). By refusing the terms of encounter a colonial context sets in motion, a politics of recognition might instead be overturned in the interests of alternative, transformative visions, of a praxis that rejects how a politics of recognition keeps relations of dominance and alterity in play.

In his book *Bound by Recognition*, Patchen Markell (2003) provocatively reframes the politics of recognition, arguing that those projects aiming to provoke more widespread recognition of marginalized groups might indeed achieve such recognition without significantly changing the relations of injustice that underwrote the act of misrecognition in the first place (see also Coulthard 2011, 36). Markell offers what he calls an "alternative diagnosis of relations of social and political subordination," one that sees such relations, "not as systematic failures by some people to recognize others' identities, but as ways of patterning and arranging the world that allow some people and groups to enjoy a semblance of sovereign agency at others' expense" (5).

Sara Ahmed (2000) advances a similar argument when she insists that it is not as though we *fail* to recognize those people we categorize as "strangers," but in fact that we instead recognize someone *as* a stranger and through those encounters where we recognize them as such, we actually *produce* them as strangers. For Ahmed, failures of recognition do not exist; instead, we recognize someone *as* something (whether it be something "like us" – a sister – or "different than us" – a stranger), and that act of recognition is also performative.

So the EDAN portraits might in fact succeed at provoking a more widespread recognition of the disappeared women as "like us" among a more normative viewing public, and yet simultaneously leave the unjust social conditions and arrangements and the normative frameworks for recognizing a life as grievable that underpin their disappearances largely intact. In other words, they seem unlikely to provoke us to consider how we are ourselves implicated in the disappearance of so many women, preferring instead to cater to dominant desires for different versions of the women that more easily fit those conventional frameworks for recognizing a life as grievable. As a result, viewers are not asked to reconsider how or why some lives remain so much more vulnerable to disappearance than others, nor to consider how some people's desires to maintain an illusion of "sovereign agency," as Markell puts it, are tightly bound to the ways that precarity and vulnerability are distributed so unevenly. As Markell insists, "what draws us to or bars us from a just relation to others is, in many instances at least, not the state of our knowledge of them, but the state of our understanding of ourselves" (2003, 35). This insight brings me back to practices of inheritance, to how such practices might spur us on from questions of recognition to relations premised both on greater justice and greater responsibility for the ways we are indelibly related to others. But there are also other dehumanized figures in the "Missing Women" story – figures that exist only in the shadows of the sorts of representations taken up in this chapter. It is to these queer(ly) shadowed figures that I turn next.

Chapter Four

Shadowing the "Missing Women" Story: "Squaw Men," Whores, and Other Queer(ed) Figures

In the decade that I have now been studying stories, images, memorials, and other representations of the women disappeared from Vancouver's Downtown Eastside, I have come across only one or two passing suggestions that any of the women might have identified with queerness in any way. In fact, although many of the women did outdoor sex work during their lives, in posthumous representations they are made to appear largely devoid of any form of sexuality – which seems to contradict the generally sex-positive and frequently very queer orientations embraced by a significant number of people who sell sex.[1] Instead, in more recent representations, descriptors like "mothers, sisters, and daughters" (noticeably, seldom "wives") have become tropes that get repeated over and over again. By contrast, the labels "whores" or "queers" have seldom, if ever, been used in a positive sense, at least not publicly, for although many of the women were labelled "prostitutes" in the mainstream press and "sex workers" in the alternative press, they have not widely been claimed as hustlers or whores in the affirmative way that such identities sometimes get used in sex-positive, queer, and sex work communities.[2] And although the odd mention is made in the press of one or two of the women's bisexuality, I have yet to come across any effort to either claim or acknowledge any of the women as queer. I could dismiss this circumstance as arising simply from a tendency to avoid speaking "ill" of the dead, but I suspect that what is at stake here is more complex – especially since significant social movements have in recent years made it difficult to view calling someone a queer or even a whore solely in a negative light. In some circles, certainly many of the circles that I move in, these are often considered transgressive, positive forms of identification. Why, then, does there appear to be an almost-complete silence about any such identifications in representations of the "Missing Women" story, even in purportedly counter-hegemonic, anti-colonialist, and queer forums and media?

The one place where sex gains traction in this story, troublingly, is through the figure of Robert Pickton. In stories about Pickton we have been told a great deal about dildos, bondage gear, handcuffs, condoms and lube, even about a blow-up sex doll (not to mention the "explosive evidence" of Pickton's fondness for frequent masturbation).[3] These reports position Pickton as the only sexual person in the story, but shadowing the mention of these objects and acts is the presumption that he paid women for kinky sex, or forced them to engage in such sex acts, or both, and that he may have a sexual preference for Indigenous women, given how they are over-represented among the women he is accused of having murdered. These accounts function in part to produce Pickton as a particular sort of figure, one that bears many resemblances to the historical figure of the "squaw man" – a term frequently applied, in the nineteenth century, to unruly, promiscuous, working-class white men who were often observed "in the company" of Indigenous women – sometimes because they "bought and sold Indian women or compelled them to live in their homes as wives or concubines" (Smith 2013, 155).[4] "Squaw men" were cast as deviant because of their non-conformity to European, particularly British, nineteenth-century social and sexual norms, and there is some evidence that their sexual and marital relationships with Indigenous women were both more likely to occur and less likely to be widely tolerated by other settlers than those of more "educated" and "genteel" white men, who some believed might contribute to "civilizing" (read: assimilating) their Indigenous wives (see Smits 1991, 38–41). Because Pickton is also repeatedly figured in the "Missing Women" story as a representative of "evil" and a vessel of responsibility for the disappearance of so many women, I believe that "sex" and "evil" have been conflated in this story to such a degree that it is difficult to also talk about the women themselves as sexual without risking degrading or dehumanizing them in the imaginations of many. But the conflation of sex with evil and degeneracy is something I want to contest, and I do so in this chapter by exploring some of the reasons why the disappeared women are more likely to be remembered today as mothers, sisters, and daughters than as queers, whores, or hustlers, arguing that we follow Andrea Smith's (2011) suggestion and shift our attention to determining how *all* these identity categories are themselves implicated in the naturalization of settler colonialism.

Before I begin my analysis of some of the queer(ed) figures that shadow the story of the "Missing Women," though, I should clarify that I am not actually interested in uncovering how many of the women might have identified in life as lesbian, bisexual, or queer, nor will I attempt to claim the loss of so many women on behalf of queer communities – which is not to say there is no value in such a project, but I am using "queer" here quite differently. Building on the work of theorists like Sara Ahmed (2006) and Jasbir Puar (2007), I am interested in how "queering" practices of representation can be used to "make strange" the commonplace assumptions that underpin what a particular representation materializes about taken-for-granted social conditions and arrangements. Ahmed uses "queer as a way of describing what is 'oblique' or 'off line" (2006: 161), while Puar insists upon the difference "between the subject being queered and queerness already existing within the subject (and thus dissipating the subject as such)" (2007: xxiv). It is the queerness that already exists and can therefore be read in the way these various figures are represented that I am interested in uncovering in this chapter. Recently, scholars such as Andrea Smith (2011), Scott Lauria Morgensen (2011), Mark Rifkin (2011, 2012), and the contributors to the 2010 special double issue of *GLQ: A Journal of Gay and Lesbian Studies* edited by Daniel Heath Justice, Mark Rifkin, and Bethany Schneider, and to the 2011 edited anthology *Queer Indigenous Studies: Critical Interventions in Theory, Politics and Literature*, have all begun to unsettle the many ways that queerness, and queer-rights struggles in particular, too often both rely upon and disavow their implication in settler colonialism. Morgensen argues, for instance, that "the imposition of colonial heteropatriarchy relegates Native people and all non-Native people of color to queered statuses as racialized populations amid colonial efforts to eliminate Native nationality and settle Native lands" (1). The "queered" status of Native-ness in a colonial heteropatriarchy might help us to understand, then, why queerness shadows the "Missing Women" story but seldom enters the story in any explicit way, for since so many of the women are already "queered" as "Native," to claim them *as* queer or on behalf of queer communities, as "our" loss, might pose problems for those queer-rights struggles that seek recognition from the colonial state. Queerness is thus always already at work in the representational practices and cultural productions that have brought the story of "Vancouver's Missing Women" to a wider public, even though it is virtually never mentioned. It is the absent presence of queerness and of these other queer(ed) figures that shadow the dominant story – the "squaw man" and the "whore" in particular – that I explore in this chapter, in the interests of disrupting the seemingly proper order of describing the women posthumously only as "mothers, sisters and daughters."

As Becki Ross and Rachael Sullivan (2012) argue, struggles over queer rights and respectability in Vancouver are inseparable from the disappearance of women from the Downtown Eastside, given how these struggles historically contributed to pushing outdoor sex workers out of the West End "gaybourhood," increasing their isolation and forcing the dissolution of the informal networks they relied upon to try to decrease their vulnerability to violence.[5] Ross and Sullivan explain that in the 1970s, "white, upwardly mobile gay West Enders sought respectability through access to privatized domesticity and consumption, and the simultaneous expansion of gay public culture through institution building and residential stability in a gentrifying neighbourhood" (606). Sex workers, by contrast, many of them also queer, or transsexual (see Ross 2012), found themselves with "little to no purchase on the terms 'community' or citizen," and they were subsequently driven out of the West End as a result of intense campaigning by residents, including many more affluent gay men (Ross and Sullivan 2012, 613). Ross and Sullivan link this dispersal of outdoor sex workers from the West End with the eventual concentration of outdoor sex work in the Downtown Eastside and the nearby "isolated, bleak, and industrial spaces where they began to go 'missing' in catastrophic numbers" (616). As they conclude:

> That white, professional, and politically ambitious gay men led the charge against prostitutes in the West End offers an unsettling twist to stories that reveal the power of binaries such as clean/dirty, civilized/uncivilized, wealthy/poor, private/public, and legal/illicit to co-construct regulatory discourses of 'self' and 'other' with often lethal effects. (614)

Those doing outdoor sex work in the West End at that time saw their status "queered" by white gay men championing a homonormativity (see Duggan 2002, Puar 2007) that attempted (and it appears largely succeeded) to drive a wedge between "respectable queers" and those engaged in the more overt, more public sexuality of sex work, who were, as Ross and Sullivan point out, also *covertly* coded as racialized others in official texts decrying their presence in the West End (615).

This history of the displacement of outdoor sex workers from the West End may help to explain why the disappeared women have not widely been claimed as "our dead" by queers in the way that the murder of a gay man like Aaron Webster was claimed and memorialized by Vancouver queer communities and in the queer press.[6] Because many prominent gay men actively advanced the further marginalization of outdoor sex workers by ousting them from the city's "gaybourhood," to claim them now as "ours" would require confronting the stark binary created between an "us" (respectable, upwardly mobile queers) and a "them" (lower-income, lower-class, often also queer or trans hustlers and whores) and grappling with its consequences. I also suspect that many of the disappeared women from the Downtown Eastside may have lived queerness not as a form of identity or affiliation with an increasingly affluent, increasingly nationalist queer community, but rather as an expression of their sexual fluidity – as Sara Ahmed describes it, "as a queer form of social and sexual contact, which is queer perhaps even before 'queer' gets taken up as a political orientation" (161). Thus, while the probability that many of them expressed their sexuality queerly is one layer of absence arising from posthumous representations of their lives, the complex ways that queerness as a form of identification is implicated in the violence they experienced is also, conveniently, made absent. It seems to me, then, that there is no easy claiming of these women on behalf of queer communities: instead, to invite the queerness that underpins representations of their lives to emerge strangely seems to require shifting our focus to the relations between settler colonialism and queerness in the present.

In her assessment of the intersections of queer theory and Native studies, Andrea Smith calls for an "identity plus" politics as a foil to those "post-identity" claims that tend to leave the dominations of "white supremacist settler colonialism" intact (2011, 61). For Smith, an "identity plus" politics, rather than focusing solely on advancing claims for recognition by marginalized communities in the way identity politics often does, instead "marks *all* identities and their relationship to the fields of power in which they are imbricated" (ibid). Smith draws upon Judith Butler's work to develop her argument here, noting that Butler has herself insisted that just because the notion of the subject can no longer be taken for granted, this does not mean it no longer has any meaning. But the radical undoing of the subject that is the premise of much of Butler's (and queer theory's) work demands that instead of taking subjects for granted as the building blocks for political action, our understanding of what it means to *be* or to become a subject is crucial to our political as well as intellectual analyses. For Smith, an adequate account of what it means to be a subject today must include an interrogation of the ways that all identities are both marked by and implicated in the maintenance of "white supremacy, settler colonialism, and heteropatriarchy" – not just historically but also in the "genocidal present" (62). Shifting to an "identity plus" politics and analytical framework therefore requires us to consider where and how an identity like "queer" gets mobilized in support of settler colonialism, for example.

To queer representations of murdered or missing women, then, requires something different than adding "queer" to the oft-cited identifications of "prostitute, addict" or to the counter-identifications of "mother, sister, daughter" so often advanced as descriptors of Vancouver's disappeared women. Instead, it requires me to interrogate how the project of settler colonialism and the many complex ways it underpins the violence the women experienced risks being erased each time these various identities and counter-identities are deployed, because they re-centre *the subject* as the place to direct our political arguments, conveniently absenting how the state, a wider public, and indeed queer complicity in settler colonialism in the present is itself indelible from the contemporary disappearance of so many women. Thus, to allow the queerness already at work in representations of disappeared women to emerge requires us to worry less about who among them "was queer" and to worry more about how queerness is taken up and positioned vis-à-vis settler colonialism – and this is increasingly cause for concern, as "gay pioneers" continue to collaborate in the displacements associated with inner-city gentrification, a practice deeply implicated in the murders of women from numerous such neighbourhoods across the country.[7]

The silence around sexuality in posthumous representations of the disappeared women is perhaps not terribly surprising, however; as Chris Finley argues, "histories of biopower deeply affected Native people's relationship to the body and sexuality ... Throughout the imposition of colonialism ... one of the methods Native communities have used to survive is adapting silence around sexuality" (2011, 31–2). In her earlier work, Andrea Smith demonstrates the many intimate links between colonialism and sexual violence, arguing that "it has been through sexual violence and through the imposition of European gender relationships on Native communities that Europeans were able to colonize Native peoples in the first place" (2005, 139). Yet Smith, Finley, and other scholars, artists and activists intent on bringing together queer and Indigenous studies and political struggles insist that this silence around sexuality must be challenged in the interests of both refusing a common confla-tion of whiteness with queerness and decolonizing our understandings of gender and sexuality (see also Driskill, Finley, Gilley, and Morgensen, eds, 2011; Morgensen, 2011; Justice, Rifkin and Schneider, eds, 2010). Given these calls, challenging the silence around sexuality in posthumous representations of the women who have been disappeared from the Downtown Eastside is an urgent task.

    And yet I must admit that the repeated public claiming of Vancouver's disappeared women (and other murdered or missing Indigenous women across the country) as mothers, sisters, and daughters – roles that seem chosen to distance the women from more overtly sexualized labels like "whore," "queer," or even "wife" – strikes me as a politically strategic practice, one that is clearly deployed to counter how the loss of these women was so consistently cast, especially in early mainstream representations, as ungrievable. I am painfully aware that in many cir-cles whores, hustlers, and queers are still categorizations of human life that remain deeply stigmatized. To many people, those of us living lives associated with any such categorizations are often unquestioningly cor-doned into the realm of "ungrievable life." As a result, those of us trying to challenge this consignment are in a difficult position – how can we begin to explain (too often in a sound bite!) to those living lives whereby unjust social conditions and arrangements are just "the way things are" that there is something to not just tolerate but indeed *celebrate* about embracing "whore" or "queer" as an aspect of one's identity? Many queer and sex-work activists are preoccupied by this question, and there are certainly no easy answers.

    There is also an important claim to kinship made through the repeti-tion of the "mothers, sisters, daughters" trope: those making this claim are doing the symbolic work of reiterating that women so often ste-reotyped as completely unattached to communities or to conventional notions of family in any way do in fact possess all these familiar human attachments. Yet while such claiming strategies might be necessary given the broader discursive context, they are also not without prob-lems: as argued in the previous chapter, a professed desire to "human-ize" also reinforces (even as it attempts to challenge) a presupposition that the subject of this humanization is actually *not*-quite-human, since effort is purportedly required in order to make her seem so. Through this reclaiming of the women as mothers, daughters, and sisters, then, I worry that some of the specific factors contributing to the women's heightened vulnerability – namely, the stigmatization of sex work and addiction, the stereotypes about Indigenous womanhood, and the negative resonances of association with the Downtown Eastside – all get reinforced, such that these facets of the women's identities are simultaneously recast as the constitutive outside of some narrow, conventional notion of normative humanness. The strategy relies on an assumption that a wider public will and should care more about the fate of these women because they were someone's mother, sister, or daughter, and in doing so it also reproduces (even as it attempts to challenge) the belief that being someone who does sex work, someone with a drug addiction, someone Indigenous, or someone from the Downtown Eastside is not enough to warrant such caring or such recognition on its own. As Geraldine Pratt has so insightfully explained:

> Empathy through normalized family loss humanizes the murdered women by locating them within narratives of the middle-class family. Not only is this a gendered and heteronormative narrative, it privatizes, individualizes, and potentially depoliticizes aboriginal women's and sex workers' specific marginality in the Downtown Eastside. (2005, 1064)

So although the assertion of kinship and a broader context for the lives of the disappeared women, one in which their relations to others mattered greatly, is one important outcome, the repetition of the "mothers, sisters, daughters" trope is also unquestionably ensnared by the cultural currency of normative gendered and sexual identities (see also Jiwani and Young 2006; Hugill 2010).

The media have been quick to take up this trope and further entrench a "grievable mothers, sisters, daughters / ungrievable prostitutes" dichotomy. For example, one well-intentioned journalist trying to draw attention to missing women from the Downtown Eastside writes, "When she disappeared, the onetime wife, mother and hairdresser was a prostitute, an alcoholic and a drug addict."[8] One could certainly read this as an attempt by this journalist to humanize the woman to whom she refers and yet, at the same time, her language implies that one cannot be all of these things at once – that once a woman becomes a "prostitute, alcoholic, or drug addict," she ceases to have any attachment, or right-of-claim, to her roles as wife, as mother, or as anything as ordinary and everyday as a hairdresser, which are securely located in her "onetime" past. Another compassionate editorial relies on similar assumptions when it proclaims, "They have all been termed prostitutes or sex-trade workers. But each one was someone's daughter, granddaughter, niece or sister. Some were mothers, even grandmothers."[9] It is the phrasing "but each one" (as opposed to "each was also") that requires interrogation. For while such phrasings might aim to recuperate the humanity of the women being remembered, they at the same time work *against* bringing to consciousness the fact that many living, breathing women still doing sex work are *also* mothers, sisters, and daughters. For example, at a 2006 workshop for journalists and reporters about media representations of women in sex work, a member of the Canadian Coalition of Experiential Women pointed out: "We really appreciate this attempt to humanize us, but you know what? We were mothers, daughters, and sisters *before* we were murdered and missing, too," and she asked that the same respectful, dignified representations that have now, at times, been granted to those women who have been disappeared or murdered also be deployed to represent *living* women who do sex work. What troubles is that in efforts to recuperate the humanity of these lives cast so often as ungrievable, we seldom hear that women could, and do, embody all these facets of identity at once, and that none of them ought to diminish our capacity to recognize the women as having lived grievable lives.

Efforts to attach the women to normative feminine roles are an attempt to also generate an acceptance of the women's status as victims, and particularly to encourage a broader public to recognize them as *innocent* victims, in order to counter the widespread tendency to see prostitutes as women who "ask for it," or "get what's coming to them." Thus, the "mothers, sisters, daughters" trope is unavoidably ensnared by the ongoing cultural currency of Madonna / whore, "good girl" / "bad girl" dichotomies (Jiwani and Young 2006, 900; see also Hugill 2010, 72–3). Because the disappeared women have been so widely associated with the whore-"bad girl" half of this dichotomy, a counter-discourse that works to recuperate the women by publicly associating them with the Madonna-"good girl" side serves a number of strategic purposes. While I suspect this strategy is a necessary one given the pervasive hold these dichotomies continue to have on the imaginations of so many people, I nonetheless think it is important to consider how efforts to reclaim the women as Madonna-"good girl" types *reproduce* the dichotomy instead of rupturing it. I have noticed that the women are only very occasionally claimed as "wives," for example, and I wonder whether this relates to a persistent desire to keep the categories of "wife" and "whore" completely incongruous; I suspect that anxiety about the potential conflation of these two categories is so pervasive that the humanizing effect of claiming the women as mothers, sisters, and daughters would actually be undermined by claiming them also as wives and attempting to bridge that significant divide.

Yet another factor to consider in relation to the "mothers, sisters, daughters" trope is the historical entrenchment, in Canadian law, policy, and culture, of a conflation between Indigenous womanhood and prostitution. As discussed in more detail in chapter 1, the complex representational practices and colonial state policies that brought this conflation about, rendering a symbolic slippage between Indigenous womanhood and "licentiousness" or "prostitution," was a very strategic way to discourage mixed-race relationships, sequester Indigenous people on reserves, and rationalize the sex discriminations of the Indian Act – in other words, to quite deliberately *separate* understandings of Indigenous womanhood from conventional familial categories like "mother, sister, and daughter," which were, in the colonial imagination, perceived to be more ideally occupied by the increasing numbers of white European women imported to help "settle" and "civilize" the burgeoning nation state. Ironically, state policies rationalized on the basis of such conflations actually worked to greatly *increase* the likelihood that Indigenous women might *need* to rely on sex work for survival. It seems to me that awareness of this history, which is of course anything but past, might very understandably lead some family members, friends, and activists responding to the contemporary disappearance and murder of so many disproportionately Indigenous women to focus on fostering representations of the women's lives that challenge, rather than reinvoke, such categorical conflations. Since racism and colonialism underpin and shape Indigenous women's participation in sex work, the likelihood that "whore" will be embraced as a positive or celebratory form of identification is deeply complicated, which helps to explain why Indigenous women's organizations have struggled over whether to support the decriminalization of sex work in Canada.

Yet Kwakwaka'wakw scholar, writer, and advocate Sarah Hunt asks us to consider whether "Indigenous women's refusal of these sexual stereotypes resulted in simultaneously distancing ourselves from women who are working in the sex trade" (2013, 87). On the one hand, she argues, it is necessary to recognize that the overrepresentation of Indigenous women in outdoor sex work speaks to how colonization has limited Indigenous women's options for survival; to speak of women "choosing" to do sex work in such a context belies the many ways that settler colonialism shapes and delimits the "choices" available. On the other hand, Hunt also points to a lack of support for women who do sex work within many Indigenous communities and links this to how "many Indigenous people have internalized the attitudes about our sexuality taught to us through residential schools and generations of dehumanization under the Indian Act" (93). Pointing out that Indigenous theories of agency are more complex and do not need to rely on the "forced vs. choice" (Doezema 1998) dichotomy that has plagued many debates about sex work, Hunt calls instead for Indigenous communities to embrace and include sex workers. Yet Hunt also reminds us that calls for both the abolition and the decriminalization of sex work rely on the colonial state to make changes in law that may have little meaningful impact for Indigenous women who sell sex, given that "Indigenous people ... are not valued within the dominant culture that created and maintains the legal system" (97). While acknowledging that decriminalization might improve sex workers' abilities to seek protection and recourse from police if they experience violence, Hunt is clear that any attempt to decolonize sex work must also look beyond these legal reforms.

Hunt's precaution about the potentially limited and limiting impact of legal reforms is founded in an awareness of how other forms of legislation, like the Indian Act, have functioned to control the bodies and sexuality of Indigenous people (84–8). The Indian Act was designed to legislate and control the sexuality not only of Indigenous women, however, but also of white men – and of lower-class white men in particular. As historian Angela Wanhalla argues, "in the newly settled Canadian West, the status of white manhood was at stake, and had to be redeemed through legal mechanisms like the *Indian Act*" (2009, 221). In the interests of sequestering "Indian" space from settler space, legislation like the Indian Act made it extremely difficult for an Indigenous woman who married a white (or other non-Indigenous) man to remain on-reserve, given that the Indigenous woman would lose her status as "Indian" and entitlement to band membership. In effect, then, the couple would be understood as "white," and the white male partner would retain his racial status. This provision of the Indian Act created severe discrimination against Indigenous women who "married out" (see, e.g., McIvor 2004, Silman and the Tobique Women's Group 1987). It also allowed for greater legislative control over white men in Indigenous spaces (such as reserves), and as such it was also perhaps imagined, at least in part, as a solution to the problem of "squaw men."

As historian Robert McDonald explains, "squaw man" was a "pejorative term that implied a departure from European cultural norms" (1996, 25). Nineteenth-century attitudes about mixed-race sexual relationships and marriages between Indigenous people and whites were "remarkably diverse," reports historian David D. Smits, but such relationships were generally much better tolerated when they occurred between wealthier men who might have a "civilizing" effect on their Indigenous partners. "Squaw man," by contrast, was a "term of opprobrium … attached to white men who married Indian women and lived with their wives' tribes" (1991, 38). Some of these men did not marry their sexual partners at all, or else quickly abandoned them, and it was generally men with less access to wealth, "cattlemen" and the like, who were so labelled.

In her book on the settlement of the California frontier, historian Stacey Smith's archival research on the figure of the "squaw man" led her to the following conclusions:

> Assumptions about class … permeated the squaw man stereotype. Squaw men allegedly came from the dregs of frontier communities. Poor, transient, and illiterate, they operated on the margins of civilized society. They were, in the strong words of one editor, "the lowest, meanest, most contemptible, worthless and abandoned trash that ever disgraced the earth." (2013, 156)

Although the roles of "squaw men" in the burgeoning economies of Canada and the United States were different (see McManus 2005), Wanhalla argues that the "Canadian squaw man was viewed with similar dislike" (221), and thus it seems likely that the image of the "squaw man" proffered by Smith offers a glimpse of how this figure was viewed by colonial officials and other more "genteel" white settlers in the Canadian West. Fast-forward a century or more, and Yasmin Jiwani and Mary Lynn Young (2006) draw our attention to how the framing of Robert Pickton's masculinity as "aberrant" and "more in line with a rural or 'hillbilly' culture" also works to reinforce the "masculine hegemony" of a more "refined" or "genteel" masculinity, given how the framing of the "Missing Women" story asks us to believe that "only *deviant* males commit such heinous sexual acts" (905, emphasis added).

But because the "Missing Women" story is so often represented as dating back only a few decades at most, the relevance of the "squaw man" figure is largely obscured, remaining only in the shadows of the "official" story. In early December 2007, for example, while a jury contemplated the evidence against Robert Pickton, an investigative journalist with the *Vancouver Sun* published a recap of the trial in a special section of the newspaper, divided into six chapters.[10] Chapter 1 is titled "The Beginning," and the remaining chapters wade through stages of the trial, concluding with a chapter on the awaited outcome, titled "Guilty or Innocent." Although useful as a summary of a lengthy and complicated legal process, this special report also neatly resituates these events within a narrative of individual culpability with a clear beginning and end that are mapped onto a very brief and recent time span. "The Beginning" of this story, in this journalist's recounting, is the birth of the joint Vancouver Police/RCMP Missing Women Task Force and its developing interest in Pickton and his property. Even the narrative summaries of the lives of the six women included in this feature begin at the moment they were last seen or reported missing – moments in time that are important to this sort of narrative recounting, but also constitute the women's lives as mattering to the story only because of when and how they were disappeared.

To be fair, the journalist included these brief synopses of the women's lives to counteract their utter lack of representation during the trial itself (the *Vancouver Sun* found that only seven of the Crown's ninety-eight witnesses, and only one of the Defence's thirty, were called to testify about the lives of the women, for example). The *Sun* and other news sources have also published different profiles of the women that do elaborate on their lives before they were disappeared. But in this special report, the details included about the women's lives are framed to fit with the narrative of individual culpability that is the trial's focus, which has the effect of adding them to the story without challenging the way the story is being told. Thus, these very narrow and recent "beginnings" seem logical in this recounting, and possibilities for contemplating other ways of understanding the timeline of this story are eclipsed.[11]

A fuller, more complex telling of this story would have to search for its beginnings much, much earlier, and elongating the timeline helps illuminate the relevance of the shadowed figure of the "squaw man." For example, media reports about Pickton frequently drew attention to his "farm-boy" roots. According to a CBC report, the Picktons were "pioneers in Port Coquitlam, with roots going back to the late 1800s."[12] Journalist Stevie Cameron similarly notes that Pickton's parents' first farm was "inherited from [his father's] family, who had homesteaded there more than a hundred years ago" (2007, 47). Pickton's mother was reportedly so reluctant to give up the family's original homestead house when their land was expropriated by the government to build the

Lougheed highway in 1967 that she had it moved, by barge, to the location of the new farm on Dominion Avenue in Port Coquitlam, where it stood until it was demolished with the property's other structures after the police concluded their forensic investigation. Defence lawyers for Pickton represented him during his trial as a simple, hard-working "farm-boy"; the media was quick to reiterate this representation, which Pickton himself perhaps sparked when he described himself during a videotaped interrogation by police as just "a plain little farm boy." As Cameron reports, during his prison conversations with an undercover officer (later offered as evidence during his trial), "it was his childhood [Pickton] wanted to talk about ... The deprivations of life at the homestead ... Living in a chicken coop, getting fresh water from a stream under the house, no fridge, working hard all his life, milking cows before and after school, slopping pigs" (2010, 476). If it is merely a coincidence that frontier mythology surfaces again here in these retellings of the life of Robert Pickton, then it is certainly a bizarre one. How does the frequent proclamation of Pickton's "farm boy" status and his homesteader life situate him in this story? The history of settler colonialism, a history that clearly held significant importance for the Pickton family, is, it seems to me, made present yet again here in this story of contemporary violence against disproportionately Indigenous women, belying its past-ness and indicating that it is thoroughly ingrained in our present.

The "farm-boy" claim figures Pickton more along the lines of a farm *hand* than farm owner, although he was of course both. Certainly his status as co-owner (with his siblings) of the farm on which he lived before his arrest provided him with a source of wealth that would be out of reach for most "plain little farm boys." Having lived most of his life on land that his family owned, Pickton only faintly resembles the transient character of the "squaw man." And yet, he has been figured (and produced himself *as* a figure) in ways that resonate very strongly with the "squaw men" of the past, through the focus on his farmhand status, the emphasis on the rough, working-class or "hillbilly" culture in which he lived, and through reports about his sexual practices that imply deviance and degeneracy. A sexual preference for Indigenous women, while not made explicit, is nonetheless implied by their disproportionate representation among the women he is accused or convicted of having murdered. The curious and surprising return of the "squaw man" figure raises a number of questions not only about how the past lives on, but also about a wider public's intense fascination with Pickton *as* a figure, helping to explain why the sheer quantity of news reports about the "Missing Women" story increased significantly after police turned their attention to him (Hugill 2010, 12–13).

To clarify, I am not at all suggesting that Robert Pickton, the individual man, is consciously re-enacting violent encounters between "squaw men" and Indigenous women. Following Gordon, I suspect that what is at stake here is "a form of haunting that does not track itself back to the individual's personal psychic life" (1997, 53). Instead, I am interested in how Pickton is produced as a figure in some of the ways the story of "Vancouver's Missing Women" gets passed on; my concern, then, is with the present-day legacies of a history of colonial conquest that is far from settled. I am concerned with how this history continues to naturalize the commission of particular forms of violence by certain subjects against certain others, to make certain forms of violence (and certain disappearances or deaths) appear unsurprising (such that they warrant little official or widespread attention until the force of their loved ones' insistence and pressure builds to a point that can no longer be ignored). My arguments here are not intended for interpretation as a search for a definitive causal explanation for the actions of an individual man, although I realize they risk appearing so. But if we identify how the colonial past is fully present in the violence at question here, might this lead us not only to questions of individual accountability for violence, which remain important, but also to much wider and more complex understandings of the "beginnings" of this story? Is it possible that Pickton's actions signal not just the individual acts of heinous violence he commited, but also something of how the past remains unsettled, of how it continues in present social arrangements and imaginings of how we are related to others, of how settler colonialism is a far-from-finished project that is continuously re-enacted in an effort to secure its permanence?

Part of the widespread revulsion towards the figure of Pickton might have to do not just with the heinous crimes of which he has been convicted, then, but also with the specific ways he has been produced as a figure in dominant retellings of the "Missing Women" story. Symbolically, through the repeated mention of his working-class farm-boy roots and the implication of his sexual relations with Indigenous women, Pickton's casting as a present-day figure of the "squaw man" helps give context to the widespread interest in and repetition of his "pioneer" roots. Widely represented as a working-class white man who strays from the cultural and sexual norms of his "respectable" Euro-Canadian lineage, we can read in the figure of Pickton a clear echo of the "squaw man" figure of the past, and this echo helps confirm him in the imaginations of many as deviant, as (sexually) perverse, and ultimately, as himself less than fully human.

In 2002, when Pickton was finally arrested and charged with the murders of several of the women disappeared from the Downtown Eastside, the "Missing Women" story began to garner the kind of national and even international attention that was until that point severely lacking. At a glance, we could easily dismiss such interest as arising largely from the spectacular arrest of a "serial killer," and thereby indicative mainly of a North American fascination with this sort of violent crime – but I am hesitant to dismiss it so easily. Instead, I suspect the entry of a "squaw man" figure helped to both familiarize the story *and* allow the story to function as another means by which a normative (white, settler, middle-class) public could reaffirm ourselves *as* normative. It also likely became easier for many to recognize the women's status as victims and to (re)frame their lives as grievable once responsibility for their deaths could be relegated *elsewhere*, to the lone man on trial (conveniently once again eclipsing the role of settler colonialism in shaping this particular story). Writing about an American fascination with the figure of Osama bin Laden after September 11, 2001, Judith Butler suggests that our interest grows in a story once the culpability of particular individuals is established:

> [This] works as a plausible and engaging narrative in part because it resituates agency in terms of the subject, something we can understand, something that accords with our idea of personal responsibility … Isolating the individuals involved absolves us of the necessity of coming up with a broader explanation for events. (2004, 5)

It is precisely any broader explanation for the myriad ways that these particular women came to be increasingly vulnerable to such violence that is made absent through such a narrow focus upon (and fascination with) the culpability of the individual figure of the "squaw man" on trial.

By investigating how Robert Pickton has been figured as a "squaw man" and an embodiment of "evil" in relation to the disappearances and deaths of the women he is accused of murdering, some readers might assume that I am seeking to rationalize or even excuse his violence. Nothing could be further from my project: questions of individual responsibility and accountability for violence must continue to be asked and answered, but must also be contemplated within a broader social framework that frequently situates perpetrators of such heinous violence as *themselves* living an ungrievable life. Judith Butler's work is again useful for thinking about what it might mean to contemplate how individuals like Robert Pickton are produced as such figures, particularly in relation to questions of individual responsibility:

> We need to distinguish, provisionally, between individual and collective responsibility. But, then we need to situate individual responsibility in light of its collective conditions. Those who commit acts of violence are surely responsible for them; they are not dupes or mechanisms of an impersonal social force, but agents with responsibility. On the other hand, these individuals are formed, and we would be making a mistake if we reduced their actions to purely self-generated acts of will or symptoms of individual pathology or "evil" ... To take the self-generated acts of the individual as our point of departure ... is precisely to foreclose the possibility of questioning what kind of world gives rise to such individuals. And what is this process of "giving rise"? What social conditions help to form the very ways that choice and deliberation proceed? Where and how can subject formations be contravened? (2004, 15–16)

Pickton's actions say something both terrible and terrifying about the kind of world that "gives rise" to such an individual, but when his casting as a contemporary figure of a "squaw man" is obscured we can learn next to nothing about this process of "giving rise" and the range of human possibilities that settler colonialism might give rise to, nor can we do much to prepare ourselves against them. I refuse to believe that nothing can be done to prepare against the heinous acts of violence that Pickton committed. Instead, I think if we take the way that Pickton has been figured in this story seriously, as a matter worthy of our attention and concern, there are indeed important things that can be learned about the ways that we are *all* in this story, too, and about how questions of justice are actually much more diffuse and complex than the spectacular trial of an individual man encourages us to believe.

So, although we must condemn Pickton's actions, to explain them only in terms of the acts of a representative of evil is to again refuse to interrogate how we are all implicated in this story, albeit differently. And while some commentators have pushed beyond this narrative of individual culpability and levelled accusations at the police, the government, or a generalized society, this still tells us little about our own differing implications in the *settler colonialism* of the present. My concern is not that we deem Pickton responsible for the violence he committed. Instead, my concern lies with the costly *way* that we judge him, and with how that judgment has, again and again, encouraged us to deflect serious attention away from the social conditions and arrangements that are also implicated in the disappearance of so many women.[13] For example, through her research in Department of Indian Affairs archives, Angela Wanhalla found that "the sexual stereotyping of women as 'squaws' played an important role in official reluctance to punish white men who offended against Aboriginal women in Canada" (224). This historical deployment of sexual stereotypes to diminish the punishment of white men who committed violence against Indigenous women uncannily resonates with the strange outcome of Pickton's trial: might Wanhalla's finding help us to understand both the long delays in any serious investigation of Pickton and his curious acquittal on *first-degree* murder charges in favour of the lesser charge of murder in the second degree?

Given how Pickton has repeatedly been figured as a vessel or flash-point for questions about justice in relation to the women who have been disappeared, it seems important to recall that the majority of the women named on the 2007 police poster remain unaccounted for. And while some might well conclude that Pickton is responsible for the disappearance of many of those women, too, certainly he cannot be held responsible for the violence and disappearances that have taken place since his arrest.[14] Further, long before Pickton was in the public eye, the *Vancouver Sun* reported that at least twenty-five different men had been charged with murdering women who did outdoor sex work in British Columbia over the past seventeen years.[15] As Don Adam, one of the lead investigators with the Missing Women Task Force, insists, "People may believe that someone with a history like Pickton is unusual ... That is untrue, as the actual number of men who brutalize sex trade workers is staggering."[16] This information alone exposes the focus on Pickton as far too narrow, since it seems that what he suggests about "the range of human possibilities that exist" (Butler 2005, 45) was suggested by others long before our attention was turned to him, and continues to be suggested by others still, today.

With the continuation of this violence in mind, the task of remembering and publicly mourning the disappeared women in ways that avoid reiterating the conflation of sex with "evil" gains new urgency. Shifting attention from the identities of the women themselves to the wider context of settler colonialism emerges as an essential aspect of remembrance practices that aim to not just remember the dead but also prevent such violence from continuing in the present. Such remembrance and public mourning cannot be performed in the interests of setting aside loss, then, or putting it in the past, "behind us," as is often mourning's intent. Instead, we might better engage in acts of public mourning designed and performed along the lines that Judith Butler imagines when she writes:

> One mourns when one accepts that by the loss one undergoes one will be changed, possibly for ever. Perhaps mourning has to do with agreeing to undergo a transformation (perhaps one should say *submitting* to a transformation) the full result of which one cannot know in advance. (2004, 21, emphasis in original)

But how might such approaches to remembrance and public mourning be initiated, enacted, and supported? To address this question, I turn in the next chapter to a consideration of various efforts to memorialize Vancouver's disappeared women.

Chapter Five

Memory's Difficult Returns: Memorializing Vancouver's Disappeared Women

Recently I was reminded that I actually first visited the Downtown Eastside in the winter of 1998, although I had no idea where I was at the time. I was not living in Vancouver then; I found myself there by chance, and one rainy day during that winter visit over fifteen years ago I did what I had done on December 6th every year since I became an undergraduate student and experienced an awakening of sorts: I gathered with other feminists to commemorate the mass murder of fourteen women in Montréal on this same day in 1989. We met at Vancouver's Science World, near the intersection of Main and Terminal streets at the southern edge of what I now know is the Downtown Eastside neighbourhood. The organizers of the commemoration were showing a new documentary about the process of building Marker of Change / À L'Aube du Changement, a permanent monument to the women murdered in Montréal on 6 December 1989, which had back then only recently been built in Vancouver's nearby Thornton Park.

Having somehow missed the national media coverage of the controversy surrounding the dedication of Marker of Change to those fourteen women murdered on December 6th and to "all women murdered by men," I remember being moved by the courageousness and dedication of the group of feminist college students who came together in 1990 and persevered over seven years to see this circle of fourteen stone benches laid permanently in the Vancouver park soil. After the film we moved to the monument itself, a short distance away, formed a circle of linked hands inside the wide ring of stone benches, lit candles, and someone spoke the names of those fourteen murdered young women, whose markers of identity – their whiteness, their status as undergraduate students at a university, the presumption of their feminism – were so similar to my own. Later, when people had dispersed, I recall that I sat on one of the benches in the light rain and reflected on the terrible weight of this loss of women whom I had never known but who died so violently, so unjustly, and could so easily, it seemed, have been me, a friend, or a woman whom I loved.

I marvel now, in hindsight, that I was able to spend that day in the Downtown Eastside without realizing (or being asked to pay close attention to) where I was, or why the particular place where I came to remember the event widely commemorated as the Montréal Massacre on that particular December 6th was significant. I do remember that in Simpson's documentary a few Downtown Eastside activists contest the decision to memorialize these fourteen relatively privileged women from nearly 4000 kilometres away in this particular neighbourhood, especially at a time when the murders and disappearances of local women were going largely unnoticed by those outside the community or those who lacked a personal connection to local women in our own lives. Yet, at the time, I felt a tad irritated by these activists' lack of support for the monument: Could they not see what an important issue this was? Did they not know, or care, that the monument was not just for these fourteen women who died so terribly but for "*all* women murdered by men," as its inscription insists? I remember my surprise at what I took to be their lack of understanding about the significance of the murders at the Polytechnique for *all women*. I was quite oblivious to my own lack of understanding about the losses happening right there in the Downtown Eastside, about their significance for all women, too. Perhaps more troublingly, I was also oblivious to how the losses of local women were being constituted as *not* mattering to all women, or to all Canadians, so very *unlike* the deaths of those fourteen women from Montréal (see Rosenberg 2000; McConney 1999; Kelley 1995; Kohli 1991).

A number of memorials have since been dedicated to Vancouver's disappeared women, some located in the Downtown Eastside and some installed elsewhere in Canada. They include permanent monuments (such as a memorial bench and boulder in CRAB Park and a wall mural in the city of Montréal), impermanent artistic or performance-based memorials (such as the memorial art of Janis Cole or Rebecca Belmore), and, perhaps most well known, the February 14th Women's Memorial March through the Downtown Eastside, which has occurred annually since 1991, making it the oldest of the memorials I could locate. The very existence of these memorials works to challenge those frameworks that facilitate the representation of the local women's lives as somehow less grievable than the lives of those 14 women from Montréal, as they attest to the necessity and importance of remembering the women and publicly acknowledging and mourning their violent deaths. Yet the process by which losses that were once widely cast as ungrievable get reframed *as* grievable losses through memorial practices, while an important undertaking, also risks reconstituting that binary of grievable/ungrievable lives, depending on the terms and frameworks mobilized for remembrance. How might a memorial avoid inadvertently re-invoking those frameworks that position certain lives as more grievable than others?

It seems to me that the kind of memorial that contributes most powerfully to challenging such frameworks is capable of enacting memory as a "difficult return." According to Roger Simon, Sharon Rosenberg and Claudia Eppert, "As a difficult return, remembrance attempts to meet the challenge of what it might mean to live, not *in* the past but *in relation with* the past, acknowledging the claim the past has on the present" (2000, 4, emphasis in original). These authors differentiate between this form of remembrance and one that deploys memory strategically to serve a particular political purpose in the present. Many of the various memorials to Vancouver's disappeared women have worked with both of these forms of memory, but those that successfully evoke remembrance as a difficult return hold the greatest potential for encouraging reflection on how we are all differently implicated in the losses they memorialize, mainly by drawing out the ways that the injustices of settler colonialism are clearly present in this contemporary story of violence, suffering and loss.

Strategic remembrance, then, tends to point us towards immediate, concrete things we can do to address an injustice. Practices of strategic remembrance usually gesture towards a brighter future, but with little or no attention to the past or to the role of past injustice in present injustice or violence. Remembrance as a difficult return, however, tends to expose how we are ourselves implicated in the injustices that contribute to the losses being remembered by evoking the social and psychic legacies of the past in the present. Such remembrance practices "unsettle and put into question the very terms of the redemptive promise of a strategic remembrance: that the future will be better if one remembers" (Simon, Rosenberg, and Eppert 2000, 3–4). As such, "remembrance as a difficult return then becomes a series of propositions of how to live with what cannot be redeemed, what must remain a psychic and social wound that bleeds" (5). This is precisely why I have come to believe that memorial practices that hold the potential to evoke remembrance as a difficult return are essential, not just to remember the many ways that Vancouver's disappeared women were and are grievable, itself an important task, but also to challenge those frameworks that cast some lives as more grievable than others in the first place.

Given that many women who have been disappeared from the Downtown Eastside remain unaccounted for, however, and given that the losses of the women who concern me are so recent, and were, at least initially, so broadly cast as ungrievable, I suspect that both of these forms of remembrance remain important, even necessary. Like Simon, Rosenberg, and Eppert, I believe that practices of strategic remembrance have a limited ability to evoke practices of inheritance, or to get us thinking about our own differing implication in the losses they mark. But as these authors also signal, "these two approaches to 'the project' of remembrance are not as disaggregated as this distinction suggests" (3). Despite their limitations, memorials that evoke strategic practices of remembrance are a necessary part of what it means to remember women who have been disappeared in the present, now, while so many Indigenous women continue to *be* disappeared and murdered and while so many people continue to disavow or remain indifferent to the wider context of settler colonialism that underpins this violence. Family, friends and community members have mobilized such practices in an effort to counter a prevailing understanding of the disappeared women as ungrievable losses. My critique of some examples of such memorials aims to flesh out both their political strengths and some of the possible limitations that I suspect might make them less likely to evoke remembrance as a difficult return.

Slightly more than a year after I attended that December 6th ceremony in Thornton Park, a permanent monument to the women being disappeared in increasing numbers from the Downtown Eastside was dedicated by several of the women's friends and family members in another park nearby. This memorial consists of a park bench located in CRAB Park, also in the Downtown Eastside, and a memorial stone that was placed in the same park a few years earlier (see figures 5.1 and 5.2).[1] Eleven of the women disappeared from the neighbourhood are named on a small plaque that graces the bench (see figure 5.3), which is also dedicated to "all other women who are missing." CRAB Park was chosen as the location for this bench because of the presence of the nearby memorial stone, which was itself intended to function, according to Downtown Eastside activist Don Larsen, like a short newspaper article at a time when women's disappearances from this neighbourhood were garnering scarcely any attention from the media or a wider public.

5.1 CRAB Park memorial bench, dedicated in 1999. Photo courtesy the author.

5.2 CRAB Park memorial boulder, installed in 1997. Photo courtesy the author.

IN MEMORY OF L. COOMBES, S. DEVRIES, M. FREY, J. HENRY, H. HALLMARK, A. JARDINE, C. KNIGHT, K. KOSKI, S. LANE, J. MURDOCK, D. SPENCE & ALL OTHER WOMEN WHO ARE MISSING. WITH OUR LOVE. MAY 12, 1999

5.3 Plaque on CRAB Park memorial bench. Photo courtesy the author.

Taken together, the stone and the bench exemplify remembrance as a strategic practice: they call on visitors to take note of the disappeared women from the neighbourhood, an important and politically necessary task at a time when those disappearances remained widely unacknowledged. They also remain important today because they offer a physical place to visit and remember the women who have been disappeared from this neighbourhood, particularly significant for those who knew the women named personally, as the CRAB Park markers remain the primary permanent, physical monument that exists thus far in the Downtown Eastside.[2] Yet, in the present (and with the benefit of hindsight not available to those who commissioned these memorials in the late 1990s), the CRAB Park memorial markers also raise several questions about their ongoing ability to provoke strategic forms of remembrance. As a result, they highlight some of the limitations of this form of memory.

In 1999, when the memorial bench was dedicated, for example, the women named were still considered missing, so it is unlikely a more fitting descriptor could have been rendered. Yet today, the phrase "women who are missing" does not tell an uninformed passerby much about the circumstances surrounding these disappearances (although one could certainly argue that few Vancouverites remain uninformed about the

"Missing Women" case and will likely connect what they know of the case to the dedication). The text of the memorial stone located near the bench avoids the word "missing" entirely, perhaps because it was dedicated before the phrase "Vancouver's Missing Women" had gained a kind of solidity in public discourse. Instead, it offers its dedication to "people" who were "murdered," many of whom, it states, were "women," and more specifically, "native aboriginal women." This adds some nuance to the text of the bench's dedication, and organizers likely intended the two to be read together. The line "many of these cases remain unsolved" on the memorial stone suggests that action is indeed needed to "solve" the disappearances, an important political statement at a time when adequate police attention was grossly lacking. Yet such language implies that the source of the problem is the lack of investigation rather than the social conditions and arrangements contributing to why women in the neighbourhood might be so vulnerable to disappearance in the first place. Someone passing by the stone today might therefore breathe a sigh of relief that "these cases" have now been "solved" by the arrest of Pickton and feel satisfied that no further action is required. So although the bench and stone undoubtedly served an important, strategic function at the time they were dedicated, their ongoing political effectiveness is limited by the spatiotemporal bounds of strategic memory.

The possible impact of these monuments on visitors is also tempered by the presence, about ten city blocks away, of the Thornton Park memorial for the women murdered at the Polytechnique in Montréal in 1989. This monument takes up the bulk of an entire park site with its circle of fourteen stone benches, each one dedicated to *one* of the women murdered in that instance, their names rising up individually from where they are carved in the side of each bench (see figure 5.4). It was of course never the intention of those commissioning any of these memorials to invite someone passing by these two parks during a walk through the Downtown Eastside today to consider the relative griev-ability implied by one memorial bench dedicated to dozens of women versus fourteen benches each dedicated to one woman, individually named, the names carved in large letters directly into the stone, but nonetheless the disparity is striking.[3] Even the raw materials of these different benches – wood, subject to carved graffiti and the rot of Van-couver's damp climate, compared to polished, engraved granite, risks implying a sense of relative value that is difficult to shake.[4]

Only a small tile in the circle of an estimated hundred or more donor tiles surrounding the stone benches in Thornton Park makes

5.4 Bench from Marker of Change in Thornton Park, Vancouver. Photo
courtesy the author.

mention of the women who have been disappeared from the neighbourhood in which this monument rests. "In loving memory of the
women killed on Vancouver's Downtown Eastside," the tile reads.
"So many women lost to us." But its obscurity, buried among so
many other tiles, restricts the possible mitigating effect of its message, for although I have visited the Marker of Change memorial
in Thornton Park many times, I was unaware of the existence of
this tile until I read about it in the Cultural Memory Group's book
(2006, 42–3). Set against the vast circle of benches dedicated to the
memory of fourteen individually named women, it is questionable
whether this tile does more than reinscribe the "differential allocation of grievability" between the women named and the local
unnamed women (Butler 2004, xiv). As Caffyn Kelley (1995) asserts,
despite its dedication to "all women murdered by men," this monument does not individually name any of the local women, disproportionately Indigenous women, who have been murdered.[5]
Sharon Rosenberg argues that Marker of Change "cannot make
explicit the presence – in name – of those women whose slain

bodies mark the grounds (the context) of Thornton Park" (2000, 82). While the women murdered in Montréal have come to be read as representative or even emblematic of violence against women in Canada (see Rosenberg and Simon 2000), and we now mark a National Day of Remembrance and Action on Violence Against Women annually on the day of their murders, to date there has been no comparable state-sponsored insistence on the importance of nationally recognizing or remembering the 1181 or more murdered or missing Indigenous women across Canada, indicative of a widespread resistance to recognizing the ongoing violence of settler colonialism. This is not to discount the important work done by the Women's Memorial March Committee in Vancouver or by the Native Women's Association of Canada's Sisters in Spirit vigils that occur across the country every October 4th, but I note that the main vigil on October 4th is usually held on Parliament Hill in the interests of trying to get Members of Parliament *to pay attention* to the issue of violence against Indigenous women, which is quite a striking difference from having the federal government itself declare a National Day of Remembrance and Action, as they did quite quickly in memory of the women murdered on December 6th.

Yet there would be a danger, too, in reading the deaths of women disappeared from the Downtown Eastside as emblematic of violence against women in Canada, just as there is a danger in not doing so – a danger inherent to the practice of emblemization itself. Sharon Rosenberg (2000) argues that when particular deaths are made to stand in for all deaths among individuals who share a specific marker of identity (i.e., "women"), a host of differences between such individuals are necessarily and troublingly downplayed or erased. The danger in arguing that the women disappeared from the Downtown Eastside should *also* be rendered emblematic of violence against women, then, lies in the potential erasure of the differences that contributed to the heightened vulnerability of these particular women in the first place. Likely we would do better to interrogate the logic of emblemization itself, as Rosenberg suggests, and instead focus on "what it might mean to *re*figure these bindings between remembrance and change, and, more broadly, between the living and the dead" (2000, 83; see also Rosenberg and Simon 2000). Differences of racialization, class, place, and history mark the deaths of women from Vancouver's Downtown Eastside, as distinct from those of the women from Montréal, and these differences also shape the vastly different public responses to those deaths, so it seems important that these differences not be erased through efforts to draw connections via gender or under the rubric of a more generic "violence against women" (on this point see also Smith 2005 and Razack 2000, 93).

Both the CRAB and Thornton Park memorials make strategic use of some of the personal names of women who have been disappeared or murdered. Listing some women's names on the plaque that graces the memorial bench in CRAB park but not others, while certainly understandable from a practical point of view given the significant constraints of space and time, might nonetheless risk again reinscribing a hierarchy of grievability, implying that those listed can in some way stand in for those who remain anonymous. It is also true that even if all the names of the women murdered were listed, an uninformed passerby would still not likely make much meaning from this remembrance practice. Questioning philosopher Edith Wyschogrod's (1985) assertion that naming the dead is necessary to an ethical practice of remembrance, Judith Butler asks: "Do these names really signify for us the fullness of the lives that were lost, or are they so many tokens of what we cannot know, enigmas, inscrutable and silent?" (1988, 69).[6] And how would one decide when all the names *had* been listed in response to the disappearance of women from the Downtown Eastside: where would the list start and stop?

And yet, this practice of naming the dead remains important, perhaps especially so in instances where the name of the person directly responsible for the deaths becomes a form of common knowledge, for so often in these instances many in the general public can recall the name of those who commit murder but not of those who have been murdered. Artists Janis Cole and Rebecca Belmore make very different uses of some of the personal names of women who have been disappeared from the Downtown Eastside in memorial art created in response to these events. Their works suggest that the inscription or recitation of names as a memorial practice has varying effects that are heavily dependent on the context, frame, or medium through which the names are communicated. Names will have little effect on transforming the legacies of unjust pasts when wider social contexts like settler colonialism remain largely untroubled through the act of naming. Through the very different uses of some of the women's names in Cole's (2009) video-art installation, *Remember Their Names* (see figure 5.5), and Belmore's (2002) performance, *Vigil*, we can develop a clearer sense of how greatly this context matters in art that aims to memorialize the women disappeared from the Downtown Eastside.

5.5 Janis Cole, *Remember Their Names*, 2009, multiple-channel video installation (detail). Reproduced with permission of the artist. Photo courtesy the author.

Cole's exhibit, *Remember Their Names*, was installed at Toronto's Trinity Square Video from 4 July to 8 August 2009, and when I visited it, my overall impression was that Cole made use of the women's personal names as a way to try to encourage a wider public to remember the individual women named on the police list of missing women, who have so often been grouped together in ways that either sweep away or over-generalize their diverse lives. Although there were many different elements to Cole's multiple-channel video installation, in this chapter I focus on those aspects that memorialize individual women (see Dean 2010a for a longer discussion of Cole's exhibit). After entering a small room with black walls and ceiling, visitors to Cole's exhibit found ourselves facing a large, oval memorial shrine on the floor containing stuffed animals, roses or other flowers, dream-catchers, cards, notes or letters, and photographs (including many childhood photographs) of some of the disappeared women. Most of these objects seemed to have been donated by family or friends of the women, as they expressed personal messages of grief or conveyed memories of primarily familial relationships. This collection of memorial artefacts productively provides viewers with a wider social context for the women's lives by highlighting how they were connected to others. A large screen was mounted behind the shrine-like oval of artefacts, and a projected image-loop began with the words "Remember their Names" in blue text across a black screen. The video then changed to an image of the poster released by the Missing Women Task Force. The poster faded, and the individual images of the women it contains were projected, along with their names, one by one onto the screen. Cole synchronized the women's poster images with their names as they are spoken in a song, "Missing," which played overhead as the images changed.[7] At the end of the video loop the poster reappeared and faded into footage of a memorial or vigil: an image appeared of candles and roses strewn on the ground and a hand-painted sign that read, "We Miss You."

The combination of memorializing artefacts on the floor, the haunting music and chanted names in "Missing," and the imagery of candles and flowers blending into the poster images on-screen seem likely to produce affective responses of sadness, grief, compassion, or empathy in most viewers. The mementos and photographs give a fuller sense of the lives lost than the images and names projected on-screen and chanted in the audio could on its own. They invite us to remember the disappeared women not just as names but through their relationships to others – as mothers, sisters, and daughters primarily, recalling the trope evoked in so many posthumous representations of their lives. We are positioned to imagine the innocence of the women's childhoods and the ordinariness of their familial or kinship connections, and as a result to begin to imagine that the disappeared women could be *any*woman, including ourselves or other women we know and care about. Although the exhibit of memorializing artefacts and an attention to the women's individual names might work to engage the empathy and concern of a wider public through their evocation of normative gendered identities and a familiar narrative of family life, there are also significant risks involved with this kind of individualizing focus. We might come to feel included in this story of loss by being invited to imagine that the disappeared women could have been *our* mother, sister, or daughter, or could have been us, could have been *any*woman. Presumably, we might, through this form of empathic identification, be moved to compassion or perhaps even action as a result of recognizing that this story could be *our* story.

But this kind of identification is a "treacherous mistake," according to Avery Gordon (1997), for not only does it require holding or "fixing" the disappeared women to those aspects of their identities that are widely presumed to be more "innocent" – their roles as mothers, sisters, and daughters and their earlier lives as children – but it also invites a repudiation of how we might each be in this story quite differently (187). Although the collection of memorial artefacts includes dream-catchers and other items that signify that many of the disappeared women were Indigenous, there is little in the exhibit that would invite viewers to consider how settler colonialism is connected to the violence they experienced. So, although Cole's title offers an important reminder in a context in which the name of the man accused of murdering many of these women is widely known and remembered while the women's names are largely forgotten by those who did not know them in life, her use of the women's names and of individual memorial artefacts to refocus our attention on their roles as mothers, sisters, and daughters risks evoking the kinds of empathic identifications that might deflect or defer consideration of our complicated and differing enmeshments with this ongoing story of disappearance and *colonial* gender-based violence.

Belmore's performance, *Vigil*, took place seven years before Cole's exhibit at the intersection of Gore and Cordova Streets in the heart of Vancouver's Downtown Eastside.[8] *Vigil* was commissioned for the Talking Stick Aboriginal Art Festival, and a video of the half-hour-long performance was transformed into a video installation for the exhibit *The Named and the Unnamed* at the Morris and Helen Belkin Art Gallery in Vancouver, with several later installations across Canada (see figures 5.6 and 5.7).

5.6 Rebecca Belmore, *The Named and the Unnamed*, 2002, video installation (detail). Collection of the Morris and Helen Belkin Art Gallery, The University of British Columbia. Purchased with the support of the Canada Council for the Arts Acquisition Assistance program and the Morris and Helen Belkin Foundation, 2005. Photo: Howard Ursuliak.

In the performance-based memorial, Belmore ritually scrubbed the streets and lit candles, engaging a viewer to assist her. She then began to shout the first names of several of the women known to be missing at the time, reading their names from where they were written in black marker up and down the flesh of her bare arms. After shouting a name, Belmore pulled a rose through her mouth, tearing her lips on the thorns and spitting the petals and leaves to the ground. She then donned a long red dress and proceeded to nail the dress to a wooden street pole, struggled to rip herself free, then nailed the dress back again until she had shredded the garment right off her body. At the end of the performance, Belmore swaggered in tank top and underwear over to a pickup truck and leaned against it as James Brown's "It's a Man's Man's Man's World" began to boom out from the truck's stereo.

5.7 Rebecca Belmore, *The Named and the Unnamed*, 2002, video installation
(detail). Collection of the Morris and Helen Belkin Art Gallery, The University
of British Columbia. Purchased with the support of the Canada Council for
the Arts Acquisition Assistance program and the Morris and Helen Belkin
Foundation, 2005. Photo: Howard Ursuliak.

There is much to comment on in this performance, but what interests me most here is Belmore's very different use of some of the wom-
en's names. By using only first names, and by inscribing those names
directly on her body, Belmore implies a proximity that invites reflection
on the possible similarities between the women named and her own
female, Indigenous body.[9] In spite of her very general use of only first
names, then, the performance resists an interpretation that would allow
us to imagine that the women named could be *any*woman; instead,
through her use of her own body and her selection of the specific place
of a Downtown Eastside street, Belmore's performance focuses attention on women racialized in particular ways through their absent presence in this particular neighbourhood. Indeed, Belmore's own body is

likely to signify very differently for her audience here on the street in the Downtown Eastside than it might in a more typical gallery space. Here, an Indigenous woman's body signifies specific forms of vulnerability and resistance to violence that Belmore's use of her own body in the performance both highlights and provocatively challenges; as Claudette Lauzon writes, "Belmore's is a body that refuses to vanish from a space in which women's bodies are *expected* to vanish without a trace" (2010, 83).

By writing the women's first names directly on her body, I would argue Belmore is challenging her audience to consider that the disappeared women could be not *any*woman, but *too many* of the Indigenous women who are over-represented in this neighbourhood. As Charlotte Townsend-Gault (2003) has argued, the names on Belmore's arms may also "draw attention to the fact that the kin-based, named, relationships of native communities were overlaid ... Place names, plant names, people's names – all overlaid, all changed" (18). This practice of naming invites reflection on a larger story of loss and disappearance, one that continues to play out in this neighbourhood and encompasses those who find themselves at the corners of Gore and Cordova witnessing Belmore's performance. Instead of drawing attention to the individual imprint of a violence potentially experienced by *any*woman, then, Belmore focuses our attention on a different kind of after-effect of violence, especially through her painful struggle to free herself from the red dress. Deploying the potent symbolism of the red dress to evoke the absent presence of the historical (but ongoing) conflation of Indigenous womanhood with "licentiousness" and "prostitution," Belmore exposes the violent effects of this reductive image, her struggle to free herself highlighting how the wider context of settler colonialism has rendered Indigenous women more vulnerable to violence through the narrow and stereotypical images of them it continues to perpetuate.

Aside from inscribing women's names on her arms, Belmore also shouted some of the first names, one by one, in a voice that is both angry and anguished. Her shouts sound as though she is both seeking and mourning those named ("seeking" because her performance took place before the remains of many of the women whose names she shouts were recovered). At one point in the performance Belmore cries out, "Frances!" and a woman some distance away appears to respond by crying out, "What?!" Belmore then shouts, "Tanya!" and another (or possibly the same) woman's voice, from slightly further away, replies

"WHAT?!" At this point in the video, the audience appears to twitter uneasily. A complex balance between proximity and distance is struck here, which has to do with the place that Belmore has chosen for her performance: the responses to the shouted names remind the mostly art-aficionado audience that there are other women in this neighbourhood contending with similar forms of vulnerability and social abandonment, but at the same time it is not *any*woman who has responded to Belmore's cries but particular women contending with specific forms of precarity, forms from which a good portion of her audience likely lives at some distance.

In Belmore's performance, the names that she shouts may not conjure images of the women's faces, and for the majority of her audience I would assume they likely don't bring to mind specific stories or memories, either. Belmore does not focus on individual women, aside from the shouting of their names, nor does she draw explicit attention to the women's roles as mothers, sisters, and daughters, and her performance thus seems less likely to lead to the forms of empathic identification I worried about with Pamela Masik's or Janis Cole's exhibits, although one could also argue that it offers less specificity about the women's unique, singular lives. Instead, Belmore's use of names is likely to make her audience feel mainly uncomfortable, because we are being asked to encounter the women not as *any*woman but as women racialized in particular ways and from this particular place, and to therefore attend to the social and psychic legacies of a colonial history that is anything but past. Belmore's imagined audience is thus not limited to a purportedly indifferent public, although she is trying to intervene in the complacency of such a public as well. But her performance addresses the diverse members of her audience in a way that is suggestive of our responsibility to look for the women and notice their absence, to attend to (and maybe, just maybe, start to better understand our relation to) the specific and complex histories of the place of the Downtown Eastside and of those who continue to call the neighbourhood home. This may radically shift how Belmore's audience, and perhaps especially those in her audience who find ourselves in Canada today as the descendants of European settlers and colonizers, recognize our place in this ongoing story of violence and disappearance. It seems plausible that viewers might come to see ourselves as implicated in this story in quite a different way from the kinds of identifications likely to be produced through Cole's work (and more mindful, too, of "the unnamed" who figure in the title of Belmore's performance-turned-video-installation, which could reference Indigenous women who continue to be violently disappeared across the country or those who have been disappeared across centuries). So, although we may not remember, or even learn, the full names of the women being remembered by this vigil, we might, through Belmore's use of their names as traces of both individual lives and wider social histories, come to grasp something significant about the collective, political, and historical dimensions of the losses being memorialized. Belmore's attention to place, her ability to evoke proximity without collapsing difference, and her use of her own body to evoke the trauma of colonial violence might invite viewers to engage in practices of inheritance that avoid some of the pitfalls of those empathic approaches to witnessing that risk collapsing the many ways that difference continues to matter. We may, in other words, experience an encounter with memory as a difficult return.

Two additional memorials offer greater insight into what it might mean to grapple, in the act of memorializing, with memory as a difficult return. The first consists of a mural dedicated to Vancouver's disappeared women painted in 2003 in downtown Montréal (see figure 5.8). It is striking that this memorial was created in Montréal, the site of those murders at the Polytechnique that are commemorated so prominently in Downtown Eastside Vancouver. The mural itself was painted on the side of the building that houses the Native Friendship Centre of Montréal and was created by a group called the Living Monument Mural Collective, composed of various people including volunteers from the Friendship Centre, the Aboriginal women's shelter, the Coalition for the Rights of Sex Workers, and Stella, a Montréal-based organization of and for sex workers (see Cultural Memory Group 2006, 171–3).[10]

The skylines of both Vancouver and Montréal are visible in the mural, so although there is no explicit mention of the murders of women at the Polytechnique, a sense of the inter-implication of these two cities is nonetheless woven into the specifically Vancouver-based deaths being memorialized here. In the sky above the two skylines, Ojibway spirit boats carry souls and a star twinkles with a piece of glass for every missing or murdered woman from the Downtown Eastside.[11] These stars bring the dead into presence, while the representation of the spirit boat moving between the two worlds of living and dead functions to rupture this divide, to suggest the untenable nature of a staunch living/dead binary, disrupting conventional understandings of living/dead

5.8 The Montréal Mural, by the Living Monument Mural Collective. Photo
courtesy Ric Knowles.

and self/other as always already entirely separable: the self standing
in front of the mural and the women represented by the twinkling stars
are bridged by the spirit boats, which might perhaps invite reflection
on the fragility of these distinctions of self/other and living/dead.

At the same time, however, the mural does not allow an easy laps-
ing into identification, or "this could have been me or someone I love,"
with the erasure of the colonial context contributing to these particular deaths that such a move might entail; its text poses a challenge to
any such slippage. In the foreground of the mural, figures representing
the artists hold a banner that reads: "We honour the more than 60 sex

workers, most of them Indigenous, who were killed or disappeared in Vancouver, BC," and below: "We pay homage to these women, victims of the comfort and indifference of a society that would sometimes rather see them as something to be eliminated. This mural is also dedicated to their friends, their children and families, to their lovers and loved ones. YOU WILL NOT BE FORGOTTEN."

There are several claims here that shatter any oversimplified assumptions one might make about the women being memorialized: the mural tells us that a group of sex workers, most of them Indigenous, are also women worthy of honour who can be victims, not of their own poor choices, or even of individual perpetrators, but of an indifferent society that views them as disposable. Instead of reclaiming the women as mothers, sisters, and daughters, the text of the mural shifts its address to the kin left to mourn these losses, and by doing so it reminds us that the women were *always* people with relationships to others that mattered greatly, that their loss was always grievable to those who knew and loved them. The YOU in the next line encompasses these mourners as well as the disappeared women, and it may be significant that friends are mentioned first in the list of those left behind who remember (and are to be remembered by others), a reminder that a commitment to never forget the dead must also be a commitment to addressing the social arrangements and conditions contributing to their deaths, which many of the women's friends continue to contend with daily. Distinctions between grief/mourning and activism thus begin to slip away, such that both become part of an everyday practice of inheriting what lives on from the women who were disappeared.

This mural strikes me as remarkable, then, for how it has the potential to evoke both remembrance as a form of strategic practice and remembrance as a difficult return at once: it is simultaneously an invocation to strategic remembrance, an indictment of a society that would dare to cast these women as "something to be eliminated," and at the same time through its imagery and mode of address it disrupts oversimplified divisions between self/other, living/dead, past/present, and grieving/activism without allowing these divisions to be dissolved entirely. Some of the differences that contributed to the women's heightened vulnerability, their Indigeneity and stigmas about sex work, are addressed directly, and the too-common representation of these forms of difference as signs of ungrievability is challenged by the mural's text. At the same time, the blending of the two skylines situates the women's disappearances as an issue of concern for others beyond the Downtown Eastside and also beyond Vancouver. The text of the mural is written in several languages: Ojibway, Inuit, Mohawk, French, and English, and it is significant that it blends Indigenous languages (frequently associated with the past) with languages imported by European colonizers (associated with the present and future). Ultimately, the mural succeeds at disrupting many of the ways the women have been cast as ungrievable losses without disavowing or re-stigmatizing the particular circumstances contributing to their vulnerability.

Although not made explicit in the mural itself, I believe this memorial also directs our attention to "an 'unworked-through past,'" and in doing so it may also succeed at evoking remembrance as a difficult return (Simon, Rosenberg, and Eppert 2000, 4). The Ojibway spirit boats may represent the fragility of distinctions between living and dead, but they also reference the significant colonial efforts to extinguish such spiritual beliefs. The blending of Indigenous and European languages also calls that past into presence, both signifying and, by representing the languages on an equal footing, resisting those massive efforts to also eliminate Indigenous languages and cultures. Resistance to colonization is thus powerfully evoked, while at the same time the violence and ongoing-ness of colonization are emphasized through reference to a contemporary tendency or willingness to see Indigenous women in particular as "something to be eliminated." This phrasing, coupled with the visual representation of the spirit boats and the presence of the different languages, provides an opening, a rupture that makes it difficult to hold the colonial past outside of or separate from our present. Such an opening invites viewers to position ourselves in this story under terms quite different from those presented by the kinds of empathic identifications usually invoked when remembrance is deployed strategically.

A final example of a memorial that holds the potential to evoke remembrance as a difficult return is found in the annual Valentine's Day Women's Memorial March (see figure 5.9).[12] Because this event takes place in the heart of the Downtown Eastside, those who contend daily with social arrangements and conditions similar to those experienced by the women who have been disappeared are a significant proportion of the mourners present. So, although the purpose of the march involves remembering the dead and the women who remain unaccounted for, the unjust social conditions and arrangements contributing to their deaths or disappearances are pressing, making any easy separation between the past (in which the particular women being

5.9 The February 14th Annual Women's Memorial March, 2012.
Photo courtesy David P. Ball.

remembered were lost) and the present (in which others continue to suffer) untenable.

Caffyn Kelley (1995) describes the Valentine's Day march as an enactment of "a different kind of memory – capable of spontaneous combustion, of furious and uncontrollable grief." The ever-present signs of injustice and unrest charge the memories brought to this march through the streets with the surging force of memory as a difficult return. Over the years, this event has strategically drawn attention to the disappearances and violent deaths of Indigenous women from the neighbourhood and demanded an official response. But beyond its strategic function, the event continues to rupture bindings of past/present, grief/activism, living/dead, and self/other, making way for the spectral presence of women who have been disappeared to return as spirit and to linger in the streets well after the marching bodies have dispersed.

"Their Spirits Live Within Us" has become this march's theme, a theme that charges those in attendance with a responsibility to bring the dead into presence, to "hold a place for their absent presence in one's contemporary life" (Simon, Rosenberg, and Eppert 2000, 4). The march itself, led by Indigenous elders, Indigenous women's groups, and family members of some of the disappeared women, winds through the streets of the Downtown Eastside, pausing to smudge sage and leave offerings like roses, cedar, and tobacco at the many spots along the way where women were either murdered or last seen (for one published ethnographic analysis of the march, see Culhane 2003). Often, as the march winds to an end, political speeches are made that highlight the injustices and inequities so visible in the Downtown Eastside. These speeches are an important, strategic aspect of the event, but for me what is so very haunting about this event is the opening offered by how the theme and numerous pauses along the way draw attention to the absent *presence* of the dead and to the ongoing responsibility we, the living, have to attend to the social circumstances of their violent and unjust deaths. This is no small charge, for as Lora McElhinney writes, the women's spirits don't always live within us easily (2007, 73). Thus, the annual repetition of the Valentine's Day march is perhaps more than anything an opportunity, an opening to learn from and reflect on what it might mean to inherit what lives on from the women who have been disappeared from this neighbourhood.

Memorials that evoke memory as a difficult return challenge us to assess our place in this story in ways quite different from those that primarily deploy memory for strategic purposes or invite us to empathically imagine the women might have been *any*woman. When memory as a difficult return is evoked, our relation to the losses being memorialized is called into question and potentially refashioned as one substantiated not on our being bystanders to those losses, but on our becoming inheritors, not of the specific or individual losses of women we did not know, but instead of what lives on from those losses. Inviting us to adopt practices of inheritance as aspects of our everyday living, such memorials seem more likely to invoke a complex sense of our differing implications in the losses they mark, compelling us to reconsider just what responsibility or justice in the wake of the disappearances and violent deaths of so many women might look like.

Reckoning (for the Present)

Since I have been advocating throughout this book that the kinds of changes needed to provoke something like justice in response to the loss of so many women from the Downtown Eastside are necessarily social or collective, it may seem a bit strange to end with a discussion of reckoning. Reckoning, as a practice, is somewhat introspective and individual, even if it can also have much broader social implications. As Avery Gordon describes it: "Reckoning is about knowing what kind of effort is required to change ourselves and the conditions that make us who we are, that set limits on what is acceptable and unacceptable, on what is possible and impossible" (1997, 202). Reckoning involves trying to discern how we can best contribute to changing or altering those social conditions and arrangements that leave some more vulnerable to violence or suffering than others. One obviously cannot change those forces on one's own, or always even know what conditions or arrangements need changing, but reckoning with how we are ourselves conditioned and, for some of us, privileged by these very forces can help us to see opportunities for intervening in them. The kind of change Gordon argues can be achieved through reckoning "is not individualistic, but it does acknowledge, indeed it demands, that change cannot occur without the encounter, without the *something you have to try for yourself*" (203, emphasis in original). Reckoning is not about a return to some idyllic or utopian past. Nor is it about delineating the future before its arrival, as though such a thing were possible. Instead, it has the potential to be both an individual and collective process of uncovering, connecting, and working to address the injustices we inherit, a coming-to-terms with what they mean in and for our everyday lives in the present – ultimately, inheriting what lives on requires reckoning with how we are all differently implicated in violence against women from the Downtown Eastside, and with what that might mean for our everyday existence.

Two recent encounters left me with many unanswered questions about what it means to really reckon with what lives on from the disappearance of so many women as an everyday practice of inheritance. The first occurred when a neighbour approached me as I sat on my front step in my east Hamilton neighbourhood. In a loud voice meant to be overheard by a woman standing quietly a short distance away, a woman we both knew was likely working that particular corner, as she did often, he said, "I talked to my buddies at the police station, they're going to do a big sweep and push all these hookers away from here." I was taken aback, and after trying to collect my thoughts for a moment, I responded, "I'd much rather see women working here, within earshot of houses, than out by the factories where the risk of violence is so much greater." Without hesitating he replied, "Women like that, when they get into cars and do what they do, they know what they're in for." Then I got angry. "I feel safer coming home at night, knowing there are other women on the street here," I retorted. "I don't want them pushed on to somewhere else – in fact, they're some of our *best* neighbours!" He stared at me blankly, then went home. The second encounter occurred at a meeting of my neighbourhood association. In response to a flyer I had helped to create and distribute alongside a small number of other local activists trying to confront a rising tide of hostility towards outdoor sex work, drug use, and other signs of poverty and marginalization in the area, a woman shouted angrily: "You can't be friendly with these people, you can't talk to them! If you do, it won't be long before you end up with an AIDS needle shoved at your throat." Although such hostility was certainly not new to me, again I was stunned into silence.

Sarah de Vries appears to have keenly felt the weight of living with full awareness that her own life was so routinely cast as a nuisance, as disposable – ultimately as ungrievable, as somehow less worthy of care and concern, in precisely the way that my neighbours conveyed. This awareness caused her to actually anticipate her own disappearance and murder and the subsequent delays in an official response or widespread public outcry. Her insights are evident in a series of startling reflections posed in her journal in December 1995:

Am I next? Is he watching me now? Stalking me like a predator and its prey. Waiting, waiting for some perfect spot, time or my stupid mistake. How does one choose a victim? Good question, isn't it? If I knew that, I would never get snuffed.

So many women, so many that I never even knew about, are missing in action.
It's getting to be a daily part of life. That's sad. Somebody dies and it's like some-
body just did something normal. I can't find the right words. It's strange. A woman
who works the Hastings street area gets murdered, and nothing.

Yet if she were some square john's little girl, shit would hit the goddamn fan.
Front page news for weeks, people protesting in the streets. Everybody makes a
stink. While the happy hooker just starts to decay, like she didn't matter, expendable,
dishonourable. It's a shame that society is that unfeeling. She was some woman's
baby girl, gone astray, lost from the right path.

She was a person.[1]

Similarly, at the end of the poem I discussed in chapter 2, De Vries
reflects on the lack of attention paid to the murder of another woman
from the Downtown Eastside and again reasserts her understanding
of – indeed, her *insistence on* – the profound injustice of the widespread
failure to recognize this woman's life as grievable:

She was somebody fighting for life
Trying to survive
A lonely lost child who died
In the night, all alone, scared
Gasping for air[2]

Reading and rereading these lines, I find I am haunted by the necessity
of trying to imagine what it must have been like to have such insight into
how one's own death might be viewed as somehow less worthy of widespread grief or concern, and then to have to face that insight yet again at the
moment of one's own murder – *in the night, all alone, scared. Gasping for air.*
At the same time, I cannot imagine it.

For Sharon Rosenberg, reckoning with our relation to people who have
died violently necessarily involves a complicated process of comporting
oneself towards the dead and simultaneously recoiling from what we cannot (bear to) know about the horrific circumstances of their dying. Drawing
on Judith Butler and Jill Bennett, Rosenberg describes the process thus:

Comporting towards a dead you through the dynamic tension of turning
towards and recoiling from, as a mode of moving outside the self in and
through making relation to a memory of those dead, involves an easing
away from the stranglehold of identity categories while not obscuring
how identity matters in contemporary [life]. (2009, 235–6)

Initially I had a strong negative reaction to Rosenberg's reliance on the language of "recoiling" because, for me, the word "recoil" used in relation to women who so frequently experienced dramatic forms of recoil from others in life was a term too laden, too over-determined (and I recall here the encounters I describe with neighbours above as prime examples of the kind of recoiling I am talking about). Of course, this is not the way Rosenberg (or Bennett) actually use the term, but I continue to worry that it is nonetheless likely to be evocative of this other use when deployed in relation to those who live and die under the weight of such social stigma. Still, as I have engaged further with what Rosenberg was trying to suggest through her use of these notions of comporting and recoiling as a practice of reckoning, I have come to see the value of the practice (even if I might choose different language to describe it).

Rosenberg argues that to engage in practices of remembrance on identity-based terms alone allows us to escape knowing something different(ly) about our relation to the violently dead, about that tie that binds the "I" and the "you." She develops this argument by analysing the contemporary trend (which began, I suspect, around 2006) towards memorializing murdered or missing Indigenous women *alongside* the women murdered during the Montreal Massacre each year on December 6th, the National Day of Remembrance and Action on Violence Against Women. Those who are more likely to recognize the women murdered at L'École Polytechnique as "like us" may well be less likely to recoil from learning about the violent deaths of other(ed) women on such a date, but simultaneously to lump these deaths together because they represent murders "of women" also risks, in Rosenberg's words, "foreclos[ing] encounters with the more complicated alterity of these dead" (235). So, although Rosenberg doesn't make this argument in quite the same way, this line of thinking returns me to one of the key arguments repeated throughout this book – namely, that when we are perhaps less likely to identify with people who have died violently because of the many ways the identity categories through which we navigate the world are constituted as quite different from theirs, it becomes all the more important to pay attention to the moment of recoil and what it suggests about both the discursive and the material effects of that (re)production of difference. Recoiling then becomes, according to Rosenberg, "a mode of *staying in relation*, as a grappling with responsibility" (236, emphasis in original), and I take her to mean here a grappling with the responsibility that arises from realizing how we are implicated in the violence experienced by others.

I propose that Rosenberg's practice of reckoning as a process of comporting and recoiling could be taken up slightly differently through a turn to the imagination, as a process of trying to imagine what it is like to live a life cast through quite different terms of identity or belonging than one's own. Simultaneously, I recognize that such an imagining will always be incomplete, but I think there is something important in the trying – that is, in risking an attempt that one knows in advance cannot ever be accomplished fully. For example, Sarah de Vries imagines the life of the murdered woman in her poem with much complexity, as someone always already fully human despite how she might have been denied such complex human-ness by many in life. But she *doesn't* grant the same complexity to the "you" who, in her poem, indifferently reads about the woman's murder in the newspaper and turns the page, all the while drinking coffee and smoking. It is entirely possible that De Vries is quite right to assume this bystander feels nothing but distance, or worse, pity, or is merely recoiling from the life and death of the woman in the newspaper with no effort at comportment, but by failing to imagine that the "you" *just might* consider herself to have some form of relation to the murdered woman, the poem risks reiterating the very terms of mattering, literally of who matters to whom, that it otherwise so strongly works against. One of the things I inherit from De Vries's poem is its alteration of *my* ways of being with others, then, which involves imagining not only what it might have been like to live the life of the murdered woman in the poem (and of course, by extension, De Vries's own life), but also to imagine that the "you" who smokes and disinterestedly turns the pages of the newspaper might possibly be challenged, encouraged, or supported to engage in a practice of inheriting what lives on from the violent loss of women like De Vries, by reckoning with how their own life and privileges might actually be implicated in the disappearance of so many women.

This brings me back to the encounters with neighbours that I described above. Now, I am actually much more comfortable thinking about recoiling as part of a practice of reckoning with my relation to these neighbours! Indeed, one could read my hesitant pauses in response to their violent articulations as moments of recoiling from what I do not want to know about them. It strikes me that the qualities of an ethical relation to the dead that have been given such texture in Roger Simon and Sharon Rosenberg's writings, among others, can also help me to navigate this relation to the living, which I am coming to see as increasingly important to my own practice of inheriting the testimony of Sarah de Vries's poem. In this instance, my own recoil from the repulsion that is evident in the words and actions of my neighbours prompts me to attend to the complicated necessity of finding ways to stay in relation rather than turn away, of my responsibility to seek opportunities to in turn attempt to support or encourage these neighbours to join the "us" that would view De Vries's testament as necessitating a reckoning with how we *see* ourselves in relation to De Vries and to other women whose identities are constituted on similar terms.

Knowing this helps me to understand why I made the mistake, when responding to my first neighbour, of accepting the terms of engagement he laid out by trying to solicit an empathic response on the basis of hailing him into an identification *first with me* and then, by extension, with the woman on the corner, by myself relying on and reiterating that troubling appeal to the generic category of "women" (i.e., "I feel safer knowing there are other women on the streets after dark"). I also attempted to distance myself from him by refusing to even be curious about his desires to "sweep and push" women doing sex work away, which it must be acknowledged is itself a way of "altering one's ways of being with others," even if not the kind we might see as desirable. I am not at all suggesting that I should have expressed support for his proposed alteration, but I do think that by framing my objection through a recourse to identity terms, and by reacting in both of these encounters with a strong recoil but no comportment towards either neighbour, I in many ways reproduced the narrow or conventional way of seeing oneself as (not) always already in relation to others to which I take exception in their own remarks.

Returning to De Vries's poem as I conclude, I take hope from the fact that although De Vries does not allow her indifferent bystander much complexity, she is nonetheless willing to *address* her, which is a mode of staying in relation across difference *through the very act of address itself*. This would seem to suggest that despite her many, many experiences to the contrary, experiences where she no doubt felt the very sort of recoil that my neighbours' comments enact, De Vries did remain hopeful that the "you" she addressed might yet be encouraged or supported to become part of an "us" that would come into being through "an attentiveness and shared reference to [her] testament," in the interests of building "a community of the living and the dead" (Simon 2006, 195). Finding ways to be in relation with others beyond the constrictions of identity but never forgetful of the ways identity matters; finding ways to stay in relation not just with the dead and with those who continue to contend with and resist the social conditions and arrangements that leave some more vulnerable to violence than others, and *also* with people like my neighbours who do continue to recoil from those whose living and dying is so frequently cast as less grievable – such challenging alterations of one's ways of being with others are the "terrible gifts" I inherit from my own reckoning with De Vries's poem.

But Sarah de Vries draws our attention to more than just the terribleness of the violent death of the woman in her poem (and, inadvertently, her own), for the lines of her poem suggest that the woman's struggles to survive actually began long before the moment of her murder. We get the impression that the woman was "trying to survive" and "fighting for life" for some time before the violent encounter in which she was killed. So, while De Vries succeeds at conveying the horror of the woman's murder, she also draws our attention back to that key issue of how we *see* the woman, not just after her death but also *in life*, and by doing so she points us to "a something to be done" (Gordon 190), which in this case includes attending to the claims not just of disappeared or murdered women but of those who continue to contend with similar forms of injustice, vulnerability, and marginalization. As one Downtown Eastside outreach worker speaking about the importance of the annual Women's Memorial March insists: "We have over 300 other days to think about the women that are still living, to think about the women that are still homeless and living in poverty." An aspect of any inheritance of what lives on from so many disappeared or murdered women, then, necessarily includes contending with the claims of those who continue to live with the greatest proximity to the violent social conditions and arrangements arising from the wider context of settler colonialism that underpins the disappearances and murders that concern me in this book. As Downtown Eastside activist Harsha Walia argues, "The only way to understand the heinous violence committed against missing and murdered women is to understand the lives and the struggles of those women who continue to survive in this neighbourhood under the same circumstances every day."[3]

Gordon insists that reckoning requires contending, individually and collectively, with something "we have lost, but never had" (Gordon 183), which in this instance must surely include a more just set of relations between Indigenous people and settler-Canadians. An acknowledgment of the colonial past's ongoing-ness in the present requires nothing less, and there can in the end be no just response to the disappearance of so many disproportionately Indigenous women from the Downtown

Eastside, or from many other neighbourhoods across the country, without a commitment to hearing the political claims of Indigenous communities and working to address the many outstanding injustices that shape these relations, injustices that deeply affect individual lives but are also social, political, economic, cultural, spiritual, and epistemological.

Given the degree to which settler colonialism is tied to this present-day violence, all of us who find ourselves living on this land now known as Canada today are implicated in the problem of seeking a just response. In addition to injustices that arise from legal, political, and economic arrangements, Miranda Fricker (2007) asks us to attend to "epistemic injustice," or injustices perpetrated on the basis of assumptions about a group of people's status as knowers or knowledge-makers. Fricker identifies two different forms of epistemic injustice: the first she calls "testimonial injustice," which occurs when a listener gives less credibility to a speaker's words based on assumptions about her identity; the second she describes as "hermeneutical injustice," which occurs when a speaker cannot be fully heard or understood due to a lack of "collective interpretive resources." As Fricker explains, "An example of the first might be that the police do not believe you because you are black; an example of the second might be that you suffer sexual harassment in a culture that still lacks that critical concept" (1). Both of these forms of epistemic injustice are evident in the disappearance of women from the Downtown Eastside, but I believe only the first form has been widely recognized or acknowledged.

Testimonial injustice is evident in this story in the way that so little credibility was afforded to those who reported their friends or loved ones missing until the late 1990s, when families presumed to be more credible knowers (white, middle-class families) began to make similar reports. This affront to some friends, families, and Downtown Eastside activists' status as knowers deepens the injustice that has occurred, and any commitment to investigate or redress the failings of police and other officials in relation to their early (lack of) response to the disappearance of women from this neighbourhood ought to also address this problem of testimonial injustice. This form of injustice has long plagued the Downtown Eastside, where residents are seldom considered to possess credible knowledge about their own lives or experiences, or about what could be done to improve those lives and experiences. The effect of widespread assumptions about poverty, race, dis/ability, addiction, sex work, and criminalization on how we interpret someone's ability to *know* require much more scrutiny, for such assumptions are undoubtedly implicated in the delayed and inadequate official response to the disappearance of women from this neighbourhood.

But hermeneutical injustice has also had a role in this story, and represents an even deeper and more long-standing history of injustice that has been linked to the violence that concerns me in this book, primarily by Indigenous scholars, writers, and activists. This form of epistemic injustice is perhaps best evidenced by Prime Minister Stephen Harper's statement, in September 2009, that Canada has "no history of colonialism."[4] The fact that Harper could make such a claim, and also that his claim would receive so little public outcry in Canada, suggests something important about how a history of genocidal, colonialist policies and practices are perceived by many non-Indigenous people in Canada: namely, as events that either did not occur, or occurred so long ago that they matter little in and for the present. Such beliefs are even consistent with Harper's recent apology for the residential school system, which worked primarily, as Jennifer Henderson and Pauline Wakeham (2009) argue, as "a part-for-whole substitution which allows the state to sidestep issues of land claims and constitutional change" (4). Widespread belief in the benign or historical nature of colonialism in Canada makes it extremely difficult to persuade a wider public that the present-day violence directed at Indigenous women is tied indelibly to an unsettled history of injustice with many, many claims on the present that are yet to be widely acknowledged, let alone reckoned with. This hermeneutical injustice must also be considered (and challenged) in any discussion about a just response to the disappearances of women from the Downtown Eastside (and across the country).

If Gordon is right when she insists that reckoning involves paying attention to "that which we have lost, but never had" (183), then one such thing surely includes a much more widespread awareness of the social and intellectual importance of Indigenous epistemologies and political thought and histories. This is a realization I have come to through reckoning with my own implication in this story, as I have (slowly, too slowly!) begun to realize that the changes in how we understand the relations between self and other and among past, present, and future that I came to believe are necessary for ending the violence, injustice, suffering, and loss that concern me throughout this book are already understandings that are extremely well developed in much Indigenous thought. For example, as an academic steeped in Western theory and criticism, I have been trained to turn to scholars like Judith Butler, Avery Gordon, or Roger I. Simon for many of the insights that drive this book, and no doubt their insights are still extraordinarily useful. But for the ideas I develop about the necessity of transforming self–other and past–present–future relations, it is also possible to draw insights from numerous Indigenous scholars, writers, and activists (as I have, belatedly, also attempted to do). My point here is not to trivialize or dismiss the very significant differences that do exist between various Western and Indigenous epistemologies, nor to suggest that either "Western knowledge" or "Indigenous knowledge" are homogeneous or monolithic, but instead to call for much more dialogue across and between these different ways of knowing and making sense of the world.

As but one example, Mi'kmaw scholar and educator Marie Battiste and Chickasaw scholar and lawyer James (Sa'ke'j) Youngblood Henderson (2000) argue that because many Indigenous languages are verb-based rather than noun-based, a sense of the relations between beings is ingrained in those languages, reflecting world views in which *relations* are central. As they explain, using the Mi'kmaw language as an example: "The Mi'kmaw language embodies relationships ... So within the philosophy of the Mi'kmaw language are the notions of how we should relate to one another and how we can retain those relationships" (89). Moving from the east to the far west coast while writing about Stó:lo world views, Lee Maracle (2007) writes: "We are called upon to pay attention to our relationship with others, to engage the world and all its beings in a responsive and responsible manner that is cognizant of the perfect right of other beings to be in relationship to us" (62). In a similar vein, Donald L. Fixico sums up these ideas thus: "In Indian thinking all things are connected, and all things are related" (2009, 560). The changed understanding of the relationship between self and other that I advocate in this book, then, as well as the notion that past, present, and future are not nearly so linear or separable as conventionally rendered, already exist in the very languages that colonialism aims (but has failed) to destroy. Epistemic justice therefore requires providing Indigenous scholars and communities with the resources needed to carry on the always ongoing work of building, preserving, reclaiming, and supporting Indigenous languages.

My concern with unsettled pasts works quite differently from the clichéd admonishment that those who fail to learn about the past are doomed to repeat it. Instead, it seems true that we can learn about the past and *still* be doomed to repeat it, because learning about the past is not the same thing as grappling with how the past is everywhere evident in the present-day making of our social world, or with how this relates to questions about justice in the present. For Wendy Brown (2001), "the future is always already populated with certain possibilities derived from the past," such that it is "haunted before we make and enter it" (150). This is a very different way of understanding the future from conventional renderings, one that significantly changes our responsibilities in the present. Instead of being responsible for autonomously creating (or failing to create) our own bright futures, for example, this reconceptualization of the future might suggest that we are instead responsible for collaborating in the present to tease out the presence of the past, such that we might better know what future possibilities it allows for and, if we are unhappy about those possibilities, to change how we recognize and respond to the past in the present.

Both Brown and Gordon (1997) argue that the goal of such interventions must be greater justice: a "more just ... future order" for Brown (140); for Gordon (working with thoughts from Derrida), "a concern for justice would be the only reason one would bother" (64). The kinds of justice these theorists have in mind are certainly not sufficiently met by changes to law enforcement, legislation, or government policy (indeed, these kinds of changes so frequently work *against* greater forms of justice, as made clear by the federal Conservatives' proposed enhancement of anti-prostitution laws happening just as I was finalizing this book). Knowing exactly what justice is or how we might recognize it is complicated and always to be determined; it is not the sort of thing that I can neatly outline here. But it involves taking stock of the past's presence in the present, of how it continues to matter now, not in the interests of provoking some one-time acknowledgment of past injustices, which secures the past squarely in the past, but instead in the interests of taking stock of how the past *lives on* in the present, all the while constraining and delimiting possibilities for the future. What justice might look like given such circumstances is hard to determine, but one thing is clear: justice is bound up with a notion of futurity that is different from a present overrun with the injustices of the past that in turn make injustice anew. As a result, a "victorious reckoning" is, as Gordon insists, a "necessarily collective undertaking" (208). It is a task that requires us to begin to reckon with the necessity of transforming our relations to others and unsettling our conventional understandings of past, present, and future – and in this case, it requires us to grapple with our differing inheritance of what lives on from Vancouver's disappeared women, which might make a more just *present*, another old idea that we have lost but never had, possible.

Notes

Preface

1 Chad Skelton, a blogger for the *Vancouver Sun*, argues that the "poorest postal code" label is applied to the Downtown Eastside mistakenly, mainly because several of Canada's First Nations reservations have much lower median incomes per household. See http://blogs.vancouversun.com/2010/02/10/is-vancouvers-downtown-eastside-really-canadas-poorest-postal-code/.

2 An analysis of the deeply flawed process or the final report of the provincial Missing Women Commission of Inquiry headed by Wally Oppal, or of the earlier Vancouver Police Department (VPD) inquiry headed by Doug LePard, is unfortunately beyond the scope of this book (mainly because such an analysis demands a book of its own). For an important series of critiques of the provincial inquiry, see Gitxsan reporter, artist, and activist Angela Sterritt's coverage for the *Tyee* and the *Dominion*, posted online at http://thetyee.ca/News/2011/10/03/DTES-Groups-Missing-Women-Inquiry/ and http://www.dominionpaper.ca/articles/4182. See also the columns written for the *Huffington Post* by Lubicon scholar and activist Dr Robyn Bourgeois, available online at http://www.huffingtonpost.ca/robyn-bourgeois/. For further information on the VPD inquiry, see http://vancouver.ca/police/media/2010/mw-spotlight.pdf. For more on the provincial inquiry, see http://www.missingwomeninquiry.ca. After the provincial government refused to fund legal counsel for numerous organizations representing women, sex workers, anti-poverty organizations, and Indigenous organizations and communities, many called for a boycott of the entire proceedings. For information about the decision by a number of organizations to collectively withdraw from participation in the provincial inquiry due to its flawed process and the provincial

government's unwillingness to cover their legal costs, see the open letter written by fifteen such organizations on 10 April 2012, available online at http://www.ubcic.bc.ca/files/PDF/OpenLetterstoMWCI_041012.pdf. At the behest of the Downtown Eastside Women's Centre and the February 14th Women's Memorial March Committee, the United Nations' Committee to End Discrimination Against Women also decided to initiate an inquiry procedure into the disappearances and murders of Indigenous women and girls in Canada in October 2011. See https://womensmemorialmarch. wordpress.com/2011/12/14/dtes-womens-organizations-release-un-submissons-details/.

3 In a version of the poster distributed in 2008, most likely the last version of the poster to be issued by the Missing Women Task Force, the six women for whose murders Robert Pickton was convicted in December 2007 are no longer listed. I explore the complexities of referring to the women as "missing" or "murdered" in much more depth in the Introduction.

4 Although the question of how best to refer to murdered or missing women might initially appear to be merely about semantics, it has very real consequences. Don Adam, former head of the Missing Women Task Force, notes for example that when his task force began to insist that the women whose disappearances they investigated were actually "murdered and we simply hadn't found their remains yet," this gave the task force access to coordination and assistance from forensics and opened up funds from victim's services to support families, neither of which were possible for an investigation of "missing" persons. See "Top Robert Pickton cop breaks his silence," available online at http://www.missingpeople.net/robert_pickton_cop_breaks_silence.htm.

5 See the website of the Women's Memorial March committee at https://womensmemorialmarch.wordpress.com/.

6 See *Missing Lives: A Special Report from the Canadian Press*. The entire collection of profiles is archived online at http://www.missingpeople.net/missing_lives_special_report.htm. The profiles that make up this special report were published in many newspapers across the country at the onset of Robert Pickton's trial. They were at one time archived online on several different news websites, but as this book was going to press I could only locate one remaining online archive on missingpeople.net (at the URL provided above).

7 Throughout this book I use the term "Indigenous" to denote and include all those with relations to the first peoples of Turtle Island (an Indigenous term for "North America"), regardless of whether or not the state would define them as "Status Indians," which continues to be a legally registered category in Canada. I am aware that there is much debate, both within and beyond

Indigenous communities, about the usefulness and meanings of terms such as "First Nations," "Native," "Aboriginal," "Indigenous," "Metis," and "Inuit," and so where possible and where relevant I am as specific about the nation or identity of the person or group being discussed as possible. Where this specificity is not possible or where I am asserting a broader generalization, I use the term "Indigenous" to encompass all the categories mentioned above.

8 See Statistics Canada's *Aboriginal Peoples Highlight Tables, 2006 Census, All Census Metropolitan Areas (CMAs) and Census Agglomerations (CAs).* Available online at http://www12.statcan.ca/census-recensement/2006/dp-pd/hlt/97-558/index.cfm?Lang=E.

9 See the Native Women's Association of Canada's "Fact Sheet: Missing and Murdered Aboriginal Women and Girls," available online at http://www.nwac.ca/files/download/NWAC_3D_Toolkit_e_0.pdf. Information about NWAC's "Sisters in Spirit" Project, an incredibly important initiative that conducted research from 2005 to 2010 on the disappearances or murders of Indigenous women in Canada, is available online at http://www.nwac.ca/sisters-spirit. Adding insult to injustice, the project's federal funding was not renewed in 2010. For a more in-depth history of NWAC's "Sisters in Spirit" campaign, see Harper (2009).

10 Walk 4 Justice has organized annual walks from Vancouver to Ottawa to raise awareness about murdered or missing women. For more information, see Angela Sterritt's report for the CBC, "Missing, Murdered Aboriginal Women Honoured in Marches," posted 14 February 2014 and available online at http://www.cbc.ca/news/aboriginal/missing-murdered-aboriginal-women-honoured-in-marches-1.2536337. For more information about the "Highway of Tears," a stretch of highway in Northern British Columbia from which Indigenous organizations and advocates estimate forty or more women have been disappeared, see http://www.highwayoftears.ca.

11 See the RCMP report, "Missing and Murdered Aboriginal Women: A National Operational Overview," available online at http://www.rcmp-grc.gc.ca/pubs/mmaw-faapd-eng.pdf.

12 See Robyn Bourgeois, "An RCMP Report Won't End Violence against Aboriginal Women," published by the *Huffington Post* on 18 May 2014, available online at http://www.huffingtonpost.ca/robyn-bourgeois/rcmp-aboriginal-women_b_5345651.html.

13 For a groundbreaking analysis of how sexual violence has been used against Indigenous women around the globe as a tool of genocide, see Smith (2005). See also Razack (2000) for an important intervention in the tendency of some feminist scholars and activists to reduce racist, colonial gendered violence to gender-based violence alone. For a compelling essay

about the connections between globalization, neoliberalism, and the intensification of discourses of disposability in relation to Indigenous women in Canada, the United States, Mexico, and Guatemala, see Erno (2010). For an analysis of a discourse of disposal in public and official discussions of outdoor sex work in Vancouver, see Lowman (2000).

14 The organizers of the annual Women's Memorial March in the Downtown Eastside cite the "increasing deaths of many vulnerable women from the DTES" and note ongoing murders of Indigenous women, including Ashley Machisknic in September 2010. See https://womensmemorialmarch.wordpress.com/. See also the blog entry of Downtown Eastside activist Jamie Lee Hamilton, "Violence on Sex Trade Workers Post Pickton," posted on 9 March 2008 and available online at http://downtowneastside.blogspot.ca/. Journalist Lori Culbert has also investigated statements about ongoing disappearances of women from the Downtown Eastside since Pickton's arrest, including Hamilton's. See "Nothing's Changed," *Vancouver Sun*, 26 February 2008 available online at http://www.missingpeople.net/nothings_changed_in_vancouver.htm. More recently, Catherine Rolfsen and Tim Lai also reported a series of attacks on women doing sex work in the Downtown Eastside. See "Police Investigate Reported Attacks on Sex Workers," *Vancouver Sun*, 23 August 2008.

15 See the CBC story, "Nathan O'Brien Search Gets Help from High-tech Gear, Helicopter," available online at http://www.cbc.ca/news/canada/calgary/nathan-o-brien-search-gets-help-from-high-tech-gear-helicopter-1.2713772.

16 See the CBC "As it Happens" radio interview with Matthew Forsyth, an Airdrie resident and coordinator of a civilian search, on Thursday, 16 July 2014. The interview can be heard online at http://www.cbc.ca/player/Radio/As+It+Happens/ID/2474212738/.

17 See "Fortney: Allen Liknes Displays Stoic Poise amid Horrific Circumstances," published in the *Calgary Herald* on 16 July 2014 and available online at http://www.calgaryherald.com/news/calgary/Fortney+Allen+Liknes+displays+stoic+poise+amid+horrific+circumstances/10035210/story.html.

Introduction

1 For a more thorough discussion of the reasons for the MOA's decision to initially host and then cancel Masik's exhibit, as well as about the controversy that erupted around *The Forgotten*, see Pinto (2013) and Moss (2012). Laura Moss also raises a compelling set of questions about the appropriateness of the MOA as the setting for the exhibit, given that it is "home to collections of centuries of Indigenous artefacts" and "has come under scrutiny in the past for the way it acquired" them (58).

2 See Ethan Baron, "B.C. Museum Cancels 'Offensive' Exhibit Featuring Paintings of Missing, Murdered Women," *Vancouver Province*, 12 January 2011; no longer available online.

3 For one media analysis that qualitatively assesses such a shift in media reportage about the disappearance and murder of Daleen Kay Bosse from Saskatchewan, see McKenzie (2010). For in-depth analyses of media coverage of Vancouver's missing women, see Hugill (2010); Jiwani and Young (2006); Janzen, Strega, Brown, Morgan, and Carrière (2013); and Pitman (2002).

4 I regret that Elle-Máijá Tailfeathers's short film *A Red Girl's Reasoning* was released too close to the date of publication of my book to allow for a serious discussion of it here. The powerful short film dramatizes the story of an Indigenous woman vigilante who revenges violence committed by white men against Indigenous women in Vancouver. I hope to discuss this important film in later work. For an interview with Tailfeathers, see http://thetyee.ca/ArtsAndCulture/2013/06/22/Radical-Art/.

5 For an elaboration of Rogoff's notion of criticality, see Rosenberg (2010).

6 A small number of women who were at one time listed on the Missing Women Task Force poster have since been located by police, and at least one of them indicated that she has no desire to be reunited with her friends and relatives. See Lori Culbert's report in the *Vancouver Sun*, "Missing Woman Found Alive," 4 December 2006, available online at http://www.missingpeople.net/missing_woman_found_alive.htm.

7 See the 2001 report by Leonard Cler-Cunningham, based on research conducted by and for the organization Providing Alternatives Counselling and Education (PACE) Society, "Violence against Women in Vancouver's Street Level Sex Trade and the Police Response." In interviews and surveys with women doing sex work the researchers found that some women named both uniform police and vice-squad members as perpetrators of violence against them. As they report, "If uniform police and Vice were combined they would have the same reported rate of attempted rape [of the sex workers surveyed] using a weapon as pimps" (63). John Lowman and Laura Fraser's (1996) report, *Violence against Persons Who Prostitute: The Experience in British Columbia*, written for the federal Department of Justice, also reports that prosecutions for crimes against "prostitutes" included "four police officers in British Columbia over the past six years (one RCMP, two VPD officers, and a reserve). In 1988 one VPD officer was found guilty of extorting sexual favors from a seventeen-year-old prostitute while he was on duty, and was sentenced to six months. In 1991 another Vancouver officer was sentenced to five years for charges of extortion, sexual assault (two counts), unlawful confinement (two counts), theft, and robbery" (cited in Cler-Cunningham and PACE, 63).

The PACE report by Cler-Cunningham is available online at
http://www.pace-society.org/library/sex-trade-and-police-response.pdf.

8 Angela Jardine's mother has been one of the people at the forefront of calls
for a formal investigation into police mishandling of the disappearances
of women from the Downtown Eastside. See Jane Armstrong, "Mother's
Pen Documents Frustration with Police," *Globe and Mail*, 15 April 2002, A5;
archived online at http://www.missingpeople.net/mother's_pen_documents-
apr_15,_2002.htm.

9 See the extensive bibliography of scholarship on Indian residential schools
compiled by the Aboriginal Healing Foundation (AHF), available online
on their archived website at http://www.ahf.ca/downloads/bibliography.
pdf. The AHF has also produced numerous publications and multimedia
resources about Indian residential schools, also available on the archived
website at www.ahf.ca. In 2014, the federal government failed to renew
funding for the Aboriginal Healing Foundation.

10 A book has been published based on the conference proceedings (see
Anderson, Kubik, and Hampton 2010). Amnesty International Canada
(2004) also builds on the findings of the 1996 Royal Commission on
Aboriginal Peoples to insist that the contemporary violence directed at
Indigenous women is a "legacy of history" (16), and geographer Adrienne
Burk (2006) links dispossession and colonization with the challenges faced
by those desiring to build monuments related specifically to losses of First
Nations peoples and cultures in the Downtown Eastside (50–1).

1 The Present Pasts of Vancouver's Downtown Eastside

1 A compelling example of the cultural work performed by the name
"Downtown Eastside" occurred in 2004 during the advancement of a
plan to revitalize an inner-city neighbourhood in Edmonton, Alberta. In
advance of the launch of this revitalization initiative, the area in question
was suddenly and repeatedly referred to by civic officials as the "Downtown
East," and soon after local news media began referring to the neighbourhood
as Edmonton's "seedy Downtown Eastside." For an analysis of the effects
of this naming, see Granzow and Dean (2007).

2 Those desiring a broader history might wish to consult Blomley (2004);
Burk (2010); Hasson and Ley (1994); Sommers and Blomley (2002);
Taylor (2003); Vidaver (2004); Boyd, Osborn, and MacPherson (2009);
Campbell, Boyd, and Culbert (2009); and the archives of the Carnegie
Community Centre's newsletter, some of which are available online at
http://carnegie.vcn.bc.ca/index.pl/newsletter.

3 For a more complex consideration of the connections between residents of Chinatown, Japantown, and the Downtown Eastside, see Cynthia Low's comments in the documentary *Survival, Strength, Sisterhood: Power of Women in the Downtown Eastside* by Alejandro Zuluaga and Harsha Walia, available online at http://vimeo.com/19877895.

4 The C-CAP report, *Disappearing Homes: The Loss of Affordable Housing in the DTES*, is available online at http://ccapvancouver.files.wordpress.com/2008/04/ccapreport08d4.pdf.

5 See local opposition to the proposed Concord Pacific condo development site at 58 West Hastings on the Save Low Income Housing Coalition's website: http://slihc.resist.ca/ and to the Pantages / Sequel 138 condo development on the DTES Not for Developers website: http://dtesnotfordevelopers.wordpress.com/aboutpantages/.

6 See the website of the police-officers-turned-filmmakers, who call themselves the "Odd Squad," at http://oddsquad.com/EN/through_a_blue_lens/. An NFB sales manager corroborates that the film is "one of the NFB's most successful productions" and has been viewed "by millions of viewers worldwide" (Al Parsons, personal communication, 30 August 2007).

7 Similarly, constructions of the neighbourhood as an "urban frontier" also legitimize a form of "anything goes" Wild West policing intended to "bring order" to a presumably disorderly space. The overwhelming documentation of extensive police brutality in the Downtown Eastside lends support to the idea that this sort of rhetoric has an effect on policing practices in the area. See Pivot Legal Society (2002), *To Serve and Protect: A Report on Policing in Vancouver's Downtown Eastside*, available online at http://www.pivotlegal.org/to_serve_and_protect.

8 Those interested in learning more about this practice, commonly referred to as "starlight tours," might begin by consulting Reber and Renaud (2003).

9 See the Native Women's Association of Canada's Sisters in Spirit Regional Fact Sheets, available online at http://www.nwac.ca/programs/sis-research. The recent RCMP report (2014) also documents much higher proportions of Aboriginal women as a percentage of all women murdered in the four western provinces (and the North). For example, while just 6% of women murdered in Ontario between 1980 and 2012 were Aboriginal, 49% of women murdered in Manitoba, 55% of those murdered in Saskatchewan, 28% of those murdered in Alberta, and 19% of those murdered in British Columbia in this same time period are identified by RCMP as Aboriginal victims (9). While a higher proportion of the overall population in the western provinces is also Aboriginal, the representation of Aboriginal people in the overall population is still significantly lower than among the women murdered in these four

provinces (drawing on data from Statistics Canada, the RCMP report notes that 16.7% of the overall population in Manitoba and 15.5% in Saskatchewan consists of persons self-identifying as Aboriginal).

10 For more background on VANDU, an important organization of and for drug users dedicated to "improving the lives of people who use illicit drugs through user-based peer support and education," see the organization's website at http://www.vandu.org. Susan Boyd, Donald MacPherson, and Bud Osborn's book *Raise Shit! Social Action Saving Lives* offers an important history of VANDU and other harm-reduction activism in the Downtown Eastside.

2 Following Ghosts

1 Robert Pickton was charged with the murder of Sarah de Vries in 2005.

2 For more on the sixties scoop, which some authors argue extended into the 1970s and is both intensified and ongoing today, see Fournier and Crey (1997), Sinclair (2007), and Dubinsky (2010).

3 This excerpt from Sarah de Vries journal is reprinted in a profile included in Amnesty International's (2004) *Stolen Sisters* report. Excerpt © Maggie De Vries. Reprinted with permission of Sarah's family.

4 This quotation is taken from Diana Melnick's profile in *Missing Lives: A Special Report from the Canadian Press* (in Dirk Meissner, "'Back Side of Hell' not a nice place to be lost, says friend," available online at http://www.missingpeople .net/missing_lives_diana_melnick.htm). Meissner's sense of what would qualify as relevant or important information about Melnick's life differs somewhat from my own, but nonetheless his point about an overall lack of information is well taken. A recent posting on the guestbook of the website Missingpeople.net provides an important counterpoint to Meissner's findings, however. A woman who states that she is Melnick's adopted cousin writes: "I looked all over the web to see if there was more information on Diana, and it is suggested that no-one knows anything about her … which is not true. For whatever reason, the family has decided not to enlighten the public, which I do respect, but I just couldn't help but want others to know, that yes she was loved and is missed and we still think of her often … and there's many of us who have been following the news from the very beginning." At one time this post was available online at http://www.e-guestbooks.com/cgi-bin/ e-guestbooks/guestbook.cgi. Message #385, but it has since been removed.

5 Sarah de Vries's poem © Maggie De Vries. Reprinted with permission of Sarah's family.

6 Victoria Freeman (2011) notes that "whether or not Indigenous historical consciousness was primarily cyclical in the past [is] a matter of considerable debate among historians of Indigenous history" (232–3). It is not my intention

to either minimize or sidestep these debates, but to engage them more fully is a project for another book. What seems important to emphasize here is that many Indigenous conceptions of time, whether cyclical or not, pose a challenge to the dominant, linear conceptions of Western thought, and place greater emphasis on space or place.

3 Looking at Images

1 The original (1999) reward poster can be viewed online at http://www .missingpeople.net/neweastside.htm.

2 See Bob Stall, "They Aren't from Kerrisdale," *Vancouver Province*, 2 April 1999. A reprint of the article can be read online at http://www .missingpeople.net/theykerrisdale.htm. Maggie de Vries's comment can be found at http://www.missingpeople.net/elm_street_article_p9.htm.

3 "Jane Doe," whose identity and therefore potential photograph are, of course, missing, is not pictured in the poster, explaining why only twenty-six photographs have this blue highlighting. By 2007, the charge for the murder of Jane Doe had already been dismissed by the court.

4 I am indebted to Anne Stone for first drawing my attention to the importance of contemplating the repetition of the poster's grid pattern during conversations we had while editing a special issue of *West Coast Line* 53 (41.1) on representations of murdered and missing women.

5 The drop in the number of women pictured reflects the fact that four women were located by police, either alive or previously deceased, between the release of the 2004 and 2007 versions.

6 I am certainly not the first person to make this point. Many activists and several of the women's friends and family members have publicly expressed concern, frustration, and anger over the use of mug-shot photographs in the police posters. Jennifer England (2004) makes a similar argument about the criminalizing effect of the poster photographs, while Geraldine Pratt (2005) argues that the cropping of the photographs and their arrangement in a grid "report[s] on the state's administration of already deviant bodies, and not on individual lives lost" (1060). See also Cameron 2010, Hugill 2010, and Jiwani and Young 2006.

7 The similarities between the police poster and a grid reproduced in Gilman's book that purports to document "the physiognomy of the Russian prostitute" (from *Archivio di psichiatria, scienze penali ed antropologia criminale* 14 [1893]) is particularly jarring. See Gilman (1985), 96–7.

8 By entering "Helen Hallmark" in Google and selecting the "Images" tab, it is possible to view the photograph of Hallmark from the police poster along

with many different images of her posted to various websites, including the ones I discuss here.

9 This alternate missing poster and image of Hallmark can be viewed online at http://www.missingpeople.net/images/Helen_Mae_Hallmark.jpg.

10 This image of Hallmark with her brother and sister can be viewed online at http://www.vanishedvoices.com/MemorialRoomHelen.html.

11 After looking at one representation of the image-grid published in the *Vancouver Sun*, Margot Leigh Butler similarly found herself "imagining the photographers who took these pictures" (2006, 162). See Butler's essay for further reflection on the significance of the photographers who took the poster photographs.

12 Artist Zoe Pawlak created oil portraits of the 26 women Pickton was accused of murdering and titled the collection *The Profession of Hurt*. Betty Kovacic painted portraits of the 50 women listed as missing by police in 2002, titling her collection *Roomful of Missing Women*. An artist known simply as Dorette created portraits in oil and pencil of 64 of the women. Deon Venter created a series of individual and grouped portraits titled *Missing*. And a group of forensic sketch artists named Project EDAN created portraits of 28 of the women, which I will go on to discuss in more detail in this chapter. I discuss Masik's *The Forgotten* project in the Introduction.

13 See Lori Culbert, "Sketches Express Softer Side of Missing Women," *Vancouver Sun*, 17 December 2005: C1. The *Sun* published all the sketches, coupled with the photographs from the police poster, over a four-page spread in the "Observer" section on this date (with the exception of the portrait of Angela Jardine, whose mother reportedly objected to its inclusion). All quotations in my discussion of the Project EDAN portraits are from Culbert's article unless otherwise indicated. The entire collection of portraits are available for viewing online at http://www.missingpeople .net/sketches_express_softer_side.htm.

14 The police poster photograph of Mona Wilson that I discuss in this paragraph can be viewed online at http://www.missingpeople.net/images/ Mona%20Wilson.jpg. It is slightly different from the one reproduced in the *Vancouver Sun* next to the EDAN portrait of Wilson.

15 The Project EDAN sketch of Mona Wilson can be viewed online at http:// www.missingpeople.net/mona_wilson.htm. I am not suggesting that the artist intentionally made Wilson appear more "white" in the sketch; instead, I am arguing that the descriptors "victim" and "softer" might be culturally conflated with whiteness to such a degree that when one sets out to draw (or for that matter to interpret) an image that we are told must represent a "softer" version of a "victim," we may unconsciously *see* or *imagine* whiteness.

16 I note the similarity that exists between a framework for the idealized victim and for the idealized, white feminine subject; see McConney (1999) and McDonald (2003) for further discussion of this line of argument.

17 See Petti Fong and Lindsay Kines, "A 'Sweetheart' Trapped by Drugs and Prostitution," *Vancouver Sun*, 26 February 2002: A1. Much of this article is recycled in Wilson's profile by the *Canadian Press* for the "Missing Lives" series.

18 See, for example, Fraser (2000), and her contribution to *Redistribution or Recognition?* (2003, with Axel Honneth), as well as Lash and Featherstone (2002), Markell (2003), Coulthard (2011), and Oliver (2001).

4 Shadowing the "Missing Women" Story

1 The overlap between queer and sex work communities is also discussed in the writings of Becki Ross (2009), Joan Nestle (1992), Amber Hollibaugh (2000), Amber Dawn (2013), and Allison Murray (1995), among others.

2 For but a few examples of this way of using the term "whore," see Michael Harris's recent article "The Unrepentant Whore," about the activism of Vancouver sex worker and activist Jamie Lee Hamilton, available online at http://thewalrus.ca/the-unrepentant-whore/. See also Gail Pheterson's (1989) edited collection, *A Vindication of the Rights of Whores*, Shannon Bell's (1995) book, *Whore Carnival*, and Annie Sprinkle's "40 Reasons Why Whores Are My Heroes" (available online at http://anniesprinkle.org/forty-reasons-why-whores-are-my-heroes/). See also Amber Dawn's (2013) memoir *How Poetry Saved My Life*, which is subtitled *A Hustler's Memoir*. Ross (2010) also points out that the newsletter published by the Alliance for the Safety of Prostitutes (an association that formed to contest the expulsion of outdoor sex workers from Vancouver's West End between 1975 and 1985) was titled the *Whorganizer* (206).

3 See Lori Culbert, "Pickton Murders: Explosive Evidence the Jury Never Heard," *Vancouver Sun*, 5 August 2010. Available online at http://www.vancouversun.com/news/Pickton+murders+Explosive+evidence+jury+never+heard/3360225/story.html.

4 I regret the necessity of repeating the term "squaw man," as I am aware of some of the history of the term "squaw" and of the violent and painful ways it frequently continues to be hurled as a sexualized racial slur towards many Indigenous women today. I am also aware of some (admittedly controversial) efforts to reclaim the term; see, for example, Abenaki scholar Marge Bruchac's "Reclaiming the Word 'Squaw' in the Name of the Ancestors," available online at http://www.nativeweb.org/pages/legal/squaw.html.

5 For additional research on the displacement of people doing outdoor sex
   work from other Vancouver strolls, resulting in their convergence in the
   Downtown Eastside, see Lowman (2000).
6 I am not at all suggesting that Aaron Webster's murder was somehow
   unworthy of the attention it received from queer communities; instead,
   I am suggesting that there is a "hierarchy of grievability" at work *within*
   communities already cast as less grievable in relation to those communities
   where more normative forms of identification are believed to prevail.
   By juxtaposing how queer communities claimed Webster as "our dead"
   but have not similarly claimed murdered or missing women from the
   Downtown Eastside – even the two or three that *have* been publicly
   identified as bisexual or transsexual – as "ours" in the same way, my
   goal is to point out the operation of this hierarchy. It is not my intention
   to critique or question the attention paid to Webster's murder, then, but
   instead to wonder why a similar attention has not been forthcoming in the
   wake of the murders of women from the Downtown Eastside.
7 For more on the relationship between queerness and gentrification, see
   Granzow and Dean (2007). For a brief and very accessible overview of
   this relationship, see Mikaila M.L. Arthur's (2004) entry "Gentrification,"
   in *glbtq: An Encyclopedia of Gay, Lesbian, Bisexual, Transgender, and Queer
   Culture*, available online at www.glbtq.com/social-sciences/gentrification.
   html.
8 See Jane Armstrong, "Missing Prostitutes: 23; Arrests: 0," *Globe and Mail*,
   5 April 1999: A1.
9 See "The Lives behind the Faces [Editorial]," *Victoria Times-Colonist*,
   31 January 2006: A10, available online at http://www.missingpeople.net/
   lives_behind_the_faces.htm.
10 See Lori Culbert's special report, "Pickton," in the *Vancouver Sun*, 1
   December 2007, Special section: E1-6.
11 The Vancouver Police Department inquiry headed by Doug LePard and
   the provincial Missing Women Commission of Inquiry headed by Wally
   Oppal both established timelines for their investigations that are similar
   to the one posited by Culbert's article. While these timelines make sense
   given the limited scope of the inquiries (both of which were mandated
   to investigate only the law enforcement responses to the "Vancouver
   Missing Women" case), they also make broader questions about justice
   difficult to perceive, let alone ask. This issue of circumventing the kinds
   of questions about social justice that could be raised by such inquiries
   through insistence on such a narrow timeline helps to explain why so
   many women's, anti-poverty, sex worker, and Indigenous groups and

organizations withdrew from and subsequently boycotted or denounced the provincial inquiry (along with the much-reported concerns about the lack of provincial funding for legal representation for many such organizations).

12 See Yvette Brend's radio story, "The Pickton Family," originally broadcast 2 January 2007 on CBC (British Columbia) Radio One's "The Early Edition." At one time the program was available online at http://www.cbc.ca/bc/features/pickton/programming.html.

13 A Canadian Press reporter noted (while the trial was ongoing) that British Columbia's solicitor general estimated "the total cost of investigating Willie Pickton and the missing women at $70 million" (cited in Cameron 2007, 171). While I am not arguing that this money should not have been spent, I do think it is worth noting the vast disparity between the amount of money spent on the investigation versus the very limited funds available to non-profit organizations that support women in the Downtown Eastside, and the even smaller amounts available to women trying to survive on social assistance (in 2013, a single person receiving social assistance in British Columbia was eligible to receive $610/month). Although I do believe that the form of justice wrought from legal proceedings is limited, this is not meant to imply that such proceedings will or should have no meaning for those who knew the women who were murdered in life. In fact, the significance that it might hold for those loved ones is reason enough to support the ongoing necessity of such proceedings. But several people who knew and loved some of the women who have been disappeared from Vancouver have also publicly expressed their concern about how the conditions for women presently living and working in the Downtown Eastside have changed little if at all in the ensuing years, and thus I suspect that for many of them, too, any sense of justice that arises from the conviction of Pickton, while important, is certainly not enough.

14 For a summary of reports of ongoing violence against women in the Downtown Eastside since Pickton's arrest, see the preface to this book, especially note 14.

15 See Lindsay Kines, "Missing on the Mean Streets: 'Who we will not see tomorrow,'" *Vancouver Sun*, 13 March 1999, http://www.missingpeople.net/missing1.htm.

16 See "Top Robert Pickton Cop Breaks His Silence," a letter by Adam published in the *Vancouver Sun*, 26 November 2010. Available online at http://www.missingpeople.net/robert_pickton_cop_breaks_silence.htm.

5 Memory's Difficult Returns

1 CRAB stands for "Create a Real Available Beach" and is itself a reminder of Downtown Eastside residents' and activists' struggles, as they had to lobby city officials to build and then maintain a park and beach accessible to Downtown Eastside residents. See Burk (2010), 47–8.

2 Wendy Poole Park, at the intersection of Main and Alexander (en route to CRAB Park for most visitors), offers another physical monument dedicated specifically to the memory of Wendy Poole, a Downtown Eastside resident who was murdered in 1989.

3 There is evidence, however, that those who lobbied for and organized the creation of the two monuments, the CRAB boulder and Marker of Change, were aware of each other's work. As Burk (2010) recounts: "The proponents of the CRAB Park boulder of course knew about Marker of Change ... Don Larson [main advocate for the CRAB monument] wrote to the Monument Project Committee informing them of his work on the CRAB Park boulder" (55).

4 For additional interpretations of the CRAB park memorial as it relates to Marker of Change and other monuments in the Downtown Eastside, see Burk (2010); Cultural Memory Group (2006); and McNeill (2008). I am indebted to Burk in particular for researching and writing histories of the creation of many of these Downtown Eastside monuments.

5 Chris McDowell, a member of the planning and organizing committee for Marker of Change, expressed her concern about the lack of attention to local women's names in a letter to other organizers on 20 May 1993. She writes: "I've been in the situation of 'explaining' to women of the Downtown Eastside why we are naming the 14 women murdered in Montreal and none of the women murdered here. What I've said is the 14 women symbolize the importance of remembering the loss of individual women ... They say that that is not true, the 14 don't mean that to them and we should name Downtown Eastside women ... Lately, I agree with them" (cited in Burk 2010, 17). Yet women from the Downtown Eastside remain unnamed in Marker of Change. Burk notes that "in the end, the [Marker of Change organizing] committee acknowledged it was unable to successfully collaborate with the Carnegie Centre ... and the Downtown Eastside Women's Centre to create a tile in memory of the local women killed," and that the existing tile was instead created with "the assistance of two women who are poets and supporters of the project" (31–2).

6 I first encountered this passage from Butler in an important critique of the limits of naming as a memorial strategy offered by Sharon Rosenberg in her essay "Violence, Identity and Public History," presented at the Canadian Association of Cultural Studies conference in 2005. In this essay, Rosenberg

argues that when one did not have a personal connection to those named while they were alive, a list of names as a memorial strategy risks being read on similar terms to statistics that calculate the numbers of dead.

7 "Missing" was commissioned by the grandfather of Andrea Joesbury, one of the women disappeared from the Downtown Eastside. The lyrics were written by poet Susan Musgrave, with guitar by Brad Prevedoros and vocals by Amber Smith. The song can be heard online by visiting http://www.missingpeople.net.

8 Since I was not in attendance at Belmore's performance I am working with published descriptions of the event, photographs, and video excerpts. I am indebted to the descriptions offered by Townsend-Gault (2004); Neville (2007); Rickard (2006); and on Belmore's website, http://www.rebeccabelmore.com.

9 This use of Belmore's body (including in many of her other performance pieces) to draw attention to histories of colonization is further discussed in Lauzon (2008) and (2010), Neville (2007), Rickard (2006), and Townsend-Gault (2004).

10 When I visited the mural in June 2007 it was significantly obstructed by graffiti, such that in places the text was no longer readable. But the mural was likely always imagined as ephemeral, its purpose and meaning dynamic rather than static or permanent. I also suspect that the *process* of creating the mural was just as significant to its creators (maybe more so) than the finished product.

11 The number of stars is reflective only of the number of women on the official list of missing women at the time the mural was created, which is a limitation of this memorial's form. But because the stars are not named, I don't find that they operate in the same overly determined or representative way as the listing of some names but not others. More images of the mural can be viewed online at http://www.missingpeople.net/montreal_mural1.htm.

12 For more information about the march, which now includes companion marches in several Canadian cities on February 14th, see https://womensmemorialmarch.wordpress.com/about/.

Conclusion

1 Sarah de Vries's journal entry reprinted with permission of Sarah's family. © Maggie de Vries.

2 These lines from Sarah de Vries's poem are reprinted with the permission of her family. © Maggie de Vries.

3 Both of the quotations in this paragraph are drawn from the documentary *Survival, Strength, Sisterhood: Power of Women in the Downtown Eastside* by

Alejandro Zuluaga and Harsha Walia, available online at http://vimeo
.com/19877895.

4 For the original press coverage, see "Every G20 Nation Wants to Be Canada,
insists PM," available online at http://www.reuters.com/article/2009/09/26/
columns-us-g20-canada-advantages-idUSTRE58P05Z20090926. For an
important rejoinder, see Harsha Walia's op-ed, originally published in the
Vancouver Sun online, and reproduced online at http://www.dominionpaper
.ca/articles/2943.

Bibliography

Ahmed, Sara. 2000. *Strange Encounters: Embodied Others in Post-Coloniality.* New York: Routledge.

Ahmed, Sara. 2006. *Queer Phenomenology: Orientations, Objects, Others.* Durham: Duke University Press. http://dx.doi.org/10.1215/9780822388074.

Alfred, Taiaiake. 2009. *Peace, Power, Righteousness: An Indigenous Manifesto.* Oxford: Oxford University Press.

Amnesty International Canada. 2004. *Stolen Sisters: A Human Rights Response to Discrimination and Violence against Indigenous Women in Canada.* Ottawa: Amnesty.

Anderson, A. Brenda, Wendee Kubik, and Mary Rucklos Hampton, eds. 2010. *Torn from Our Midst: Voices of Grief, Healing and Action from the Missing Indigenous Women Conference.* Regina: Canadian Plains Research Centre.

Asfour, John Mikhail, and Elee Kraljii Gardiner. 2012. "Introduction." In *V6A: Writing from Vancouver's Downtown Eastside,* ed. John Mikhail Asfour and Elee Kraljii Gardiner, 1–14. Vancouver: Arsenal Pulp Press.

Barman, Jean. 2005. *Stanley Park's Secret: The Forgotten Families of Whoi Whoi, Kanaka Ranch and Brockton Point.* Madeira Park, BC: Harbour Publishing.

Barman, Jean. 2006. "Taming Aboriginal Sexuality: Gender, Power, and Race in British Colombia, 1850–1900." In *In the Days of Our Grandmothers: A Reader in Aboriginal Women's History in Canada,* ed. Mary-Ellen Kelm and Lorna Townsend, 270–300. Toronto: University of Toronto Press.

Barthes, Roland. 1981. *Camera Lucida: Reflections on Photography.* New York: Hill and Wang.

Battiste, Marie Ann, and James (Sákéj) Youngblood Henderson. 2000. *Protecting Indigenous Knowledge and Heritage: A Global Challenge.* Saskatoon: Purich Publishing Ltd.

Bell, Shannon. 1995. *Whore Carnival*. Brooklyn, NY: Autonomedia.

Bennett, Jill. 2005. *Empathic Vision: Affect, Trauma, and Contemporary Art*. Stanford, CA: Stanford University Press.

Bergland, Renée L. 2000. *The National Uncanny: Indian Ghosts and American Subjects*. Hanover, NH: University Press of New England.

Blomley, Nicholas K. 2004. *Unsettling the City: Urban Land and the Politics of Property*. New York: Routledge.

Boyd, Colleen E., and Coll Thrush, eds. 2011. *Phantom Past, Indigenous Presence: Native Ghosts in North American Culture and History*. Lincoln: University of Nebraska Press.

Boyd, Susan C., Bud Osborn, and Donald MacPherson. 2009. *Raise Shit! Social Action Saving Lives*. Black Point, NS: Fernwood.

Brown, Wendy. 2001. *Politics Out of History*. Princeton, NJ: Princeton University Press.

Brown, Wendy. 2005. *Edgework: Critical Essays on Knowledge and Politics*. Princeton, NJ: Princeton University Press.

Burk, Adrienne L. 2003. "Private Griefs, Public Places." *Political Geography* 22 (3): 317–33. http://dx.doi.org/10.1016/S0962-6298(03)00035-0.

Burk, Adrienne L. 2006. "In Sight, Out of View: A Tale of Three Monuments." *Antipode* 38 (1): 41–58. http://dx.doi.org/10.1111/j.0066-4812.2006.00564.x.

Burk, Adrienne L. 2010. *Speaking for a Long Time: Public Space and Social Memory in Vancouver*. Vancouver: UBC Press.

Butler, Judith. 1988. "*Spirit in Ashes* [Book review]." *History and Theory* 27 (1): 60. http://dx.doi.org/10.2307/2504962.

Butler, Judith. 2004. *Precarious Life: The Powers of Mourning and Violence*. London: Verso.

Butler, Judith. 2005. *Giving an Account of Oneself*. New York: Fordham University Press. http://dx.doi.org/10.5422/fso/9780823225033.001.0001.

Butler, Judith. 2009. *Frames of War: When Is Life Grievable?* London: Verso.

Butler, Margot Leigh. 2003. "On 'Implicatedness.'" *W6*: n.p.

Butler, Margot Leigh. 2006. "'I'm in There! I'm One of the Women in That Picture.'" In *Killing Women: The Visual Culture of Gender and Violence*, ed. Annette Burfoot and Susan Lord, 155–76. Waterloo, ON: Wilfrid Laurier University Press.

Cameron, Emilie. 2008. "Indigenous Spectrality and the Politics of Postcolonial Ghost Stories." *Cultural Geographies* 15 (3): 383–93. http://dx.doi.org/10.1177/1474474008091334.

Cameron, Stevie. 2007. *The Pickton File*. Toronto: A.A. Knopf Canada.

Cameron, Stevie. 2010. *On the Farm: Robert William Pickton and the Tragic Story of Vancouver's Missing Women*. Toronto: A.A. Knopf Canada.

Campbell, Larry, Neil Boyd, and Lori Culbert. 2009. *A Thousand Dreams: Vancouver's Downtown Eastside and the Fight for Its Future*. Vancouver: Douglas & McIntyre.

Cariou, Warren. 2006. "Haunted Prairie: Aboriginal 'Ghosts' and the Spectres of Settlement." *University of Toronto Quarterly* 75 (2): 727–34.

Carnegie Community Action Project. 2008. *Disappearing Homes: The Loss of Affordable Housing in the Downtown Eastside*. Vancouver: Carnegie Community Centre Association.

Carter, Sarah. 2006. "Categories and Terrains of Exclusion: Constructing the 'Indian Woman' in the Early Settlement Era in Western Canada." In *In the Days of Our Grandmothers: A Reader in Aboriginal Women's History in Canada*, ed. Mary-Ellen Kelm and Lorna Townsend, 146–69. Toronto: University of Toronto Press.

Cler-Cunningham, Leonard, and PACE Society. 2001. *Violence against Women in Vancouver's Street Level Sex Trade and the Police Response*. Vancouver: PACE Society.

Compton, Wayde. 2012. "Seven Routes to Hogan's Alley: 2. A Home." In *V6A: Writing from Vancouver's Downtown Eastside*, ed. John Mikhail Asfour and Elee Kraljii Gardiner, 114–19. Vancouver: Arsenal Pulp Press.

Coulthard, Glen S. 2011. "Subjects of Empire: Indigenous Peoples and the 'Politics of Recognition' in Canada." In *Home and Native Land: Unsettling Multiculturalism in Canada*, ed. May Chazan, Lisa Helps, Anna Stanley, and Sonali Thakkar, 31–50. Toronto: Between the Lines Press.

Culhane, Dara. 2003. "Their Spirits Live within Us: Aboriginal Women in Downtown Eastside Vancouver Emerging into Visibility." *American Indian Quarterly* 27 (3 & 4): 593–606. http://dx.doi.org/10.1353/aiq.2004.0073.

Cultural Memory Group. 2006. *Remembering Women Murdered by Men: Memorials across Canada*. Toronto: Sumach Press.

Dawn, Amber. 2013. *How Poetry Saved My Life: A Hustler's Memoir*. Vancouver: Arsenal Pulp Press.

Dean, Amber. 2010a. "Can Names Implicate Us? The Memorial-Art of Rebecca Belmore and Janis Cole." *Public: Art, Culture, Ideas* 42 (*Traces*), ed. Chloe Brushwood Rose and Mario di Paolantonio, 101–12.

Dean, Amber. 2010b. "Inheriting What Lives On from Vancouver's Disappeared Women." In *Not Drowning but Waving: Women, Feminism and the Liberal Arts*, ed. Susan Brown, Jeanne Perreault, Jo-Ann Wallace, and Heather Zwicker, 351–68. Edmonton: University of Alberta Press.

Dean, Amber. 2010c. "Space, Temporality, History: Encountering Hauntings in Vancouver's Downtown Eastside." In *The West and Beyond: New Perspectives on an Imagined Region*, ed. Sarah Carter, Alvin Finkel, and Peter Fortna, 113–32. Athabasca, AB: Athabasca University Press.

Dean, Amber. 2010d. "Inheriting What Lives On: The 'Terrible Gift' of Sarah de Vries' Poetry." In *Torn from Our Midst: Voices of Grief, Healing and Action from the Missing Indigenous Women Conference 2008*, edited by A. Brenda Anderson, Wendee Kubik, and Mary Rucklos Hampton, 168–81. Regina: Canadian Plains Research Centre.

Dean, Amber. 2013. "Public Mourning and the Culture of Redress: Mayerthorpe, Air India, and Murdered or Missing Aboriginal Women." In *Reconciling Canada: Historical Injustices and the Contemporary Culture of Redress*, ed. Pauline Wakeham and Jennifer Henderson, 181–98. Toronto: University of Toronto Press.

Dean, Amber, and Anne Stone, eds. 2007. *West Coast Line 53* 41 (1), Special issue, "Representations of Murdered and Missing Women."

Deloria, Vine, Jr. 2003. *God Is Red: A Native View of Religion*. 30th anniversary edition. Golden, CO: Fulcrum Publishing.

Derrida, Jacques. 1994. *Specters of Marx: The State of the Debt, the Work of Mourning, and the New International*. New York: Routledge.

De Vries, Maggie. 2003. *Missing Sarah: A Vancouver Woman Remembers Her Vanished Sister*. Toronto: Penguin Canada.

Doezema, Jo. 1998. "Forced to Choose: Beyond the Voluntary vs. Forced Prostitution Dichotomy." In *Global Sex Workers: Rights, Resistance, and Redefinition*, ed. Kamala Kempadoo and Jo Doezema, 34–50. New York: Routledge.

Driskill, Qwo-Li, Chris Finley, Brian Joseph Gilley, and Scott Lauria Morgensen, eds. 2011. *Queer Indigenous Studies: Critical Interventions in Theory, Politics, and Literature*. Tucson: University of Arizona Press.

Dubinsky, Karen. 2010. *Babies without Borders: Adoption and Migration across the Americas*. Toronto: University of Toronto Press.

Duganne, Erina. 2007. "Photography after the Fact." In *Beautiful Suffering: Photography and the Traffic in Pain*, ed. Mark Reinhardt, Holly Edwards, and Erina Duganne, 57–74. Williamstown, Chicago: Williams College Museum of Art and the University of Chicago Press.

Duggan, Lisa. 2002. "The New Homonormativity: The Sexual Politics of Neoliberalism." In *Materialising Democracy: Towards a Revitalized Cultural Politics*, ed. Russ Castronovo and Dana D. Nelson, 175–94. Durham, NC: Duke University Press. http://dx.doi.org/10.1215/9780822383901-007.

England, Jennifer. 2004. "Disciplining Subjectivity and Space: Representation, Film and Its Material Effects." *Antipode* 36 (2): 295–321. http://dx.doi.org/10.1111/j.1467-8330.2004.00407.x.

Erno, Kim. 2010. "Political Realities: The Impact of Globalization on Indigenous Women." In *Torn from Our Midst: Voices of Grief, Healing and Action from the Missing Indigenous Women Conference 2008*, edited by Brenda

A. Anderson, Wendee Kubik, and Mary Rucklos Hampton, 57–68. Regina: Canadian Plains Research Centre Press.

Ferris, Shawna. 2007. "'The Lone Streetwalker:' Missing Women and Sex Work-Related News in Mainstream Canadian Media." *West Coast Line 53* 41 (1): 14–25.

Finding Dawn. 2006. Directed by Christine Welsh. Montreal: National Film Board of Canada.

Finley, Chris. 2011. "Decolonizing the Queer Native Body (and Recovering the Native Bull-Dyke): Bringing 'Sexy Back' and Out of Native Studies' Closet." In *Queer Indigenous Studies: Critical Interventions in Theory, Politics, and Literature*, edited by Qwo-Li Driskill, Chris Finley, Brian Joseph Gilley, and Scott Lauria Morgensen, 29–41. Tucson: University of Arizona Press.

Fix: The Story of an Addicted City. 2002. Directed by Nettie Wild. Vancouver: Canada Wild Productions.

Fixico, Donald L. 2009. "American Indian History and Writing from Home: Constructing an Indian Perspective." *American Indian Quarterly* 33 (4): 553–60.

Fournier, Suzanne, and Ernie Crey. 1997. *Stolen from Our Embrace: The Abduction of First Nations Children and the Restoration of Aboriginal Communities.* Vancouver: Douglas & McIntyre.

Francis, Margot. 2011. *Creative Subversions: Whiteness, Indigeneity, and the National Imaginary.* Vancouver: UBC Press.

Fraser, Nancy. 2000. "Rethinking Recognition." *New Left Review* 3: 107–20.

Fraser, Nancy, and Axel Honneth. 2003. *Redistribution or Recognition? A Political-Philosophical Exchange.* London: Verso.

Freeman, Victoria. 2011. "Indigenous Hauntings in Settler-Colonial Spaces: The Activism of Indigenous Ancestors in the City of Toronto." In *Phantom Past, Indigenous Presence*, edited by Colleen E. Boyd and Coll Thrush, 209–54. Lincoln: University of Nebraska Press.

Fricker, Miranda. 2007. *Epistemic Injustice: Power and the Ethics of Knowing.* Oxford: Oxford University Press. http://dx.doi.org/10.1093/acprof:oso/9780198237907.001.0001.

Gelder, Ken, and Jane M. Jacobs. 1998. *Uncanny Australia: Sacredness and Identity in a Postcolonial Nation.* Carlton South, Vic.: Melbourne University Press.

Gilman, Sander L. 1985. *Difference and Pathology: Stereotypes of Sexuality, Race, and Madness.* Ithaca: Cornell University Press.

Gordon, Avery. 1997. *Ghostly Matters: Haunting and the Sociological Imagination.* Minneapolis: University of Minnesota Press.

Goulding, Warren David. 2001. *Just Another Indian: A Serial Killer and Canada's Indifference.* Calgary: Fifth House Publishers.

Granzow, Kara, and Amber Dean. 2007. "Revanchism in the Canadian West: Gentrification and Resettlement in a Prairie City." *Topia: Canadian Journal of Cultural Studies* 18: 89–106.

Harper, Anita Olsen. 2009. "Sisters in Spirit." In *Restoring the Balance: First Nations Women, Community, and Culture*, ed. Eric Guimond, Gail Guthrie Valaskakis, and Madeline Dion Stout, 175–99. Winnipeg: University of Manitoba Press.

Harris, R. Cole. 1997. *The Resettlement of British Columbia: Essays on Colonialism and Geographical Change.* Vancouver: UBC Press.

Hasson, Shlomo, and David Ley. 1994. *Neighbourhood Organizations and the Welfare State.* Toronto: University of Toronto Press.

Henderson, James (Sa'ke'j). 2000. "Postcolonial Ghost Dancing: Diagnosing European Colonialism." In *Reclaiming Indigenous Voice and Vision*, ed. Marie Battiste, 57–76. Vancouver: UBC Press.

Henderson, Jennifer, and Pauline Wakeham. 2009. "Colonial Reckoning, National Reconciliation? Aboriginal Peoples and the Culture of Redress in Canada." *English Studies in Canada* 35 (1): 1–26. http://dx.doi.org/10.1353/esc.0.0168.

Hill, Susan M. 2009. "Conducting Haudenosaunee Historical Research from Home: In the Shadow of the Six Nations–Caledonia Reclamation." *American Indian Quarterly* 33 (4): 479–98.

Hirsch, Marianne, and Valerie Smith. 2002. "Feminism and Cultural Memory: An Introduction." *Signs* (Chicago) 28 (1): 1–19. http://dx.doi.org/10.1086/340890.

Hollibaugh, Amber L. 2000. *My Dangerous Desires: A Queer Girl Dreaming Her Way Home.* Durham, NC: Duke University Press.

Hugill, David. 2010. *Missing Women, Missing News: Covering Crisis in Vancouver's Downtown Eastside.* Halifax: Fernwood.

Hunt, Sarah. 2013. "Decolonizing Sex Work: Developing an Intersectional Indigenous Approach." In *Selling Sex: Experience, Advocacy, and Research on Sex Work in Canada*, ed. Emily Van Der Meulen, Elya M. Durisin, and Victoria Love, 82–100. Vancouver: UBC Press.

Hunt, Sarah. 2014. "More than a Poster Campaign: Redefining Colonial Violence." In *The Winter We Danced: Voices from the Past, the Future, and the Idle No More Movement*, edited by The Kino-nda-niimi Collective, 190–3. Winnipeg: ARP Books.

Jacobs, Beverley, and Andrea J. Williams. 2008. "Legacy of Residential Schools: Missing and Murdered Aboriginal Women." In *From Truth to Reconciliation: Transforming the Legacy of Residential Schools*, ed. Marlene Brant Castellano, Linda Archibald, and Mike DeGagne, 121–40. Ottawa: Aboriginal Healing Foundation.

Janzen, Caitlin, Susan Strega, Leslie Brown, Jeannie Morgan, and Jeannine Carrière. 2013. "'Nothing Short of a Horror Show': Triggering Abjection of

Street Workers in Western Canadian Newspapers." *Hypatia* 28 (1): 142–62. http://dx.doi.org/10.1111/j.1527-2001.2011.01256.x.

Jiwani, Yasmin, and Mary Lynn Young. 2006. "Missing and Murdered Women: Reproducing Marginality in News Discourse." *Canadian Journal of Communication* 31 (4): 895 –917.

Johanson, Reg. 2007. "Homes Not Game Shows." *West Coast Line 53* 41 (1): 96–7.

Justice, Daniel Heath, Mark Rifkin, and Bethany Schneider, eds. 2010. "Sexuality, Nationality, Indigeneity." Special double-issue of *GLQ: A Journal of Gay and Lesbian Studies* 16.

Justice, Daniel Heath, Mark Rifkin, and Bethany Schneider. 2010. "Heaven and Earth: From the Guest Editors." A special double-issue of *GLQ: A Journal of Gay and Lesbian Studies* 16: 1–3.

Kavanagh, Sarah Schneider. 2011. "Haunting Remains: Educating a New American Citizenry at Indian Hill Cemetery." In *Phantom Past, Indigenous Presence*, ed. Colleen E. Boyd and Coll Thrush, 151–78. Lincoln: University of Nebraska Press.

Kelley, Caffyn. 1995. "Creating Memory, Contesting History: Inside the Monstrous Fact of Whiteness." *Matriart* 5 (3): 6–11.

Kohli, Rita. 1991. "Violence against Women: Race, Class and Gender Issues." *Canadian Women's Studies* 11 (4): 13–14.

Lash, Scott, and Mike Featherstone, eds. 2002. *Recognition and Difference: Politics, Identity, Multiculture*. London: Sage.

Lauzon, Claudette. 2008. "What the Body Remembers: Rebecca Belmore's Memorial to Missing Women." In *Precarious Visualities: New Perspectives on Identification in Contemporary Art and Visual Culture*, ed. Olivier Asselin, Johanne Lamoureux, and Christine Ross, 155–79. Montreal, Kingston: McGill-Queen's University Press.

Lauzon, Claudette. 2010. "'In the Presence of the Absent': Rebecca Belmore's Art of Witness." In *The Politics of Cultural Memory*, ed. Lucy Burke, Simon Faulkner, and Jim Aulich, 76–91. Newcastle upon Tyne: Cambridge Scholars Publishing.

Lowman, John. 2000. "Violence and the Outlaw Status of (Street) Prostitution in Canada." *Violence Against Women* 6 (9): 987–1011. http://dx.doi.org/10.1177/10778010022182245.

Lowman, John, and Laura Fraser. 1996. *Violence against Persons Who Prostitute: The Experience in British Columbia*. Department of Justice Canada: Research, Statistics and Evaluation Directorate.

Maracle, Lee. 2007. "Oratory on Oratory." In *Trans.Can.Lit: Resituating the Study of Canadian Literature*, ed. Smaro Kamboureli and Roy Miki, 55–70. Waterloo, ON: Wilfrid Laurier University Press.

Markell, Patchen. 2003. *Bound by Recognition*. Princeton, NJ: Princeton University Press.

Marker of Change: The Story of the Women's Monument. 1998. Directed by Moira Simpson. Vancouver: Moving Images.

McConney, Denise S. 1999. "Differences for Our Daughters: Racialized Sexism in Art, Mass Media and Law." *Canadian Women's Studies* 19 (1/2): 209–14.

McDonald, Jean. 2003. "Hyper Exposed and Virtually Anonymous: Vancouver's Missing Women in the Prime Time News." *Journal for the Arts, Sciences, and Technology* 1 (2): 115–19.

McDonald, Robert. 1996. *Making Vancouver: Class, Status, and Social Boundaries, 1863–1913*. Vancouver: UBC Press.

McElhinney, Lora. 2007. "Memorial March, 2007." *West Coast Line 53* 41 (1): 70–3.

McIvor, Sharon Donna. 2004. "Aboriginal Women Unmasked: Using Equality Litigation to Advance Women's Rights." *Canadian Journal of Women and the Law* 16: 106–36.

McKenzie, Holly. 2010. "'She Was Not into Drugs and Partying. She Was a Wife and Mother': Media Representations and (Re)Presentations of Daleen Kay Bosse (Muskego)." In *Torn from Our Midst: Voices of Grief, Healing and Action from the Missing Women Conference 2008*, edited by A. Brenda Anderson, Wendee Kubik, and Mary Rucklos Hampton, 142–61. Regina: Canadian Plains Research Centre Press.

McManus, Sheila. 2005. *The Line Which Separates: Race, Gender, and the Making of the Alberta-Montana Borderlands*. Edmonton: University of Alberta Press.

McNeill, Laurie. 2008. "Death and the Maidens: Vancouver's Missing Women, the Montreal Massacre, and Commemoration's Blind Spots." *Canadian Review of American Studies* 38 (3): 375–98.

Morgensen, Scott Lauria. 2011. *Spaces between Us: Queer Settler Colonialism and Indigenous Decolonization*. Minneapolis: University of Minnesota Press.

Moss, Laura. 2012. "Is Canada Postcolonial? Re-Asking through 'The Forgotten' Project." *TOPIA: Canadian Journal of Cultural Studies* (27): 47–65.

Murray, Alison. 1995. "Femme on the Streets, Butch in the Sheets (a Play on Whores)." In *Mapping Desire: Geographies of Sexuality*, ed. David Bell and Gill Valentine, 59–66. New York: Routledge.

My Name Is Scot. 2012. "Skid Road (Establishing Footage)." In *V6A: Writing from Vancouver's Downtown Eastside*, edited by John Mikhail Asfour and Elee Kraljii Gardiner, 135–39. Vancouver: Arsenal Pulp Press.

Native Women's Association of Canada. 2010. *What Their Stories Tell Us: Research Findings from the Sisters in Spirit Initiative*. Ohsweken and Ottawa, ON: Native Women's Association of Canada.

Nestle, Joan. 1992. *The Persistent Desire: A Femme-Butch Reader*. Boston: Alyson
Publications.

Neville, Charo. 2007. "Rebecca Belmore: *Vigil* and *The Named and the Unnamed*,
2002." *West Coast Line 53* 41 (1): 52–6.

Oleksijczuk, Denise Blake. 2002. "Haunted Spaces." In *Stan Douglas:
Every Building on 100 West Hastings*, ed. Reid Schier, 96–117. Vancouver:
Contemporary Art Gallery / Arsenal Pulp Press.

Oliver, Kelly. 2001. *Witnessing: Beyond Recognition*. Minneapolis: University of
Minnesota Press.

Oppal, Wally T., and the British Columbia Missing Women Commission
of Inquiry. 2012. *Forsaken: The Report of the Missing Women Commission of
Inquiry*. Victoria: Government of British Columbia.

Pearce, Maryanne. 2013. "An Awkward Silence: Missing and Murdered Vulnerable
Women and the Canadian Justice System." PhD diss., University of Ottawa.

Perry, Adele. 2001. *On the Edge of Empire: Gender, Race, and the Making of British
Columbia, 1849–1871*. Toronto: University of Toronto Press.

Peters, Evelyn J. 1998. "Subversive Spaces: First Nations Women and the City."
Environment and Planning D 16 (6): 665–85. http://dx.doi.org/10.1068/d160665.

Pheterson, Gail. 1993. "The Whore Stigma: Female Dishonour and Male
Unworthiness." *Social Text* 37, A Special Section Edited by Anne McClintock
Explores the Sex Trade: 39–64.

Pinto, Meg. 2013. "Pamela Masik and *The Forgotten* Exhibition: Controversy
and Cancellation at the Museum of Anthropology." *Museum Anthropology* 36
(1): 4–17. http://dx.doi.org/10.1111/muan.12001.

Pitman, Beverley A. 2002. "Re-Mediating the Spaces of Reality Television:
America's Most Wanted and the Case of Vancouver's Missing Women."
Environment & Planning A 34 (1): 167–84. http://dx.doi.org/10.1068/a34134.

Pivot Legal Society. 2002. *To Serve and Protect: A Report on Policing in
Vancouver's Downtown Eastside*. Vancouver: Pivot Legal Society.

Pon, Gordon, Kevin Gosine, and Doret Phillips. 2011. "Immediate Response:
Addressing Anti-Native and Anti-Black Racism in Child Welfare."
International Journal of Child, Youth, and Family Studies 2 (3/4): 385–409.

Pratt, Geraldine. 2005. "Abandoned Women and Spaces of the Exception."
Antipode 37 (5): 1052–78. http://dx.doi.org/10.1111/j.0066-4812.2005.00556.x.

Puar, Jasbir K. 2007. *Terrorist Assemblages: Homonationalism in Queer Times*. Durham,
NC: Duke University Press. http://dx.doi.org/10.1215/9780822390442.

Razack, Sherene H. 1998. "Race, Space, and Prostitution: The Making of the
Bourgeois Subject." *Canadian Journal of Women and the Law* 10: 338–76.

Razack, Sherene H. 2000. "Gendered Racial Violence and Spatialized Justice:
The Murder of Pamela George." *Canadian Journal of Law and Society* 15 (2):
91–130. http://dx.doi.org/10.1017/S0829320100006384.

Reber, Susanne, and Rob Renaud. 2003. *Starlight Tour: The Last, Lonely Night of Neil Stonechild*. Toronto: Random House Canada.

Reder, Deanna. 2010. "What's Not in the Room? A Response to Julia Emberley's *Defamiliarizing the Aboriginal*." *Topia: Canadian Journal of Cultural Studies* 23–4: 406–15.

Regan, Paulette. 2010. *Unsettling the Settler Within: Indian Residential Schools, Truth Telling, and Reconciliation in Canada*. Vancouver: UBC Press.

Rickard, Jolene. 2006. "Rebecca Belmore: Performing Power." In *Rebecca Belmore: Fountain* [Catalogue], 68–76. Kamloops, BC: Kamloops Art Gallery, The Morris and Helen Belkin Art Gallery.

Rifkin, Mark. 2011. *When Did Indians Become Straight? Kinship, the History of Sexuality, and Native Sovereignty*. New York: Oxford University Press.

Rifkin, Mark. 2012. *The Erotics of Sovereignty: Queer Native Writing in the Era of Self-Determination*. Minneapolis: University of Minnesota Press.

Rogoff, Irit. 2005. "Looking Away: Participations in Visual Culture." In *After Criticism: New Responses to Art and Performance*, ed. Gavin Butt, 117–34. Oxford, UK: Blackwell. http://dx.doi.org/10.1002/9780470774243.ch6.

Rosenberg, Sharon. 2000. "Standing in a Circle of Stone: Rupturing the Binds of Emblematic Memory." In *Between Hope and Despair: Pedagogy and the Remembrance of Historical Trauma*, ed. Roger Simon, Sharon Rosenberg, and Claudia Eppert, 75–89. Lanham, MD: Rowman and Littlefield.

Rosenberg, Sharon. 2003. "Neither Forgotten nor Fully Remembered: Tracing an Ambivalent Public Memory on the 10th Anniversary of the Montreal Massacre." *Feminist Theory* 4 (1): 5–27. http://dx.doi.org/10.1177/14647001 03004001001.

Rosenberg, Sharon. 2004. "Memorializing Queers / Queering Remembrances: Encounters with Loss and the Problematics of Identity." *Torquere: Journal of the Canadian Lesbian and Gay Studies Association* 6: 1–11.

Rosenberg, Sharon. 2005. "Violence, Identity and Public History: Thoughts on What Is Inextricable, but Must Be Otherwise." Conference paper presented at Canadian Association of Cultural Studies Conference, University of Alberta.

Rosenberg, Sharon. 2007. "Distances and Proximities: (Not) being there." *West Coast Line 53* 41 (1): 60–3.

Rosenberg, Sharon. 2009. "Meditations on Turning towards Violently Dead." In *Democracy in Crisis: Violence, Alterity, Community*, ed. Stella Gaon, 220–40. Manchester: Manchester University Press.

Rosenberg, Sharon. 2010. "Facing Losses / Losing Guarantees: A Meditation on Traumatic Ignorance as a Constitutive Demand." In *The Future of Memory*, ed. Richard Crownshaw, Jane Kilby, and Antony Rowland, 245–63. Oxford: Berghahn Books.

Rosenberg, Sharon, and Roger I. Simon. 2000. "Beyond the Logic of Emblemization: Remembering and Learning from the Montreal Massacre." *Educational Theory* 50 (2): 133–55. http://dx.doi.org/10.1111/j.1741-5446.2000.00133.x.

Ross, Becki L. 2009. *Burlesque West: Showgirls, Sex and Sin in Postwar Vancouver.* Toronto: University of Toronto Press.

Ross, Becki L. 2010. "Sex and (Evacuation from) the City: The Moral and Legal Regulation of Sex Workers in Vancouver's West End, 1975–1985." *Sexualities* 13 (2): 197–218. http://dx.doi.org/10.1177/1363460709359232.

Ross, Becki L. 2012. "Outdoor Brothel Culture: The Un/Making of a Transsexual Stroll in Vancouver's West End, 1975–1984." *Journal of Historical Sociology* 25 (1): 126–50. http://dx.doi.org/10.1111/j.1467-6443.2011.01411.x.

Ross, Becki, and Rachael Sullivan. 2012. "Tracing Lines of Horizontal Hostility: How Sex Workers and Gay Activists Battled for Space, Voice, and Belonging in Vancouver, 1975–1985." *Sexualities* 15 (5–6): 604–21. http://dx.doi.org/10.1177/1363460712446121.

Royal Canadian Mounted Police. 2014. *Missing and Murdered Aboriginal Women: A National Operational Overview.* Ottawa.

Rymhs, Deena. 2006. "Appropriating Guilt: Reconciliation in an Aboriginal Canadian Context." *ESC: English Studies in Canada* 32 (1): 105–23. http://dx.doi.org/10.1353/esc.2007.0068.

Schick, Carol. 2010. "Media: A Canadian Response." In *Torn from Our Midst: Voices of Grief, Healing and Action from the Missing Indigenous Women Conference 2008,* edited by A. Brenda Anderson, Wendee Kubik, and Mary Rucklos Hampton, 133–41. Regina: Canadian Plains Research Centre Press.

Sekula, Allan. 1986. "The Body and the Archive." *October* 39: 3. http://dx.doi.org/10.2307/778312.

Shier, Reid. 2002. "Introduction." In *Stan Douglas: Every Building on 100 West Hastings,* 10–17. Vancouver: Contemporary Art Gallery / Arsenal Pulp Press.

Silman, Janet, and the Tobique Women's Group. 1987. *Enough Is Enough: Aboriginal Women Speak Out.* Toronto: Women's Press.

Simon, Roger I. 2005. *The Touch of the Past: Remembrance, Learning, and Ethics.* New York: Palgrave Macmillan.

Simon, Roger I. 2006. "The Terrible Gift: Museums and the Possibility of Hope without Consolation." *Museum Management and Curatorship* 21 (3): 187–204. http://dx.doi.org/10.1080/09647770600202103.

Simon, Roger I. 2013. "Towards a Hopeful Practice of Worrying: The Problematics of Listening and the Educative Responsibilities of Canada's Truth and Reconciliation Commission." In *Reconciling Canada: Historical*

Injustices and the Contemporary Culture of Redress, ed. Pauline Wakeham and Jennifer Henderson, 129–42. Toronto: University of Toronto Press.

Simon, Roger I. 2014. *A Pedagogy of Witnessing: Curatorial Practice and the Pursuit of Social Justice*. Albany, NY: SUNY Press.

Simon, Roger I., Sharon Rosenberg, and Claudia Eppert, eds. 2000. *Between Hope and Despair: Pedagogy and the Remembrance of Historical Trauma*. Lanham, MD: Rowman & Littlefield Publishers.

Sinclair, Raven. 2007. "Identity Lost and Found: Lessons from the Sixties Scoop." *First Peoples Child and Family Review* 3 (1): 65–82.

Smith, Andrea. 2005. *Conquest: Sexual Violence and American Indian Genocide*. Cambridge, MA: South End Press.

Smith, Andrea. 2011. "Queer Theory and Native Studies: The Heteronormativity of Settler Colonialism." In *Queer Indigenous Studies: Critical Interventions in Theory, Politics and Literature*, ed. Qwo-Li Driskill, Chris Finley, Brian Joseph Gilley, and Scott Lauria Morgensen, 43–66. Tucson: University of Arizona Press.

Smith, Neil. 1996. *The New Urban Frontier: Gentrification and the Revanchist City*. London, New York: Routledge.

Smith, Stacey L. 2013. *Freedom's Frontier: California and the Struggle over Unfree Labor, Emancipation, and Reconstruction*. Chapel Hill: University of North Carolina Press.

Smits, David D. 1991. "'Squaw Men,' 'Half-Breeds,' and Amalgamators: Late Nineteenth-Century Anglo-American Attitudes toward Indian-White Race-Mixing." *American Indian Culture and Research Journal* 15 (3): 29–61.

Sommers, Jeff, and Nicholas K. Blomley. 2002. "The Worst Block in Vancouver." In *Stan Douglas: Every Building on 100 West Hastings*, edited by Stan Douglas, Reid Schier, and Contemporary Art Gallery, 19–58. Vancouver: Contemporary Art Gallery and Arsenal Pulp Press.

Sontag, Susan. 1990. *On Photography*. New York: Anchor Books.

Sontag, Susan. 2003. *Regarding the Pain of Others*. New York: Farrar, Straus and Giroux.

Stone, Anne. 2004. "Objective Hazard." In *Biting the Error: Writers Explore Narrative*, ed. Mary Burger, Robert Gluck, Camille Roy, and Gail Scott, 78–84. Toronto: Coach House Books.

Stone, Anne. 2009. "Bearing Partial Witness: Representations of Missing Women." *Review of Education, Pedagogy & Cultural Studies* 31 (2): 221–36. http://dx.doi.org/10.1080/10714410902827259.

Suzack, Cheryl. 2010. "Emotion before the Law." In *Indigenous Women and Feminism: Politics, Activism, Culture*, ed. Cheryl Suzack, Shari M. Huhndorf, Jeanne Perreault, and Jean Barman, 126–51. Vancouver: UBC Press.

Taussig, Michael T. 1999. *Defacement: Public Secrecy and the Labor of the Negative.* Stanford, CA: Stanford University Press.

Taylor, Paul. 2003. *The Heart of the Community: The Best of the Carnegie Newsletter.* Vancouver: New Star Books.

Thobani, Sunera. 2007. *Exalted Subjects: Studies in the Making of Race and Nation in Canada.* Toronto: University of Toronto Press.

Through a Blue Lens. Directed by Veronica Mannix. 1999. Montreal: National Film Board of Canada.

Thrush, Coll. 2011. "Hauntings as Histories: Indigenous Ghosts and the Urban Past in Seattle." In *Phantom Past Indigenous Presence*, ed. Colleen E. Boyd and Coll Thrush, 54–81. Lincoln: University of Nebraska Press.

Townsend-Gault, Charlotte. 2003. "Have We Ever Been Good?" In *Rebecca Belmore: The Named and the Unnamed*, 9–50. Exhibition catalogue. Vancouver: The Morris and Helen Belkin Art Gallery.

Townsend-Gault, Charlotte. 2004. "Feeling Implicated." In *The Challenge of Native American Studies*, ed. Barbara Saunders and Lea Zuyderhaudt, 53–66. Belgium: Leuven University Press.

Van Alphen, Ernst. 1999. "Colonialism as Historical Trauma." In *Grey Areas: Representation, Identity and Politics in Contemporary South African Art*, ed. Brenda Atkinson and Candice Breitz, 269–81. Johannesburg: Chalkham Hill Press.

Vancouver, City of. 2006. *2005/06 Downtown Eastside Community Monitoring Report.* Vancouver: City of Vancouver.

Van Kirk, Sylvia. 2006. "Colonized Lives: The Native Wives and Daughters of Five Founding Families of Victoria." In *In the Days of Our Grandmothers: A Reader in Aboriginal Women's History in Canada*, ed. Mary-Ellen Kelm and Lorna Townsend, 170–99. Toronto: University of Toronto Press.

Van Wagenen, Aimee. 2004. "An Epistemology of Haunting: A Review Essay." *Critical Sociology* 30 (2): 287–98. http://dx.doi.org/10.1163/156916304323072116.

Vidaver, Aaron, ed. 2004. "Woodsquat," a special issue. *West Coast Line 41* 37 (2/3).

Wanhalla, Angela. 2009. "Rethinking 'Squaw Men' and 'Pakeha-Maori': Legislating White Masculinity in New Zealand and Canada, 1840–1900." In *Re-Orienting Whiteness*, ed. Leigh Boucher, Jane Carey, and Katherine Ellinghaus, 219–34. New York: Palgrave-Macmillan.

Watts, Vanessa. 2013. "Indigenous Place-Thought and Agency amongst Humans and Non Humans (First Woman and Sky Woman Go on a European World Tour!)." *Decolonization: Indigeneity, Education & Society* 2 (1): 20–34.

Williams, Carol. 2003. *Framing the West: Race, Gender and the Photographic Frontier in the Pacific Northwest*. Oxford: Oxford University Press.

Williams, Patricia J. 1991. *The Alchemy of Race and Rights*. Cambridge, MA: Harvard University Press.

Woolford, Andrew. 2001. "Tainted Space: Representation of Injection Drug-use and HIV/AIDS in Vancouver's Downtown Eastside." *BC Studies* 129: 27–50.

Wyschogrod, Edith. 1985. *Spirit in Ashes: Hegel, Heidegger, and Man-made Mass Death*. New Haven: Yale University Press.

Index

Note: Page numbers in **bold** refer to figures.